ENGLISH PAINTING

ENGLISH PAINTING

From Hogarth to the Pre-Raphaelites

BY

JEAN-JACQUES MAYOUX

PREFACE BY

SIR ANTHONY BLUNT

SKIRA

RIZZOLI
NEW YORK

First published 1975
First paperback edition 1989

Published in the United States of America in 1989 by
RIZZOLI INTERNATIONAL PUBLICATIONS, INC.
597 Fifth Avenue/New York 10017

Printed in Switzerland

Library of Congress Cataloging-in-Publication Data

Mayoux, Jean-Jacques.
    [Peinture anglaise. English]
    English painting: from Hogarth to the Pre-Raphaelites / by
    Jean-Jacques Mayoux: preface by Sir Anthony Blunt.
        p.   cm.
    Translation of: Peinture anglaise.
    Bibliography: p.
    ISBN 0-8478-1015-1:
    1. Painting, English.   2. Painting, Modern — 17th-18th centuries —
    England.   3. Painting, Modern — 19th century — England.   I. Title.
ND466.M3913 1989
759.2 — dc 19   88-23912
                                                          CIP

CONTENTS

Preface

It would be very nearly true to say that fifty or a hundred years ago French art critics and art historians only wrote about French art and never looked outside the borders of France, and that foreigners were not encouraged to take part in the game. There were, of course, exceptions: Géricault and Delacroix had discovered the British painting of their own day – particularly Constable, Wilkie and Lawrence – and some, but not many, of the critics had followed their lead, and when Monet came to England in 1900 he was influenced by the late works of Turner. Ruskin wrote about French Gothic – and Proust even translated him – and in 1882 Ernest Chesneau produced a history of English painting which can still be read with interest and profit. But on the whole the French continued to think that English painting was second-rate, and the English – with the exception of Sir Richard Wallace – found French painting either stiff and affected (Poussin) or frivolous and slightly immoral (Boucher). In literature, it may be said in parenthesis, the situation was different. Voltaire had called attention to the existence of English literature; the Romantics had used Shakespeare as a stick to beat Racine; Taine produced his Histoire de la Littérature Anglaise *and the Symbolists admired Blake. The English hardly returned the compliment and, although John Morley wrote with enthusiasm about the Encyclopédistes, it was more on account of their philosophical and political ideas than for their style; so that, when in the 1920s Lytton Strachey ventured to place Racine among the great writers of the world, it was a novelty – and something of a shock – for the English public.*

Now all this is changed. French art, of all periods from the Middle Ages to the twentieth century, is a favourite subject among university students; the exhibitions of French painting held in London have attracted vast crowds; and English art historians such as Dr Joan Evans have written extensively about French art of the Middle Ages, and others have worked on the painting and architecture of later periods.

In France, too, things have changed. Scholars such as Jean Bony have turned their attention to English medieval art; English scholars have been invited to organize exhibitions of French art in Paris, and to catalogue, for instance, the English paintings in the Louvre. What is perhaps even more startling is that contemporary English art has begun to be accepted in France and that exhibitions of Moore, Sutherland and Bacon have attracted thousands of Parisians. In fact close collaboration and friendliness have replaced the aloofness and suspicions of the past, and it is in this new atmosphere of cooperation that we welcome M. Mayoux's history of English painting.

M. Mayoux has devoted his life to the study of English literature and held the chair of English at the Sorbonne from 1951 till his retirement in 1973; but on the side, so to speak, he has always indulged his love of English painting, and this volume is the result of long study and deep understanding.

One of the most striking features of the book is the degree to which M. Mayoux has been able to get inside English painting and to see it with English eyes, but this is not to say that the book is just like other histories of English painting. It has its own distinctive French flavour, which comes out most clearly in the evocative descriptions which the author gives of individual paintings. Such a method is an old and sound tradition in French criticism and is here applied to good effect. Secondly, M. Mayoux has his own personal likes and dislikes, which are not necessarily the same as ours. He dismisses Gainsborough's fancy pieces as sentimental, just as most Englishmen find the moralizing and sensual paintings of Greuze distasteful. When he writes of the Pre-Raphaelites his views are again strong. Of Holman Hunt's A Converted British Family Sheltering a Christian Priest from the Druids *he writes: 'It seems to me that it would be difficult to do anything more bogus than this picture.' But about the* Scapegoat *he has a magnificent phrase: 'The guilty beast is arrested in an everlasting trance.' Sometimes he pulls our leg – gently and in a friendly way – as when, describing Millais's* Order of Release, *he refers to 'the inevitable joyful dog, which ever since Opie and Gainsborough had been bounding from picture to picture to welcome its master.'*

It is, however, with Turner that M. Mayoux is most completely at home. His descriptions of the later pictures, his analyses of their qualities, dramatic, poetic and formal, are memorable, and his summing up of the artist's achievement helps us to see Turner more clearly in the perspective of European painting as a whole. This approach is not only applied to Turner, however, and one of the great merits of the book is that it sees English art as forming part of that of the whole European community.

Anthony Blunt
London, April 1975

Introduction

English painting has long been overshadowed by the Continental schools, and some amends seem called for: such is the spirit in which this survey is modestly offered. Some surprises, it is hoped, will be in store for the reader among the illustrations, chosen from the wealth of fine work produced in the century and a half extending from the birth of Hogarth to the death of Turner. But if there are some fine British painters, is there, one may ask, a British school of painting? In England itself, apparently, there was room for doubt less than two centuries ago, for in his fourteenth presidential Discourse delivered at the Royal Academy in 1788, Sir Joshua Reynolds, the most famous of living English painters, declared: 'If ever this nation should produce genius sufficient to acquire to us the honourable distinction of an English school, the name of Gainsborough will be transmitted to posterity, in the history of the art, among the very first of that rising name.'

Despite his false modesty – for of course he was also thinking of another founder of that school: himself – Reynolds' reservations were justified. In view of the long-continued flowering of the Dutch and Flemish schools up to that time, it is amazing that another branch of the same West Germanic stock should have produced such very different fruit. In England, it must be admitted, the achievements of late medieval and Renaissance painting were slender indeed: it is not by chance that the attribution 'French' was peevishly scratched off the Wilton Diptych at the National Gallery – a picture which in France would never have aroused envy, nor any sense of wounded pride. This slender achievement is the more surprising because it did not spring from any lack of taste or interest. In the Induction to *The Taming of the Shrew*, two centuries before Reynolds' fourteenth Discourse, Christopher Sly is shown all the luxuries of aristocratic life, among which were pictures:

> Adonis painted by a running brook,
> And Cytherea all in sedges hid,
> Which seem to move and wanton with her breath...
> We'll show thee Io as she was a maid,
> And how she was beguiled and surpris'd,
> As lively painted as the deed was done.
> Or Daphne roaming through a thorny wood,
> Scratching her legs that one shall swear she bleeds...

This seems to show that at the end of the sixteenth century the English aristocracy had a decided taste for mythological painting and looked to it for a certain suggestive magic. But where in the England of that day was the painter who could satisfy such a taste? Hans Eworth, perhaps, but he was not English. Under Richard II, a Bohemian strain had made its appearance (he had married Anne of Bohemia). Under Mary, Antonio

Moro was summoned from Spain and became Sir Anthony More. Under Henry VIII, who as a Protestant looked to the North, Holbein became the court painter. Under Charles I, after various Flemings and the great Rubens himself, it was Van Dyck who settled in London, dying there just before the Civil War broke out; and it is with Van Dyck in fact that the history of modern British painting begins, for he founded the tradition of grace and prestige that attaches to its most popular and appealing form, portrait painting. He was followed by a Dutchman, Sir Peter Lely, who contrived to enjoy the favour first of Cromwell, then of Charles II. After Lely and his insipid *Beauties* formerly at Windsor Castle, came a German, Sir Godfrey Kneller, who painted the even more insipid *Beauties* at Hampton Court. True, there were a few good English painters among their contemporaries. William Dobson was one; he portrayed the leaders of the King's party, and their tense faces, steady, serious gaze and dramatic but unemphatic gestures have a force which still strikes the imagination. But Dobson died at thirty-six and was never the dominant figure that Kneller was to be, on the threshold of the period with which this book is concerned. Coming to England a decade or so before the Glorious Revolution of 1688, Kneller was exactly the painter required by the bourgeois monarchy. He took no interest in the pretty women to be seen at court, but left a large body of portraits of the leading worthies of that day, many of them members of the Kit-Cat Club, whom he immortalized in small portraits of a standard size (36 by 28"), since known as Kit-Cat. Of course the full-length portrait in the tradition of Van Dyck continued to exist, with the drapery and the column against which the subject nobly leans, and indeed there was a great future in store for it. But the Kit-Cat Club would have none of it: head and shoulders sufficed, with an abundance of wig, and even more of conventionality. Evidence of class or social group counted for more than individuality, but just enough of the latter is provided for these worthies to be as distinctly present on the walls as they must have been in the club room. Most vitally present of all is the bookseller Jacob Tonson (1717); he wears no wig and already, not being a person of quality, he has an engaging Hogarthian head, with a darting eye.

Kneller, whose point of view was thoroughly middle-class, enjoyed a brilliant career and became the first painter in England to be made a baronet. But one and the same period was traversed by currents which were not strictly contemporary. The middle-class England then in the making preserved that vision of grandeur which had presided over the architectural creations of Inigo Jones, Wren and Webb, and which required a Rubens for the great allegorical decorations of the Banqueting House in Whitehall. Even though it was no longer a question of the Royal Palace at Greenwich, but of Greenwich Hospital, the walls and ceilings of the old seamen's home had to be decorated, as did those of St Paul's. And the fashionable decorators were there to do the job; they had come from Italy and France after Antonio Verrio, despite little or no talent, became the most highly paid painter in England, and was immortalized in a couplet by Pope. But, a sign of the times, at least one Englishman, James Thornhill, entered the field of decorative painting, enjoying its profits and glory, and going far to redeem the national honour. His foreign competitors were no longer mediocrities. The Frenchman Louis Laguerre was skilful and inventive and his English rival learnt much from him. The Venetian Sebastiano Ricci needs no presentation here; he has his place in the history of Venetian painting, and not only as a transmitter of Veronese. But Thornhill knew where to turn for commissions and how to appeal to patriotic sentiments.

And it was he who was called upon to decorate the dome of St Paul's with grisaille panels and the ceiling of the Painted Hall at Greenwich Hospital. If these works are looked at closely, he is seen to be weak in design: his bodies all too readily verge on the monstrous, the arms especially, and a look at his *Venus Arming Aeneas* in the Tate Gallery shows that it is not just a question of scale. It is precisely in his large-scale decorations, high overhead, that one is struck by his good qualities: his vitality and energy of movement, dynamically projecting limbs whose uncouthness goes unnoticed, setting up a rhythm and investing everything with a fine glow of colour. His concerns were typical of his time, in an England which, standing between the past and the present, was trying to bring forth a living art even by way of academic forms. His notes show him wondering how to dress William of Orange, then George I, in pictures commemorating their arrival. What did they look like? The truth seems to have been that they did not look so very glorious. They must therefore be idealized. But how far? To the extent of going back to antiquity? Thus the question is raised which occurs again half a century later with *The Death of General Wolfe*.

Thornhill would have liked to decorate Kensington Palace, but he failed to secure this commission. It was awarded not to a foreign intruder, but to a noted architect named William Kent, the protégé of Lord Burlington. Kent was a good architect and furniture designer, but a poor painter. Thornhill was understandably resentful, and his quarrel with Kent was continued by his son-in-law William Hogarth, who was not the man to let personal enmities die down.

Sir James Thornhill was, as I have said, representative of the times; for he stormed a bastion of art hitherto securely held by foreigners and managed to bring to it a certain national spirit. After this success, an artist of vigorous powers and aggressive temper seemed to be needed, a genuine creator with a strong sense of social values, in order to bring together in clear, emphatic form, at this crucial moment, the tendencies which were to characterize the British school.

1

Hogarth, Painter of Everyday Life and Prophet of Living Art.
Sir James Thornhill, Hogarth and the Temptation of the Grand Style.
Attitudes, Conflicts and Struggles of Hogarth. A Baroque Aesthetic.

WILLIAM HOGARTH was born in Smithfield, in the heart of London, on 10 November 1697. He was the son of a schoolmaster from Westmorland who had come to London to seek his fortune and whose most ambitious venture was the compilation of a Latin dictionary which never found a publisher. In London his father led the wretched life of a literary hack, and the careful researches of Ronald Paulson[1] have shown that he spent five years in the Fleet Prison for debt, until he was released after the passing of a special act of Parliament to free debtors. In those days, and until the time of David Copperfield, such prisons were open to the debtor's family, who made their home there in a picturesque squalor which must have impressed itself upon the mind of an artist always sensitive to the grotesque side of life, and which may have hardened his heart.

In the autobiographical notes written late in life, Hogarth says nothing of this period, from his tenth to his fifteenth year, just as Dickens long refrained from speaking of similar experiences. Hogarth merely says that at fifteen he was apprenticed to a silver engraver, where he learned to cover tankards and salvers with heraldic motifs, arabesques and grotesques. The discipline of hand and eye which he acquired here served him well when he came to engrave the lines of strenuous movement, rendering them with admirable ease and trenchancy.

By 1720, when he was twenty-three, he had set up on his own as an engraver, working chiefly as an illustrator for the booksellers. The paintings in St Paul's and Greenwich Hospital were constantly in his mind and he dreamed of becoming a painter. It was not until the end of his life that he described his youthful ambitions, in unverifiable but highly suggestive terms. He dreamed not just of painting but of painting in the grand style. For there were years of humiliation to make up for, and they were the impressionable years of childhood. The father having so signally failed to prosper, is it surprising that the son in his hurt pride should have gone in quest of something more glorious with which he might identify himself, even though that identification was founded on a misjudgment of his own powers?

Since he speaks in his reminiscences of his most recent quarrel (with Churchill and Wilkes in 1762), it shows that he was writing of his childhood and youth when it was already a long way off and it was, therefore, doubtless romanticized to some extent, though

Sir James Thornhill (1676-1734)

Sketch for the Ceiling of the Painted Hall at Greenwich Hospital, c. 1708. Oil on canvas. (38 × 26″).

Victoria and Albert Museum, London.

the facts may be accurate enough: 'Mimicry, common to all children, was remarkable in me.' Here, admirably stated, was his point of departure: a power of empathy which enabled him to achieve an almost physical identification with external reality and to render its essence to striking effect.

At twenty-one he can hardly have fixed his aims so clearly as he later imagined, looking back through the haze of memory. But he had aims nevertheless. He was eager to improve his technical skill as an artist, having lost precious years in the drudgery of silver-plate engraving; and eager to enjoy life as well. Realizing that he would have to teach himself, he set out to constitute a method of his own, based in part on his congenital laziness, but also on his rugged individualism, his refusal to accept any formal discipline or conventions. 'For want of . . . care and patience I despaired of . . . having the full command of the graver, for on these two virtues the beauty and delicacy of the stroke of graving chiefly depends.' So he had to do without this beauty and delicacy. In painting the student is set to copying. But Hogarth felt that he had already copied all too much as a prentice engraver – those heraldic motifs and all too many others besides. 'It occurred to me that there were many disadvantages' in 'continually copying prints and pictures.' He rebelled at the idea of copying works in which he could detect no very superior merit. This was characteristic of him. But, more interestingly, as he pointed out himself, even in drawing from the living model one is merely copying what one sees and this is not the way to become an artist. 'For', he wrote, 'as the eye is often taken off the original to draw a bit at a time, it is possible to know no more of the original when the drawing is finished than before it was begun.'

This seems to me one of Hogarth's most significant and revealing remarks. Nikolaus Pevsner, in his book *The Englishness of English Art*, suggests that a tendency towards the linear may be considered as one of the peculiarities of that Englishness. What is it that the copied line, repeatedly broken off and resumed, has lost? Not perhaps its 'plastic' value, but certainly its continuity and its 'plasmatic' value – that dynamic thrust and vitality which can only come when the whole is grasped by a single act of the imagination. Only thus can the living form be recreated. Here it comes back to the need for empathy, the necessity for the artist to find in his own body an intuition of that form, just as he has lodged it in his head by a trained effort of memory: to 'fix forms and characters in my mind, and, instead of *copying* the lines, try to read the language, and if possible find the grammar of the art, by bringing into one focus the various observations I had made.' What he aimed at mastering were typical interplays and combinations of lines. There was no question of building up for himself a collection of individual forms; he sought rather, by a free and flexible association of their elements, to recreate an equivalent of those forms. 'Laying it down', he wrote, 'first as an axiom, that he who could by any means acquire and retain in his memory perfect ideas of the subjects he meant to draw, would have as clear a knowledge of the figure as a man who can write freely hath of the twenty-four letters of the alphabet and their infinite combinations.' 'A sort of technical memory' is how he describes this process of reconstructing in the mind what he had seen and analysed with the eye.

'Thus, with all the drawbacks which resulted from the circumstances I have mentioned, I had one material advantage over my competitors, viz. the early habit I thus acquired of retaining in my mind's eye, without coldly copying it . . ., whatever I intended to imitate.' So that 'be where I would, while my eyes were open, I was at my studies' and 'even my pleasures became a part of them.' Hogarth contrasted his method, based on a constant fidelity to life, with the characteristic procedures of conventional art in the eighteenth century. 'Whatever I saw, whether a remarkable incident or a striking object, became more truly to me a picture than one that was drawn by a camera obscura.' The vogue of the camera obscura at that time as an illusionist device is well known. Hogarth's truth was not illusion.

Hogarth was attracted by the grotesque and bizarre, and he was quite conscious of this bent of his mind: 'And thus the most striking objects, whether of beauty or deformity, were by habit the most easily impressed and retained in my imagination.'

What he had rejected, all that had been mapped out in art and had only to be tamely followed, the works of the past which even in his apprentice days he had been loath to copy, all this he naturally belittled. 'I grew so profane as to admire nature beyond pictures... I saw or fancied delicacies in the life so far surpassing the utmost efforts of imitation that when I drew the comparison in my mind I could not help uttering blasphemous expressions against the divinity even of Raphael Urbino, Correggio and Michael Angelo.'

This view, too, is characteristic of the Englishness of certain artists, if not of English art as a whole. Life, after all, with its untold potentialities and mysteries, extending *ad infinitum* beyond the insights of even the most imaginative vision, far outranges art. But this view would seem to apply more aptly to the philosopher than to the artist, and indeed, from Hogarth to Constable and beyond, it was a source of confusion, as also of piquant contradictions. Meanwhile, however reluctant Hogarth may have been to submit to the conventional methods of technical training, in 1725 he began attending an art school recently opened by Sir James Thornhill. There, amidst the appurtenances of art, he found at least one object which in his eyes represented the values and attractions of life: Thornhill's daughter, Jane, with whom he eloped in 1729. It was several years before the angry father acknowledged his son-in-law.

Hogarth painted two self-portraits: one full length, in side view, seated at his easel painting the comic muse; the other full face, in bust length, with his pug dog and his easel, the latter marked with a serpentine line and inscribed 'The line of Beauty and Grace.' He was a short, plain-faced man. The self-portrait with his pug, in the manner of a good Kit-Cat canvas, brings him vividly to life, with his large round head encased in a fur cap, the deep scar on his forehead of which he was proud (as are all egoists of any distinctive mark), his large, wide-open eyes with their lively, forthright glance, his short thick nose, firm mouth and wilful chin – a 'sort of knowing jockey look' as Leigh Hunt said of him. He prided himself on being well dressed and was fond of creature comforts. According to J.T. Smith in his *Life of Nollekens*, he had no objection to fulfilling his professional obligation of observing human behaviour in places of ill fame: 'My father knew Hogarth well, and I have often heard him declare that he revelled in the company of the drunken and profligate.' That he was sociable and outspoken one can readily believe. Pugnacious, stubborn and arrogant, he was always getting into quarrels. The first was with the architect William Kent. It was Lord Burlington, Kent's patron, who introduced into England the new Italian style of Palladian architecture, which Hogarth, in his sturdy Englishness, heartily disliked, more especially as it was regular architecture *par excellence*. To enrage Hogarth even more, William Kent had the presumption to design an altarpiece in an Italian style for St Clement Danes. Hogarth considered Pope as part of the Lord Burlington coterie; the poet was author of an epistle, 'Of the Use of Riches', in which he spitefully attacked Lord Chandos for his lavishness and bad taste. Hogarth's two prints on *Burlington Gate* (1724 and 1731) satirize their pretensions and malevolence. The fact that Pope's ideas of good and bad taste were very similar to his own mattered little to Hogarth; in the eighteenth century, ideas counted for much less than names and cliques. Very little was needed in the way of provocation for Hogarth to have a fling at the adversary.

It is a point worth emphasizing that he depended much more for a living on his prints than on his painting, partly perhaps because he made so many enemies among patrons and collectors. Prints, on the other hand, were bought by that broad, anonymous, middle-class public to which Hogarth had addressed himself from the beginning and with which he entered so readily into communication. To earn a living he had to obtain a fair price for his prints, but as soon as an artist achieved some popularity the pirates stepped in and flooded the market with cheap counterfeits. Hogarth himself describes the situation: 'The first plate I published, called the *Taste of the Town*...² had no sooner begun to take run but I found copies of it in the printshops selling for half the price whilst the originals were returned to me again. I was obliged to sell my plate for what these pirates pleased to give me, as there was no place of sale but at their shops.'

John Nichols, in his *Anecdotes*, identified eight counterfeit sets of *A Harlot's Progress* (1732). In 1735 Hogarth completed the admirable set of eight prints after his paintings of *A Rake's Progress*. But he did not put them on sale at once. In an open letter to an MP, Hogarth gave a circumstantial account of the piracies of the printsellers and proclaimed the artist's right to the due reward of his labours. He called for a law protecting him against pirates. His initiative was successful and the Engravers' Act, giving the artist the exclusive right to reproduce his designs, came into force on 15 June 1735.

For him this was only a beginning. He now took up the cudgels against the cosmopolitanism of both patrons and dealers, their rooted preference for an art of the past whose hollow vanities and popish religiosity had no connection with the needs of contemporary England. In June 1737 he addressed a letter under the pseudonym of 'Britophil' to the *St James's Evening Post* in which he defended the work of his father-in-law Sir James Thornhill and struck a blow against the dealers: 'It is their interest to depreciate every English work, as hurtful to their trade, of continually importing ship-loads of dead Christs, Holy Families, Madonnas and other dismal dark subjects, neither entertaining nor ornamental.'

With his keen eye for satire he drew a picture of the scene between dealer and customer which is as good as a stage play. The customer bluntly observes: 'That grand Venus, as you are pleased to call it, has not beauty enough for the character of an English cook-maid.' Here are the unmistakable accents of that sturdy, insular, middle-class nationalism portrayed by Dickens. The dealer, Mr Bubbleman, exclaims: 'Sir, I find that you are no connoisseur; the picture, I assure you, is in Alesso Baldminetto's [*sic*] second and best manner.' Then, 'spitting in an obscure place, and rubbing it with a dirty handkerchief,' Bubbleman skips to the other end of the room and exclaims: 'There's an amazing touch! A man should have this picture a twelvemonth in his collection before he can discover half its beauties.' The overawed customer is thus duped into buying it: he 'gives a vast sum for the picture... and bestows a frame worth fifty pounds on a frightful thing... not worth so many farthings.'

Not only paintings were imported but painters as well. 'If a painter comes from abroad, his being an exotic will be much in his favour; and if he has address enough to persuade the public that he has brought a new discovered mode of colouring, and paints his faces all red, all blue, or all purple, he has nothing to do but to hire one of these painted tailors as an assistant... and my life for his success.' Such was the Frenchman J. B. Van Loo, who arrived from Paris at this very time, in 1737, and soon monopolized the portrait market in London.

In 1745, to sell his pictures of the *Harlot*, the *Rake*, the *Four Times of Day* and the *Strolling Actresses*, he organized an auction of his own, without the interference of the picture dealers. But it was an ill-devised affair, the stimulus of competitive bidding being replaced by bids recorded in writing in a book, and it yielded poor results. On the admission ticket he engraved a 'Battle of the Pictures' satirizing the pompous subjects of the Old Masters, St Andrew, the Flaying of Marsyas, the Rape of Europa, the pictures all stacked up in an interminable series behind their respective prototypes. The moral was that such art is but the mechanical repetition of a stereotype, the original inspiration being gone for ever. Hogarth rightly saw that an art divorced from the society around it must be lifeless. Why, he asked himself, did art flourish in Greece and stagnate in England? In Greece civic sense and religion combined to give the artist his due place and due honour, and such was no longer the case.

A living art was the reverse of all that and he proposed, not only his own, but that which he hoped to bring into existence. For this, schools were needed and he helped to establish one after his father-in-law's death in 1734, donating to it all the objects he had inherited from Sir James. His idea was for a school run on co-operative lines. He was community-minded, but no great democrat. He saw no point in teaching everyone to draw. 'Giving lads of all ranks a little knowledge of everything is almost as absurd as it would be to instruct shopkeepers in oratory, that they may be thus enabled to talk people into buying their goods.' Tuition was therefore not to be free. He was alive to the danger of encouraging vocations which, socially speaking, were useless or unnecessary. 'Men will be rendered miserable which might have lived comfortably enough by almost any manufactory, and will wish that they had been taught to make a shoe, rather than thus devoted to the polite arts.'

Opposed to any popularized schooling of artists, he was also opposed to the creation of an Academy on the French model, which he regarded as a mere school of imitation serving to maintain a tradition and impose a set code of rules. He agreed with Voltaire that the academy in France had produced nothing but 'mannerists and imitators'. Not surprisingly for a self-educated artist, he saw no point in making the journey to Italy and poring over the art of the past; this approach did not stimulate genius but merely cut it off from nature.

He was an inveterate xenophobe. He never went to Italy. But France, the ridiculous and hated rival of old England, was just across the water and in 1743 he made the trip to

Paris. He found (as most people do) what he expected to find: 'a farcical pomp of war, parade of religion and bustle with very little business – in short, poverty, slavery and insolence, with an affectation of politeness.' In 1748 he took advantage of a lull in the long struggle for supremacy between France and England to make a second trip. At Calais, his eye was caught by the heraldic devices on the fortified English Gate, a relic of the English occupation of the town. While he was sketching them, a soldier laid hands on him and he was arrested as a spy; though soon released, he was sent back by the first available ship. As soon as he got home he took his revenge by painting *Calais Gate* or *The Roast Beef of Old England* (Tate Gallery). As always with Hogarth, everything tells in this subtle and suggestive tissue of relationships. The 'farcical pomp of war' is summed up in two lean and ragged soldiers with bowls of thin soup, while an inn servant passes by, staggering under the weight of a sirloin of beef on which a fat, sleek friar, licking his lips, lays a finger. Just behind them, the vertical chains of the drawbridge overhang the figures ominously; chains of servitude, they also suggest the hangman's rope. Beneath the gateway can be seen the spikes of the portcullis. On the cross at the top of the gate is a crow. In the distance beyond it is a religious procession, with a cross, a surpliced priest and kneeling worshippers. Slumped in the foreground, in the shadow of the arch framing the picture on the right, with an onion beside him, is a plaided Jacobite wringing his hands and lamenting the fate that, since the '45, has brought him to such a pass. Just across from him, called perhaps by the Scotsman, three hideous crones huddle together (undoubtedly an allusion to the witches in *Macbeth*), three fishwives showing off amidst their wares a monstrous, leering skate. Above them is the figure of Hogarth sketching the gate. For him, roast beef epitomized the superiority of England and English liberty, as opposed to the darkness of superstition and the shackles of oppression. It is as if the figures were engaged in a ballet centring on the sirloin, which has just arrived from England for the English inn at Calais, the Lion d'Argent. As so often with Hogarth, even in his outside scenes, the light is not quite sunlight, the contrasts are over-emphasized and the white highlights smack of artifice.

The xenophobic satire of this picture has its counterpart in the domestic satire of the *March to Finchley* (Thomas Coram Foundation for Children, London), which shows the English guards at Tottenham Court Turnpike marching northwards to put down the Jacobite rising of 1745. Again the rendering of sunlight in this open-air scene is not quite natural. But a power that can only be described as epic – it being understood that an epic of this period can only be a burlesque epic – pervades this work by the man whom his friend Fielding aptly called 'a comic history-painter', for he here commemorates one of the mass movements of modern times in a spirit which, harking back to those of ancient times from the Trojan War on, is yet a spirit of robust parody. The warrior's leave-taking as seen here is indeed a far cry from Hector's solemn leave-taking of Andromache. One woman, pressing her hand against her swollen belly, clings to the leading soldier's right arm, while another, presumably with more legitimate claims on him, tugs fiercely at his left arm. On the right a tipsy guardsman has collapsed in a puddle, while one of his mates tries to revive him with a swig from the can and a cavalry officer's satchel with the royal monogram GR lies in the mud. The middle distance, too, is enlivened with picturesque incidents, like the milkmaid kissing a soldier and inadvertently emptying her pail into a hat. Every detail tells, clear and sharp. From the windows of the house on the right, at the sign of King

Charles, the girls who have entertained the soldiery wave good-bye. In the distance the troops can be seen marching away in good order, but the eye continually reverts to the three admirably balanced groups in the foreground, skilfully if somewhat artificially lighted. Satirical in his xenophobia, he was equally satirical in his patriotism. This strikes a balance, but it irritated George II, to whom the work had been naïvely offered, so that Hogarth sarcastically dedicated it 'To His Majesty the King of Prussia, an encourager of Arts and Sciences.'

Like the progressive artists and architects of today, Hogarth felt that a painter should work for society and that society should help him to do so by exhibiting his works in public buildings. The great hospitals, St Bartholomew's for example, gave him just such an opportunity. In 1739 a philanthropic seaman, Captain Thomas Coram, obtained a royal charter for the establishment of his Foundling Hospital. A governor of it from the start, Hogarth saw it as a further opportunity for painters to exhibit and publicize their work. At his prompting, artists donated portraits and history paintings to the Foundling Hospital. Here, independent of any academic setting, was 'the first permanent public museum of English art' (Lawrence Gowing). The first periodic exhibitions were those sponsored by the Society of Artists from 1760 onwards.

Many of Hogarth's ideas seem to have been the fruit of a compensatory aggression. As such, they were apt to be confused and contradictory. His ideas about 'the grand style' are a case in point. He realized how much it had always depended on the social system, on Christianity in particular, or rather on Catholicism, whose traditional imagery had been rejected by Anglicanism. The great religious subjects had therefore been ousted and mythological subjects, which in Catholic countries had always been coupled with them, accordingly lost their *raison d'être*. Nonetheless, almost in the same breath he deplored the fact that this grand style received no encouragement in England, though the English excelled in it, or would, if their religion gave any scope for it. He carries his argument now in one direction, now in another. But here the influence of his spiritual father, Thornhill, is probably at work, and the rankling of old grievances goaded his instinctive jealousy and arrogance to seek revenge.

So after making his mark with the *Harlot's Progress* and confirming it with the *Rake's Progress* (c. 1733, Sir John Soane's Museum, London), he determined to enter a new field. 'The puffing in books about the grand style of history painting put him upon trying how that might take...' Accordingly in 1735-36, undaunted by his inexperience, he painted his vast *Pool of Bethesda*, 'with figures seven foot high', for the great staircase at St Bartholomew's Hospital. Its contradictions are evident. Except for the central figure, which must be one of the feeblest effigies of Christ in existence, the Gospel scene turns into a faintly sinister comedy enacted by grimacing housewives, while the rich woman's attendants – she is Hogarth's sole nude, and not a very appealing one – keep the poor folk away from the healing waters. The colour scheme is reminiscent of a cheap holy picture. If Hogarth had continued in this manner, he would be a forgotten man. He seems here to be masquerading as a feeble northern imitator of Raphael – the Raphael of *St Peter and St John Healing the Sick* and of the cartoons then at Hampton Court.

He also painted *The Good Samaritan* for St Bartholomew's. Ten years later, in 1746, for the Foundling Hospital, he turned again to a biblical theme, *Moses Brought to Pharaoh's*

Daughter. It was an apt theme for the Hospital and he showed a sensitive touch in his handling of it. A charming little Moses, clinging to a handmaiden's skirts, gazes shyly at Pharaoh's daughter who, reclining in royal ease, holds out her hand to him. Reminiscent of Van Dyck and Raphael, the scene is pervaded by a luminous sheen, reaching into the green shadows diffused around the figures, and sustaining a subtle colour scheme. But it is no masterpiece. He fails to quicken these traditional forms, as great religious painters have always quickened them, from the primitives to Delacroix and beyond, with those personal emotions and that heightened reality which alone can renew such familiar, ever-recurring figures. Horace Walpole's comment remains all too true: 'The burlesque turn of his mind mixed itself with the most serious subjects.'[3]

Though this picture and the *Pool of Bethesda* may have their admirers, there seems no point in dwelling further on Hogarth's efforts in this field. That he entered it at all was due to the characteristic pugnacity of the man and a curiously indirect method of justifying his usual style of painting: if I have chosen my familiar style, he seems to be saying, I have done so freely and not because I am unable to adopt another, which is supposed to be more difficult, but in fact is not – judge for yourself. And so one can. For it is evident that, were it not for the solid tradition of grand-style subjects on which Hogarth unconsciously bases himself, he would probably lapse into parody. An itch to attempt the grand style came over him periodically. In 1748 it led to a disconcerting outburst of vulgarity. The grand-style picture of that year, verging as usual on parody, was *Paul Before Felix*. But, as if to show that this was the real thing, he went a step further and made an etching of it, 'in the true Dutch taste', entitled *Paul Before Felix Burlesqued* – 'designed and etched', he wrote, 'in the ridiculous manner of Rembrandt.' For that manner, says his commentator, he had a sovereign contempt. But how could he help adding character to his own Dutch manner – the worried look of Felix, the dismay of the high priest, a spreading sense of agitation and an overwrought emotionalism. It is not character that is expressed in those pictures which commemorate great moments in human history or religious legend, but a mysterious confrontation transcending any single personality. Even the character of Judas, in pictures of the Last Supper, is conveyed by a purse or the colour of his hair rather than by a grimace or a facial feature or any evident meanness. Before this mystery, Hogarth's imagination stops short. He proves himself to be a genuine and robust descendant of the Flemish masters. Thus is he seen, nowadays, but not thus did he see himself; for if, on the walls of the rooms in his pictures, Italian religious and mythological paintings are often ridiculed, nonetheless, in the last scene of *Marriage à la Mode* (National Gallery) the tasteless mediocrity of the parvenu's home is indicated by the crude still lifes hanging on the wall – and they are in the Flemish manner.

There is, however, one link between Hogarth and the grand style and that is the serpentine line set forth in the 1745 self-portrait and extolled in *The Analysis of Beauty* of 1753. As early as 1745 the antiquary, George Vertue, noted that Hogarth was apt to hold forth on the inimitable beauty of the serpentine curve. Never was a painter of social satire so preoccupied with aesthetics, so obsessed by theories and by this one in particular. *The Analysis of Beauty* is, in a sense, a eulogy of the serpent considered as an aesthetic symbol and he presented it with one of those strikingly apt quotations which he was never at a loss for, unlettered though he was.

So varied he, and of his tortuous train
Curl'd many a wanton wreath in sight of Eve,
To lure her eye,

three lines from Milton which, with reference to the serpent, define a sensuous, wanton beauty and which associate the moving, living S-curve with the shifting play of mood and desire. Line should not perhaps be taken literally, as with Blake, to mean the contour of a body. Nonetheless, they both shared the same belief in the virtue of the essential, dynamic line; both aimed at rendering a principle and a purpose rather than any visible manifestation. In an oil sketch like *The Dance (The Happy Marriage VI)*, linear vision is present by implication: it has been left to the spectator's eye to supply and retrace the lines.

Hogarth was full of ideas, but when it came to sorting them out and writing them down he needed the help of his friends. One was Dr Benjamin Hoadly, whom he portrayed at least three times. Another was Dr Kennedy, who supplied him with the passage from Lomazzo quoting Michelangelo to the effect that a figure should always be 'pyramidal, serpent-like and multiplied by one, two and three'. 'The greatest grace and life a picture can have is that it expresses motion', wrote Hogarth. 'Now there is no form so fit to express this motion as that of the flame of fire... an element most active of all others.'

In illustrating his *Analysis*, Hogarth figured the serpentine curve not as a plane but as a volume unfolding inside a pyramid or coiling round a cone. It is difficult to trace this idea to any one source, for it is found in one form or another in Leonardo, Alberti, Du Fresnoy and Roger de Piles. Alberti dwells on the virtue of ascending spirals, as of licking flames, and like Hogarth he applies it to hair. Du Fresnoy cites serpents and flames as suggesting and symbolizing vital movement.

So Hogarth took up arms against the straight line and those who used it in representing the human figure, and like his predecessors he connected the serpentine curve with the baroque aesthetic of movement: 'The serpentine line which, as it dips out of sight... and returns again... not only gives play to the imagination, and delights the eye... but informs it likewise of the quantity and variety of the contents.'

He owed something – though he never acknowledged it – to the ideas of Francis Hutcheson, an early eighteenth-century philosopher who, in his system of aesthetics, had made much of the concepts of unity and variety. To join the two terms indissolubly together and yet give to variety a primacy whose importance had escaped Hutcheson, Hogarth coined the term 'composed variety'.

A certain animosity, a pervading spirit of dissent, seems to underlie the exposition of his ideas. It comes out in his chapter on symmetry. Is symmetry pleasing to the eye? No, but it is to the mind, to the judgment. What the eye demands is a subtler equilibrium, attainable by turning the object and thereby breaking up its uniformity: 'Thus the profile of most objects, as well as faces, are rather more pleasing than their full fronts.' And he praises the grace of a head turned a little to one side or somewhat inclined, as is seen so often in his portraits (that of the exquisite Mrs Garrick, for example).

Any necessary symmetry should be countered by dissymmetry and vice versa. The oval should be preferred to the circle, the triangle to the square and the pyramid to the cube. He prefers the odd number, as the ancients did. As far as architecture is concerned, buildings should be 'varied and picturesque'. Ranged against him in this were Lord Burlington, Kent and the Palladians, with their strict and static system of proportions. Hogarth was all for diversity and movement, for unexpected elements advancing or receding. He saw the diversity he liked in the gothic of Westminster Abbey, and in the discreet baroque of Wren, St Paul's or St Mary-le-Bow, the latter perhaps the church 'the most elegantly varied... of any in Europe'. By the picturesque he meant an aesthetic of sensation and tension sustained by the imagination. His views on the subject are set forth in the curious chapter devoted to 'intricacy'. In using this term he seems to have had in mind not so much an aspect of things as a particular relation of subject to object induced by tantalizing design and elusive movement. Intricacy gives pleasure because it 'leads the eye a wanton kind of chase'. It keeps the mind alert: that is the essential point. 'Pursuing is the business of our lives... Every arising difficulty... enhances the pleasure.' In pursuit and exertion lies the pleasure of the chase. 'Even cats will risk the losing of their prey to chase it over again', and 'the eye hath this sort of enjoyment in winding walks.' Hogarth's way of seeing things, as gradually revealed in the pages of his book, is pre-eminently sensual. It had been so from childhood. He describes his reaction, when 'very young', to the 'beguiling movement' of a country dance: 'my eye eagerly pursued a favourite dancer through all the windings of the figure... bewitching to the sight.' And he goes on: 'The beauty of intricacy lies in contriving winding shapes... This principle also recommends modesty in dress, to keep up our expectations, and not suffer them to be too soon gratified.' It is the suspense of the strip-tease that is the essential; the end result is an anti-climax. Here is his definition of that principle: 'Intricacy in form, therefore, I shall define to be that peculiarity in the lines which compose it that leads the eye a wanton kind of chase.' This notion may be said to underlie the English garden with its winding walks, the figures of the dance, and all Romantic art. Hogarth has indeed some good things to say and it is 'a richer and subtler book than current ideas of it lead one to expect' (Lawrence Gowing). It deepens one's understanding of his work. In Italian comedy 'the attitudes of the harlequins are ingeniously composed of certain little, quick movements of the head, hands and feet, some of which shoot out as it were from the body in straight lines, or are twirled about in little circles.' One sees what Hogarth means by lines.

In the chapter on proportions, he refuses to see beauty in terms of this 'mathematical' notion – he disliked Dürer. Instead, he extols the 'living machines of nature' (one of them man) which are all the more beautiful for the variety and complexity of the movements they have to perform. Fish, 'as they have fewer motions than other creatures, so' are their forms less remarkable for beauty.'

While on the one hand Hogarth defines the picturesque in conjunction with beauty, on the other he foreshadows the sublime which, in 1756, became one of the categories used by Edmund Burke in his famous essay.[4] The grandiose was no concern of his, but he emphasized the broad sweep of an Oriental costume or state robes; and it is clear that he aimed at this majestic effect when he portrayed *Benjamin Hoadly, Bishop of Winchester* (Tate Gallery), whose costume and ornaments so nobly fill the canvas.

Hogarth, however, was not concerned with style for its own sake. The style whose principles he formulated was a rococo derivative of baroque and, in his mind, applicable to life; it was as well suited to furniture design as to painting.

He was not to get off so lightly from this venture into aesthetics and literature. He had many enemies, and his own rashness left him continually open to their attack. His attempts seemed comic in the eyes of others, and in 1754 Paul Sandby – who will be dealt with here only as a watercolour landscapist, but who was a recognized figure in English painting – issued a series of prints ridiculing the line of beauty, which was shown running over the leg, wooden leg and crutch of a cripple.

For some reason Hogarth gave over the pugnacious independence he had maintained all his life, and in his old age he rallied to the new sovereign George III and his prime minister Lord Bute; even before that, in 1757, he had accepted the appointment of Serjeant Painter to the King. Acting in the ministerial interest he published his satirical print *The Times* (1762) and this brought him into collision with the two demagogues Wilkes and Churchill. They retaliated fiercely, and Sandby joined in the fun with a telling satire on *The Line of Buty*. Hogarth's last years were embittered by these conflicts, and he died in 1764, prematurely aged by the vexations they brought upon him.

When Charles Lamb said, 'Other pictures we look at, his prints we read,' he had in mind the prompt and ready recognition of the objects represented. This is not what is regarded as the most important element today, but rather the artist's personal touch. Of course there is no question of confusing intention and effect, but it can do no harm to understand what the intention was. I will, therefore, review his work as it developed in the course of his career. Having married Thornhill's daughter in 1729, he began painting, as he says himself, small conversation pieces ('from 10 to 15″ high') which, however, did not prove to be very profitable. This was a standard type of picture in the England of that day, a group of figures psychologically interrelated. Not many of Hogarth's seem to have survived. *The Sleeping Congregation* of 1728 (it is 21″ high) may be one. The *Conquest of Mexico*, however, of 1731-32 attains the respectable size of 57¼″. It is a conversation piece and something more, for it represents child actors performing Dryden's *Indian Emperor or The Conquest of Mexico* in the ornate setting of a private theatre. Children acting before adults and other children, such is the subject and in effect it touches the theatre only by way of parody. The result is a fresh and forthright piece of painting, proficiently enhanced with glazing and transparencies, creating a living presence with the minimum of modelling; there is little attempt to indicate shading, but the full luminosity of flesh and fabric is brought out; above all, though faced with a complicated problem of placing, he succeeds admirably in relating all the figures involved. Ten years later, in the *Graham Children*, he did not succeed so well.

The conversation piece, set sometimes out of doors, sometimes indoors, was held by the English at that time to be characteristic of their homely simplicity, but its Dutch affiliation is unmistakable. The most *telling* conversation pictures in the world are the silent ones of Vermeer, and Hogarth is no Vermeer, nor even a Terborch. Impatient of talk, he wants action, and naturally enough he sees it, on canvas, as an imitation and in a sense an illustration of the stage. And so he painted *A Scene from The Tempest, Falstaff Examining his Recruits* and above all the main scene of *The Beggar's Opera* by John Gay which, produced in 1728, was then at the height of its popularity: an entertaining satire of contemporary society and indeed a challenging exposure of its corruptions. From 1728 to 1731 Hogarth painted six versions of the scene from *The Beggar's Opera* in which the two women plead for the life of Macheath, the highwayman. Before being given a Marxist slant by Brecht, Gay's satire had become a celebration of anarchic values. In Brecht, the society from which, after all, Macheath had sprung was inevitably affected by his existence; in England, that society hastened to take to its heart its glorious outlaw, as medieval society had done in the case of Robin Hood; forty years later even the bourgeois-minded Boswell could indulge in a reverie in which he identified himself with the highwayman.

The Tate Gallery version of *The Beggar's Opera* is a superb composition on a monumental scale, the first in which the young painter showed his powers. He had not yet arrived at the views set forth in *The Analysis of Beauty* and the composition is almost symmetrically arranged round the central figure of the hero, whose bright red coat lights up the canvas, and whose fine presence is in no way diminished by the irons shackling his legs. Four figures grouped round Macheath occupy the centre of the stage: on his right the fat jailer puts out his hand towards his kneeling daughter, the deep blue of her dress set off by a large yellow sash, her angular, graceless attitude and her father's lumbering figure contrasting with the elegantly dressed informer Peachum on the other side, and *his* daughter, the charming Polly, all in filmy white, who is interceding on behalf of Macheath. The black line of the latter's hat leans to this side, pointing straight at Polly.

The room, with its dim barred windows and steep staircase on the right, provides a monumental setting; and Hogarth showed a sure touch in distributing the lights and shadows. Comparison of the different versions of this subject reveals how much he had learned about painting in the space of three years. In the first version the right-hand wall, instead of coming forward, seems to slip away; it is no surprise to find later that some of his didactic prints suffer from faulty perspective. Other early pictures show that he was not yet master of his brush; in them, indeed, he gives the impression of being a naïve painter.

He was passionately fond of the stage. One of his best friends was David Garrick, whom he portrayed as Richard III, the actor's first successful role in 1741. Later, in 1757, he painted Garrick and his wife in an exquisite conversation piece.

But stage action, however enthralling, is life at second hand. It was life at first hand, with which he himself was thoroughly familiar, that Hogarth now set himself to record. He turned his thoughts, he wrote, 'to a still newer way of proceeding, viz. painting and engraving modern moral subjects'. For 'painters and writers never mention in the historical way any intermediate species of subjects between the sublime and the grotesque.' He therefore decided to 'compose pictures on canvas similar to representations on the stage; and farther hope that they will be tried by the same test, and criticized by the same criterion.' 'My picture is my stage', he wrote, 'and men and women are my players, who by means of certain actions and gestures are to exhibit a dumb show.'

Here then was the great project (perhaps less clearly and consciously conceived than he says) which Hogarth carried out superbly and which made him the greatest popular painter of all time. Making periodic incursions into the grand style like forays into enemy territory, this art of his was always deliberately couched in a popular key, wholly and readily recognizable as such and intentionally didactic. 'Subjects of most consequence are those that most entertain and improve the mind and are of public utility... If this be true, comedy in painting stands first as it is most capable of all these perfections'. 'Ocular demonstration will convince sooner than ten thousand volumes.'

In his emphasis on the didactic, however, how far was he acting on his own impulse? Of course, being good-natured and confident, like many people at that time, that mankind was moving into a better age, he honestly sought to help men forward and believed that the best way of doing so was to show them life as it is with all its pitfalls and follies. What Dickens was to be in the nineteenth century, the spokesman of a whole class, Hogarth was already a century earlier, and for the same section of society – the productive middle class, then at the start of its formidable rise and not yet cut off from life by a petrifying moral code. Rather, it was elaborating that code, for in 1735, in the London area alone, the Society for the Reformation of Manners instituted proceedings in 99 380 cases. No wonder

William Hogarth (1697-1764)
Scene from the Beggar's Opera VI, 1729-31. Oil on canvas. (22½ × 29⅞″). Tate Gallery, London.

there was a demand for 'moral subjects'. But looking more closely one is aware of an element of cunning that runs through nearly the whole of Hogarth's œuvre: a plural but convergent reading of each work is put forward, but there are divergent, underlying readings. One commentator went so far as to suggest that, for controversial subjects on which he had produced a picture, Hogarth kept in reserve an alternative version in case the wind turned.

He had no lack of ideas. One of his early pictures, *The Christening* (1729-30), is full of those innuendoes and implications that characterize so much of his work. A tissue of ironies contradicts the apparent relations between the figures making the scene in effect an anti-conversation. The seated mother is accepting another man's attentions. The father is admiring himself in a looking glass. The clergyman holding the baby ogles the pretty girl beside him, while a meddling child upsets the basin of water. Here, connecting the moods and feelings of these people, runs a serpentine line indeed. From now on Hogarth, like a good comic writer, kept these 'ideas' in mind and made the most of them; some reappear in the *Harlot's Progress*, some in *Marriage à la Mode*.

George Vertue describes the development of the *Harlot's Progress*. 'He began a small picture of a common harlot, supposed to dwell in Drury Lane, just rising about noon out of bed, and at breakfast... this whore's deshabillé careless and a pretty countenance and air – this thought pleased many. Some advised him to make another to it as a pair, which he did. Then other thoughts increased and multiplied by his fruitful invention, till he made six different subjects which he painted so naturally... that it drew everybody to see them.' He went on to engrave six plates from them, and these attracted nearly 1200 subscribers at a guinea a set.

Here, in 1731, was the first 'cartoon strip'. The six paintings were sold in 1745 to Alderman William Beckford. They perished ten years later in a fire at Fonthill, Beckford's house, judging by the prints, an irreparable loss.

Of the colours, therefore, nothing is known, but Hogarth never surpassed the expressive power of these six prints. The procuress ensnaring the country girl on her arrival in London is an unforgettable figure. Cupidity, cynicism and cruelty lurk in the very movement of her mouth. Everything about this face, even the beauty patches, tells of corruption and vice. What chance has an innocent girl against the wiles of this practised bawd? She is doomed from the start to degradation, victimization and death, and in tracing her downward path Hogarth leaves the moral implications to speak for themselves. Pity is shown, but discreetly shown. It makes itself felt in the fourth scene in Bridewell where, as in a circle of the *Inferno*, the women prisoners are set to beating hemp with wooden mallets under the eye of a cruel guard. Urging Mary to work harder, he threatens to shackle her hands with a carcan, which has already been applied to another prisoner, while a woman behind her steals her kerchief. Mary stands out as the only gentle soul among these hardened, sneering wretches.

This is drama in the manner of the Japanese Kabuki. Everything is true and topical, and instantly recognizable as such in a town which was still a close-knit community where people knew each other. Any Londoner of that day would have been able to identify the procuress as Mother Needham, the magistrate as Justice Gonson, and Mary as Mary Hackabout, a notorious woman of the town who had just been taken in a round up by the police.

Beginning with this first series of story-pictures, Hogarth's satirical art has a double orientation: an obvious moral lesson remorselessly driven home, and an implied criticism not only of manners but also of taste. In plate two, where Mary quarrels with her Jewish protector, the walls are hung with large religious paintings. These, then, were among the status symbols of the ladies of the town and, the spectator is invited to conclude, that is the only place worth putting them. A Negro boy with a plumed turban brings in the kettle, and when Mary kicks over the tea table to enable her lover to make off in the general confusion, a pet monkey scurries away under a shower of scalding water. All this represents the bogus luxury of a bogus, unproductive class. In plate three she has become the mistress of a notorious thief and the religious paintings, except for a vague *Sacrifice of Abraham*, have been replaced by two prints, one representing Macheath, which is predictable enough; but the other – a malicious touch, this – represents Dr Sacheverell, the rabble-rousing preacher who some years before had been at the centre of the factional strife between Whigs and Tories.

With Hogarth, the need to express his sense of popular epic alternated with his genius for the dramatic. This gave rise to large pictures like *Southwark Fair*, which owes something to Jacques Callot's *Impruneta Fair*. But Hogarth differs from Callot in this, that whatever the crowd he assembles he organizes it in distinct groups animated by separate tensions and specific occupations, while at the same time marking it by concentrated shafts of light. Often it is one figure in his compositions towards whom the attention of the others is directed and who thus directs the spectator's gaze.

Hogarth was at the height of his powers when, about 1733, he painted the eight pictures of *A Rake's Progress*, admirable small-size canvases ($24\frac{1}{2} \times 29\frac{1}{2}''$). In the second picture, which shows the rake's levée, the unreality of the scene is marked. The rake, whose foolishness is inscribed in his face, seems lost amidst a roomful of parasites and turns in bewilderment towards an unsavoury-looking ruffian standing behind him. Not even the kneeling jockey holding the cup won by his horse is in his line of vision. Each of the other figures – the musician at the harpsichord, the fencer pointing his sword, the landscape gardener, etc. – sums up his trade with an apposite gesture, like so many signboards, each standing alone in a dimension of his own. The play of light links up their varied movements, holding them together in a dominant tonality of green and blue.

The third picture, the Tavern Scene, is the most brilliant of the series, and indeed one of Hogarth's finest paintings. A lozenge-shaped composition resting on an inverted triangle, unstable, high-keyed and vibrant, it reposes in the foreground on a green mass, full of rococo twists and turns, made up of the clothes already thrown off by the buxom girl who is now about to pull off her shoes and stockings. The befuddled rake has fallen backwards, partly on a chair, partly on the lap of a girl who has already relieved him of his watch, which she hands to an accomplice. From brunette to blonde, from one bonnet to the next, along a succession of heads turning this way and that, Hogarth as usual leads the eye beginning with the girl undressing in the left foreground, proceeding to the rake on the right and circling back by way of the girls sitting behind the table. One girl, standing on a chair at the apex of the upper triangle, seems to be setting fire to a map of the world. Of the figures of Roman emperors on the wall, all have been mutilated except one, that of Nero. The bourgeois painter exposes the destructive forces of profligacy and decadence. Sensuali-

William Hogarth (1697-1764)

A Rake's Progress, Scene II : The Rake's Levée, or Surrounded by Artists and Professors, c. 1733. Oil on canvas. (24½ × 29½").
Trustees of Sir John Soane's Museum, London.

A Rake's Progress, Scene III : The Tavern Scene, or The Orgy, c. 1733. Oil on canvas. (24½ × 29½"). ▷
Trustees of Sir John Soane's Museum, London.

ty at this table is taking a turn for the worse. Two rivals face each other on either side of the loving couple: one brandishes a knife, while the other spews a mouthful of gin into her face. Hogarth, perhaps with his friend Hayman, had seen these things. He had frequented these evil haunts, as a journalist goes in search of the truth. But he must have contrived to

mingle duty with pleasure. Whatever the anecdote represented, the painter's sensuality is obvious from his painting itself.

Most of these genre scenes deal with stock subjects. Hogarth must have seen at least a print of Jan Steen's picture, now in the Louvre, of similar doings in an evil haunt; in it a youth has his head on one prostitute's lap, while another hands his watch to an old bawd. The two later prints *Beer Street* and *Gin Lane* were based on two subjects by Bruegel, *Lean Fare* and *Rich Fare*.

An ironic genre scene like the *Rake's Marriage* and a dramatic incident like his *Arrest* have less of the characteristic dynamism of the series than the powerful collective scenes, almost epic in scale, which are set in a gaming house, a prison and a madhouse; all three make play with rich chiaroscuro effects, the last showing an even more singular mastery than the tavern scene. The figures are more widely distributed in the dim space of a large room, forming three groups, each representing a different mood of what might be called picturesque insanity: three madmen on the left, one receiving a gleam of light on an unfeeling forehead; two fine ladies in brightly coloured dresses, looking about them with amused curiosity and fluttering their fans among these living dead; and the foreground group around the naked, inert, bewildered rake, in whom Paulson sees a reference to the stock figure of Christ deposed from the Cross; this last is by no means unlikely, for a spirit of mischievous parody is often present in Hogarth, directed not at religion but at religious painting. The girl whom, in the first picture, the young heir and future rake had deserted in her pregnancy, sending her away with a handful of guineas, now reappears, having followed him at a distance like a shadow. She kneels beside him, relieving what are doubtless his last moments with her tender and compassionate care. She is the most 'sentimental' figure in the series and thus not a little tedious.

The paint, applied with the easy freedom and fluency of watercolours, yet nonetheless rich and creamy, renders the fabrics particularly well, setting them off with gleaming highlights and coloured shading. Though his brushwork is sometimes a little contrived for the sake of his public, it is all the more important to give their due to his natural gifts. His sketches are most worthy of attention; *The Staymaker*, for example, with its mixture of bland colours bathed in a muted light.

The Four Times of Day, painted in 1736-37, does not tell a connected story. Each scene has its own figures and its appropriate action. *Morning* is one of the few canvases by Hogarth in which the lyricism of a given time and place is caught, despite the prim silhouette of the old maid (in whom Fielding recognized his Bridget Alworthy) walking to church in the dim light of a snowy morning, while revellers sally forth from an all-night tavern and humble folk warm themselves at an open fire. The satire is at its sharpest in *Noon*, showing Huguenots coming out of the French church. With what skill and gusto Hogarth sets out groups and incidents, breaks up what is almost a crowd into distinct and separate episodes, giving rise to his usual ironies, mishaps and misunderstandings. Symbolism finds due expression at the hour of noon, and everybody seems to be eating or handling food. He even includes a blasphemous touch of grim humour concerning the inn, whose name was 'At the Sign of Good Food' and whose sign shows John the Baptist's head on a platter; amidst this confusion of appetites a Negro is shown running his hand over the milkmaid's breast.

At the same period, in 1737, he painted a picture whose loss is as irreparable as that of the Harlot paintings: *Strolling Actresses in a Barn*, a work which, though on an ampler scale, brings to mind a *Capricho* by Goya. It perished in a fire at Littleton Park in 1874, but luckily the admirable print made by Hogarth himself still exists. This large composition is the most whimsical and baroque of all his works. The serpentine line appears here with sensual connotations worthy of his successor Rowlandson, but handled more intensely. It sets off the swelling breasts of Flora and Diana, indeed it brings out with startling effectiveness the whole person of Diana – a happy combination of loose garments and smooth flesh rendered with precisely drawn movements. This barn, where the actresses are preparing for a performance of *The Devil to Pay in Heaven*, is packed to the very rafters with a variety of heraldic monsters and dragons which must have turned Hogarth's thoughts back to his early days as a silver-plate engraver. How absurd and delightful is the incongruity between the humble, untidy reality of these figures and the grandiloquence of the roles they are dressing for. Cupid, with wings and quiver on his back, has climbed a ladder to fetch a pair of stockings. The eagle of Jupiter is spooning pap into the mouth of a terrified infant. Night is darning Juno's stocking on an overturned wheelbarrow. Horace Walpole, who had no very high opinion of Hogarth's painting, regarded this picture as his masterpiece.

About 1743 came *Marriage à la Mode*. It is impossible to treat these pictures as pure art, as if they did not tell a story. He was right to see these series as his miniature theatre, a succession of scenes disposed with an astonishing sense of stagecraft. Take *The Marriage Contract*, in the Earl's drawing room. Two groups claim one's attention. On the left, bride and groom turn their backs on each other; the Viscount admires his own face in a mirror and his bride toys with her ring while receiving the attentions of the lawyer's clerk. On the right, the bride's father, a miserly, snub-nosed alderman, his shapeless legs encased in thick stockings; then the lawyer and the arrogant old Earl with a heap of the alderman's gold in front of him. His legs are well turned despite the gout, his coronet figures on his crutches, and with an imperious forefinger he points to his family tree – an unanswerable argument. Through the window just over his head can be seen the half-finished mansion in the Palladian style on which he has squandered his fortune. On the wall are portraits of his ancestors and large Italian-style compositions. Two dogs, apparently on the same leash, ignore each other. When the rake married a one-eyed spinster, a dog in a corner beside them could be seen making up to a one-eyed bitch. These suggestive parallel touches are characteristic of Hogarth.

His criticism of taste is constantly associated with the criticism of manners. To realize this, one need only note the grotesque *objets d'art* cluttering the mantelpiece in the young couple's house and the monstrous clock in the most absurdly expansive vein of rococo; or, in *The Countess's Morning Levée* (c. 1743), the miscellaneous collection of objects brought home from an auction and sorted out by a grinning Negro boy, not to mention the mythological paintings on the wall. Dutch painting is in turn criticized in the last scene showing the Countess's suicide in the home of her alderman father, who has relapsed into avarice after having spent so much on acquiring a lord for son-in-law. The walls of the room are hung with mediocre still lifes and, so that there should be no mistake, the commentator notes that no blame should attach to Mr Hogarth for these vulgar pictures: 'He obviously means to heap ridicule on these coarse and grotesque absurdities of the Dutch painters.'

This 'stage' of his, presented in terms of painting, calls of course for a dramatic art. In other words, contrary to the nature of visual art, it involves the time element. It involves time as measured by the clock, and not only the indefinable temporality in which Vermeer's figures live. In early Italian paintings, two successive actions of the same figure were often set out in the same picture. Hogarth is more skilful in organizing time-lags within the same painting between characters involved in the same action. For example, in the fifth scene, the killing of the young Earl by his wife's lover, the wounded Earl collapses (his body sagging in its fall, as Paulson notes again, like that of Christ in a Descent from the Cross),

William Hogarth (1697-1764)
Marriage à la Mode II : Shortly after the Marriage, c. 1743. Oil on canvas. (27½ × 35¾").
National Gallery, London.

while the lover escapes through the window on one side and the Watch bursts into the room on the other. In itself the simultaneity of the three actions is absurd. Actually, in a single *scene,* Hogarth concentrates the matter of a chapter in a novel, doing so by devices which are also a part of his genius. And then to back up these pictures and these series there were all the overtones that still fascinated Charles Lamb and that are now lost (and that, by way of compensation, leave the present-day spectator free to concentrate on the painting): the innumerable allusions, all that was topical, familiar, recognizable; the fact, for instance, that the rake was arrested on St David's day, for the picture includes a Welshman wearing a leek on his hat. Names were connected with every one of the eleven drunkards in *A Midnight Modern Conversation* (*c.* 1731, Collection of Mr and Mrs Paul Mellon, Upperville, Va), and this was one reason for the great popularity of this painting, which was copied so often that it is no longer quite certain which is the original.

About 1754, for the last time, Hogarth satirized public affairs with the four large paintings (40 × 50″) of *An Election* (Sir John Soane's Museum, London). Satirical hits at election practices, and all the corruption involved in them, provided a constant theme in both literature and caricature. Hogarth raised such satire to an exceptional level once again in close connection with contemporary history. The slogan 'Give us back our eleven days', for example, alludes to the adoption of the New Style calendar, which had shortened the year 1752 by eleven days. It was also the year of the tumultuous Oxford contest. Hogarth had never been more Flemish, but probably no Fleming has equalled the power of such a

William Hogarth (1697-1764)
Marriage à la Mode IV: The Countess's Morning Levée, c. 1743. Oil on canvas. (27¾ × 35¾″). National Gallery, London.

composition as *An Election Entertainment* and the sureness with which the multitude of figures is distributed, separated by their individual concern with their food, yet joined together by broad rhythmic patterns: a swirling movement and two triangles linked at their base, the lower one pointing downward, the upper one culminating in the female fiddler standing on a chair. This layout is comparable to that of the Tavern Scene in the *Rake's Progress*, the girl with a candle occupying the same position.

Chairing the Member (c. 1754) is laid out in the form of a pyramid, but a pyramid that is toppling over, drawn irresistibly to the left by the scampering sow and piglets and by the bent leg, pointing in the same direction, of the brawler who, with his stoutly plied staff, has inadvertently fetched one of the bearers a stunning blow on the head, thus depriving the chaired member of much-needed support. Something is happening at every point, and the eye is carried from one incident to the next, only lingering afterwards on the wealth of amusing details crammed into the picture.

But Hogarth, one soon discovers, wants to have it both ways, and this satirical pageant of the England of his time is not perhaps to be taken too seriously. In the second scene, *Canvassing for Votes*, open attempts at bribery are going on and a mob is pulling down the sign of the Royal Crown. But at the Lion in the foreground the effigy of the animal before the inn door is about to devour a fleur-de-lis. Whatever the mob's hostility to the crown, the British lion asserts itself and prevails.

William Hogarth (1697-1764)
A Midnight Modern Conversation, c. 1731. Oil on canvas. (30 × 64½″). From the Collection of Mr and Mrs Paul Mellon, Upperville, Virginia.

William Hogarth (1697-1764)

An Election: The Polling, c. 1754. Oil on canvas. (40 × 50″). Trustees of Sir John Soane's Museum, London.

Fielding saw in Hogarth the comic historian of contemporary manners. It is only recently that his genius for portraiture has been recognized and appreciated. He disliked the work of the established practitioners. Their portraits were too much like still lifes, too much like statues, motionless, idealized, overdressed in fine clothes. In art he objected to all that was static, so that landscape held no attraction for him. Life and movement were all in all to him.

A painter of genius cannot be confined to a set formula, not even his own, and the striking thing about Hogarth's first memorable portrait is its terrible immobility. This is his

William Hogarth (1697-1764)

An Election: Chairing the Member, c. 1754. Oil on canvas. (40 × 50″). Trustees of Sir John Soane's Museum, London.

picture of *Sarah Malcolm* (National Gallery of Scotland, Edinburgh) in the condemned cell at Newgate, a small canvas showing the murderess full length, sitting at a table, her arms crossed behind a rosary. Hogarth had paid her a visit two days before her execution, and he has conveyed remarkably well the sensations that must have been running in her head, such as are described by Moll Flanders in pretty much the same circumstances. Obduracy and fear are written in her features, her head is turned slightly to one side, as with tight-lipped composure she gazes vacantly before her. It is a fine piece of painting, the face with its pinkish headcloth laid in with deft touches of paint stands out in the gloom of the cell.

1740 is the date of the portrait of *Captain Thomas Coram* (Thomas Coram Foundation for Children, London), which he may have meant as a challenge to Van Dyck and his successors. One cannot help feeling that this portrait represents Hogarth quite as much as its ostensible subject, for his intentions are obvious and it is characteristic of him that he should wish to glorify a man of good will and at the same time to parody the men of pomp whose style of portraiture he disliked, such as Rigaud with his portrait of the financier *Samuel Bernard*. The whole tradition of the stately Van Dyck portrait is summed up in the column, the drapery and the expanse of sea visible in the left background. Portrayed in full length, a dignified figure in his long red coat, the philanthropic captain is anything but pompous; with his short legs and good-humoured smile, he has an irresistible air of kindly simplicity. In his right hand he holds the Royal Charter, obtained in 1739, of his hospital for foundlings. Having made his fortune in America as a shipwright and sea captain, first at Taunton, Massachusetts, then in Boston, he had returned to London and set up as a merchant at Rotherhithe. In the way of business he was continually walking from Rotherhithe to the City of London, and the sight of dead or abandoned children in the streets of the East End so much distressed him that he devoted his fortune and energies to their relief. The picture parodies the stock symbols and gestures of the grand style; for example, the globe, alluding not to empire but to world travel.

The portrait of *Bishop Hoadly* (c. 1743, Tate Gallery) is a demonstration rather than a parody. It anticipates the theories set forth in the *Analysis* concerning the 'awful dignity' of dress. Hence the ample lawn sleeves, their bluish white profusion setting off the complacent serenity of the face, and the easy sweep – quite unlike the figure of Captain Coram – of the black silk robes in their truly episcopal stateliness.

The portraits of women, which he did in his forties, are perfectly straightforward; an admirable example is that of *Mrs Salter* (1744, Tate Gallery). In it Hogarth reverts to pure modelling, almost in the academic manner, and transcends it in the immediacy and directness of this face, the awareness of human contact lighting the eyes, the openness of the features. He had never proved himself so fine a colourist, so fine a painter, as in the rendering of these graceful fabrics. His distinctive originality found even freer scope in the depiction of his six *Servants* (1750-55, Tate Gallery), and over these faces his brush plays to happiest effect. There is magic in his picture of the *Shrimp Girl* (c. 1745, National Gallery), which time has turned into Hogarth's Mona Lisa. No one can fail to respond at once to the radiance of her femininity, to the way in which this face, triumphantly overcoming – as Hogarth meant it to overcome – the immobility of the still-life portrait, is borne forward towards an invisible interlocutor, with all the intensity of her dark eyes, her parted lips, her moist, sensuous mouth. More than that: in this sketch one sees the painter at work, in the act of plying his brush; one sees this all but perfect face emerging from what is formlessness and becoming painting; a whitish impasto will be an ear, a bluish scumble will be the tie holding her bonnet.

If this is Hogarth's masterpiece as a sketch, his masterpiece in finished portraiture is probably the tender conversation piece of *David Garrick and his Wife* – Garrick seated at his writing desk, pen in hand, his young, attractive wife behind him, playfully reaching over his head with a dancing movement to snatch the pen from his hand. Never had Hogarth applied himself with such loving care to the rendering of embroideries, lace,

William Hogarth (1697-1764)

◁ *Captain Thomas Coram*, 1740. Oil on canvas. (94 × 58"). With acknowledgments to the Governors and Guardians of the Thomas Coram Foundation for Children, London.

Hogarth's Servants, c. 1750-55. Oil on canvas. (24½ × 29½"). Tate Gallery, London.

William Hogarth (1697-1764)

The Shrimp Girl, c. 1745. Oil on canvas. (25 × 20¾″). National Gallery, London. ▷

Hogarth's Servants (detail), c. 1750-55. Oil on canvas. Tate Gallery, London.

delicate fabrics, pearl bracelets, all in the most delightful harmonies of blue and ochre. Mrs Garrick's face is one of the most subtly expressive ever painted by Hogarth.

One leaves him with regret. He produced an enormous body of work, of which only the merest sampling can be given here. Our time ranks him very high; his own did not. James Barry questioned whether he could really be called an artist at all. Horace Walpole set little store by him: 'As a painter he had but slender merit.' As a social

Joseph Highmore (1692-1780)
Pamela Telling a Nursery Tale, c. 1743-45. Oil on canvas. (30 × 32″). Fitzwilliam Museum, Cambridge.

chronicler, however, he had his admirers from the very beginning: the Swiss Rouquet, the German Lichtenberg, and among his countrymen John Nichols, and then John Ireland, who appreciated that he was head and shoulders above such men as Jervas, Highmore, Hudson and Hayman.

Joseph Highmore (1692-1780), a pupil of Kneller, came under Hogarth's influence, even though he was five years older. But he always retained a charm of his own, whose appeal lay perhaps in a certain hesitancy and timidity. His individual portraits, though warm and attractive, and handled with dainty precision, are less interesting than his conversation pieces, such as *Mr Oldham and his Guests* (undated, Tate Gallery). It is a neat, effective composition, striking a graceful balance between two heads put together and two set apart; from it, through the familiar symbols of pipe, bowl and flagon, there radiates a sense of cordial friendship, kindly fellow-feeling and modest contentment with life. One of the figures, with its stubby nose and pursed lips, borders on caricature in its humanity and verisimilitude. The delicate modelling is very different from Hogarth's handling. Before being to some extent rediscovered, Highmore was best known for his series of twelve paintings illustrating Richardson's *Pamela*, sentimental like the novel itself, bright and

Francis Hayman (1708-76)

The Milkmaids' Garland, or Humours of May Day, c. 1735. Oil on canvas. (54 × 92″). Victoria and Albert Museum, London.

attractive in colour, admittedly mannered, with oddly elongated figures; yet something more than a sedate variant on Hogarth's more exuberant vision. Highmore infused into English art the elegant style of the French engraver Gravelot, who worked in London from 1732 to 1745.

Francis Hayman (1708-76), Hogarth's junior by eleven years, is closer to him in temperament, though he too learned much from Gravelot, as he subsequently imparted something to Gainsborough, in whom one finds a reflection of certain of Hayman's awk-

Arthur Devis (1711-87)
Sir George and Lady Strickland in the Grounds of Boynton Hall, 1751. Oil on canvas. (46 × 35 ½").
Ferens Art Gallery, Kingston upon Hull Corporation.

ward touches, like the shambling legs pointed out by Horace Walpole. The surprising charm of his painting goes hand in hand with a mannerism much more marked than in Highmore – a fanciful combination of the French and English traditions, as in *The Milkmaids' Garland or Humours of May Day* (c. 1735, Victoria and Albert Museum), a naïve *fête galante* whose dancing figures, despite their modest station, are endowed with an unreal grace. Gainsborough, in painting his own milkmaids, never forgot those of Hayman.

Arthur Devis (1711-87) was a painter of upper middle-class life. One looks with pleasure at his *James Family* (Tate Gallery). If the landscape were a little better defined and integrated, the water a little more aquatic and the group a little more at ease, this scene would anticipate the charm of Gainsborough's *Mr and Mrs Andrews*. The latter indeed is almost matched by *Sir George and Lady Strickland in the Grounds of Boynton Hall* (reproduced on page 44). True, the Andrews couple, despite their biscuit-like consistency, stand in a real world, whereas this scene by Devis has nothing to do with reality; it is a thing of enchantment. It is bathed in the unworldly light of a dream – the gentleman in blue and the lady in pink and green are engaged in a dumb show whose meaning is unclear. The colouring, as so often in the case of these minor artists, is delightfully fresh. A rich and vital flowering of portraits, conversation pieces and genre scenes of all kinds thus took place around Hogarth, though not necessarily under his aegis.

2

The Classical Phase and the Discovery of the Grand Style.
From Portraiture to History Painting:
Ramsay, Reynolds, Romney, Raeburn, Opie, Lawrence, Copley, West, Barry.

HOGARTH was the prophet of the Old Dispensation. Between him and the radical reformation represented by Reynolds, comes a modest harbinger in the person of Ramsay.

Allan Ramsay (1713-84) was a friend of Hume, Johnson, Rousseau and Voltaire. His fine portrait of Rousseau, with his intense, uneasy gaze, is famous, partly because Rousseau found himself unrecognizable in it and accused the artist of having turned him into a cyclops. A cultivated Scot with engaging manners, Ramsay was only twenty-three when he left on his first journey to the Continent in 1736. For the next two years he spent most of his time in Rome studying painting. In France he was attracted by the work of Maurice Quentin de La Tour and the pastellists, and their influence is marked in many of his portraits, particularly in that of his second wife, *Margaret Lindsay* (1754-55, National Gallery of Scotland, Edinburgh). The composition is all his own and it is striking: the young woman's mood is suggested by the slight movement inclining her towards the right side of the picture, thus forming a sharp angle with the forthright vertical on the left. After working for some years in both London and Edinburgh, and after a second journey to Italy in 1754-57, he settled in London in the latter year. He cheerfully accepted Reynolds' ascendancy, and in fact it proved no hindrance to his career, for on the accession of George III, of whom he had done a fine portrait as Prince of Wales, nicely combining the stately and the familiar, he was appointed Painter in Ordinary in preference to Reynolds. He painted the King again, superbly, in his coronation robes. Though Reynolds favoured the company of literary men, Ramsay was by far the most cultivated painter of his time; indeed, from 1770 on, he virtually gave up painting and devoted himself to literature.

He is an interesting painter, all the more so for the fact that it is difficult to place him. Was it lack of energy or lack of shrewdness that prevented him from arriving at a style of his own? Is the superiority of his female portraits due to the fact that with them he felt able to express a certain grace and strength of feeling? Yet his male portraits show considerable force and have, moreover, a soundness of design superior perhaps to that of Hogarth himself: especially in a portrait like that of *Dr Mead* (1747). Here, it is true, a certain stiffness lingers on, that old starchiness that Hogarth abhorred and the new age dreaded. So Ramsay duly went in search of ease and naturalness, an everyday simplicity, and ten years

Allan Ramsay (1713-84)

Portrait of Margaret Lindsay, the Painter's Wife, 1754-55.

Oil on canvas. (30 × 25"). National Gallery of Scotland, Edinburgh.

later he contrived to impart something of these qualities even to the ceremonial portrait of the Prince of Wales. But if Reynolds reflected on the use he might make of the full-length portrait of *MacLeod of MacLeod* (1748, Dunvegan Castle), which Ramsay had posed, contradictorily, in a 'natural' exterior, he must have concluded that, since painting is not nature, there was a lesson to be learnt here.

Two pictures which demonstrate Ramsay's contrasting styles are, on the one hand, the simple, 'natural' portrait of *Lady Mary Scott* (1760, Castle Ashby), gloriously coloured, with the subdued yet surprisingly sonorous harmony of the pink dress and the blue background, and, on the other hand, the extraordinary portrait of *Lady Mary Coke with a Theorbo* (1762, Marquess of Bute) in the Van Dyck manner, quite artificial, all in contrasted light. Even in his own day Ramsay's work met with varying judgments, for his style, thanks to his classical training in Italy and the influence of the French School in Rome, was a mixture of quasi-grandeur and discreet subtlety. Edward Edwards, the chronicler of the English painting of that day, considered that he lacked both the vigorous execution and the brilliant colouring of Reynolds, but achieved 'a calm representation of nature that much exceeds the mannered affectation of squareness which prevails among his contemporary artists... Unfortunately he was too much interested in literature.'

Joshua Reynolds, unlike Hogarth, came of a good middle-class family. He was born on 16 July 1723 at Plympton, in Devon, where his father the Reverend Samuel Reynolds, a former Fellow of Balliol, was headmaster of the Grammar School. From father to son the men of the family had taken holy orders, becoming either clergymen or schoolmasters. Not particularly precocious, nor impelled by any irresistible vocation, he decided at the age of seventeen to study art. Apparently from reading the *Theory of Painting* by Jonathan Richardson, he gained a lofty notion of the profession. It was from thence, perhaps, that the principles of pictorial idealism entered both into his art and into the *Discourses* of the future president of the Royal Academy. In 1740 he went to London and became the pupil of a fashionable portrait painter, Thomas Hudson, from whom, by 1743, he had learned his fill. He then returned to Devonshire and settled at Plymouth, where he spent the next six years, apart from occasional stays in London. He came under the influence of the painter William Gandy, of Exeter, the son of a pupil of Van Dyck; a dissolute but lively artist, Gandy is remembered for having declared that the pigments of a picture should have the textural richness of cream and cheese. Some of Reynolds' canvases seem to be in accordance with this excellent recipe.

At Plymouth he contented himself with the local clientele for portrait painting and tried his hand at landscape. His slow, belated growth seemed to have come to a stop when in 1749 he met Commodore Keppel, of whom he made several admirable portraits in the course of the next thirty years. Keppel liked the young man and, hearing that he wished to visit Italy, invited the artist to accompany him to the Mediterranean on board his ship, the *Centurion*. Reynolds sailed with him in May 1749, and after spending a month at Port Mahon in Minorca, he found passage on a ship bound for Leghorn. From there he made his way to Rome, eager to study the masterpieces and already in awe of Michelangelo, whose name was to be the last word in the last of his *Discourses*. His first sight of Raphael, however, in the Vatican, left him with a feeling of disappointment. This, he concluded, was his own fault, and with characteristic diligence he set about correcting his faulty taste until he, too, shared the universal admiration of Raphael. It cost him dear: while copying the Raphaels throughout the winter in the chilly, draughty rooms of the Vatican, he caught a severe cold which resulted in deafness.

Neither then nor later, however, was he the pedant that is sometimes imagined. His outstanding gifts are apt to be overlooked because his inflexible will repressed them. The sketchbooks of this period are full of spirited caricatures. What the caricaturist seeks to bring out is character, and Reynolds, when he wished, displayed this gift in a high degree.

In the spring of 1752, after several studious years in Rome, he set out for northern Italy. In Florence he appreciated the monumental grandeur of Masaccio. In Parma he was dazzled by Correggio, to the point of being obsessed by him for the rest of his life. In Bologna he studied the Carracci and pondered over eclecticism. Distrustful of inspiration, he wished to give his art something of a scientific basis, carefully, almost statistically working out the distribution of light and shadow on his pictures: one quarter light, one quarter shadow, the rest in half-tones, with Rubens on the side of light and Rembrandt on the side of shadow. A visit to Venice brought the influence of Titian strongly to bear on his work, though he said little about it.

He returned to England in October 1752. Early in 1753 he settled in London with his sister, who kept house for him, his rather cold nature readily adapting itself to bachelorhood. Then began the publicity campaign of the great society painter – a showy carriage, liveried lackeys, reception halls the walls of which were hung with Old Masters. Success came quickly. In 1755 his clients for the year numbered one hundred and twenty, and they had to pay the price for their portraits. Following the baneful practice that had sprung up with Van Dyck and Kneller, he relied on studio assistants for the draperies. To his pupils, among them Northcote, who became his biographer, he gave as little instruction as possible; they were not allowed to see him at work. There is much in his career that strikes one today as unpleasant; needless to say, he had few friends among his fellow painters, apart from Allan Ramsay, who was ever indulgent. However, as early as 1753 he had met Dr Johnson, the pontiff of literary classicism, and their great friendship lasted for more than thirty years, until the Doctor's death. It was at Reynolds' suggestion that the Literary Club was established in 1764, with Johnson, Goldsmith, Burke and Garrick. It served his interests, even if that was not the main reason for his setting it up, though it must be said that Johnson had occasion to protest that he was not disposed to make a show of himself. Honours came in plenty, and when the Royal Academy was founded in 1768 he was naturally offered the presidency. He pronounced his first *Discourse* at the age of forty-five, on 10 December of that year. In 1769 he was knighted. In 1773 he was made a doctor *honoris causa* of the University of Oxford. Goldsmith expressed his disgust at the scheming and mutual toadying to which he then lent himself, even prostituting his art in not very edifying allegories. On Ramsay's death in 1784, the appointment of King's painter was bestowed on him and he grumbled at the salary: 'The King's rat-catcher is better paid.' In 1789 his sight began to fail and within a few months he was blind in one eye. Thereafter he ceased to paint. In 1790 Fuseli was elected a member of the Academy in preference to his own candidate. He accordingly handed in his resignation and it was politely accepted. On the 10th of December 1790 he delivered his farewell *Discourse*, the fifteenth, a tribute to Michelangelo.

As early as 1753, in the portrait of his attendant *Giuseppe Marchi* (Burlington House), dressed in a turban and Turkish costume à la Rembrandt, his art had appeared cultured, full of memories and allusions (Titian, Bassano), and yet strongly personal. From that same year dates the brilliant, life-size portrait of his friend *Commodore The Hon. Augustus Keppel* (National Maritime Museum, Greenwich), whose exploits at sea had made him the hero of the day. Making an imperious gesture with his arm, Keppel stands against the sea, the element which he dominated; but his gesture and pose are, as has already been seen, those of Norman, twenty-second laird of MacLeod (1748, Dunvegan Castle); and, as Ellis K. Waterhouse[5] has pointed out, Ramsay had borrowed that gesture and pose from the Apollo Belvedere. Thus, by an almost abrupt mutation, the middle-class art of portraiture rose to a higher plane of cultural prestige. The imitation is manifest: in both cases, the warrior's right hand is made to stand out with intense highlights against a rocky hillside replacing the pillar of the Van Dyck tradition. Reynolds contrived to treat the rugged rock-face as chipped stone, which makes a nobler effect and lends itself to vivid painting. Both men have the sea on their left hand; but MacLeod's sea is a studio backdrop, distant and sluggish. Reynolds had genius enough to join together the rough sea, the man and the clouds behind him. In a blue tonality the light in Reynolds' portrait impinges on the figure vividly, from his face to his leg, and emphasizes the movement; with Ramsay the light impinges only on the face, making it seem artificial.

The Keppel picture marks a decisive mutation in portraiture, giving it a new function and a new status; it marks the transition from subjective revelation to objective formulation. Ramsay, the cultivated Scot, must be credited with the initiative behind that mutation; but without the ambitious drive of Reynolds it might never have taken place.

Reynolds, at the age of thirty, had made a promising start. Why did so little come of it? Few painters have been so severely judged, even by those who recognize his outstanding gifts. This is no doubt because he fails to inspire any sympathy or warmth of feeling. Elie Faure likened his mentality to that of a grisette cloyed with foolish dreams, and denounced him for dragging the mantle of Rembrandt through gutters running with scent and caramel. George Moore deplored his child subjects, which he likened to leering monkeys. In his showy carriage he paraded through the streets of London with his sister Fanny, but in the end he dismissed her from his house, and when he died she spoke of him as a grim tyrant. The attendant and handyman he brought back from Italy with him, Giuseppe Marchi, he treated ungenerously. In a review some years ago of Derek Hudson's book on Sir Joshua, the late Sir Harold Nicolson drew attention to the portrait of him painted by his friend and admirer, Angelica Kauffmann. Though she is not a great, nor even a good artist, Nicolson makes a telling point. Unlike the series of skilful and on occasion touching self-portraits which Reynolds made, Angelica's portrait of him is a revelation all the more cruel for being perfectly unconscious: the shifty eyes, the sly, dishonest mouth, the intimations of cunning and meanness, all give due warning.

He was consumed with ambition. He could conceive of no other art but one that intelligently followed the line laid down by himself. That line, it seemed to him, was marked out for eternity, but eternity is capricious. Reynolds thought he could side with eternity from the outset by ignoring the trivia inseparable from present, immediate, everyday things. Such was the classicist's point of view, which is familiar enough. But painting depends for its life on craftsmanship, on the material support, on the pigments. Unfortunately, neither in Italy nor afterwards in London did Reynolds learn to respect his colours. He embarked on fantastic experiments with pigments and bitumen, so that after two centuries his cracked and darkened pictures are not always very nice to look at, still less to examine at close quarters, even when one's interest is aroused. He was a painter, it is true, who wished to serve both God – his God – and Mammon. His first concern was to get rich, and in fact fame and wealth were both ends in themselves and mutually conducive means.

Being the painter of a certain class, the dominant oligarchy, he thus came to see things and people as it wished them to be seen, in its service, in the service of what dominated in that class: man, the male sex. To see the men of that class as they wished to be seen was not too serious; such is the fate of portraiture. To see their wives and children as they wished them to be seen was, however, very serious, for it involved a falsification, a veritable corruption of vision.

Everything stems from the same principle of suggestion conveyed by a hidden yet revealed symbolism. The Apollo Belvedere behind the gesture of Commodore Keppel represented a discovery. It meant that the innocent imagination was unwittingly programmed simply because it found itself in the presence of a manifest but inexplicable undertone. But if, instead of being thus borne along, the spectator's imagination recoils and refuses, then all the artist's skill will have gone for nought. Such is the case with *Robinetta*, a little girl whom Reynolds, on the strength of her name or nickname, wished to be seen with an emblematic robin, in accordance with a sentimental association of ideas. Such is the case with the *Strawberry Girl*, a doleful, ageless creature, sinking back dispiritedly, incapable of telling us whether she is carrying fruit or a message. Such is the case with *Miss Bowles*, where the dog plays so strong a part in the appeal to sentiment. Reynolds had stopped at Parma all right. The pity is, not that he was smitten with Correggio, but that he seems to have gone from place to place picking up a certain number of prestigious recipes. So much so that a complete mental block sets in, making it impossible for the spectator to accept any child of his as representing the *Age of Innocence* or the *Infant Samuel* or *St John the Baptist* (after Guido Reni).

Childhood with him is rendered as grown-ups desire it; it is expected to give rise to melting smiles, even if innocence as thus conceived lapses into an expression of idiocy. Too much stress is laid on the symbolism of the attribute – lamb, strawberries, bird. The *Children with a Butterfly Net* (1775, Lord Faringdon) may be compared with Gainsborough's two daughters chasing a butterfly. Gainsborough portrays naïveté and movement prompted by unthinking desire; Reynolds portrays a set and lifeless pose. Yet, for all that, the appeal of the five *Heads of Angels* in the National Gallery is difficult to resist. Though perhaps a little too ideally beautiful, these five children's heads are very well painted, borne into a

Sir Joshua Reynolds (1723-92)

Commodore The Hon. Augustus Keppel, 1753-54. Oil on canvas. (94 × 58″). National Maritime Museum, Greenwich. ▷

Lady Jane Halliday, 1779. Oil on canvas. (94 × 58¼″). The National Trust, Waddesdon Manor. ▷▷

vague empyrean by little wings; one is almost tempted to compare them with the six heads of Hogarth's *Servants*, and the comparison would not be wholly gratuitous. There is something in Mrs Thrale's famous phrase about Reynolds: a 'heart too frigid' and a 'pencil too warm'. One cannot forget his ambition and the formulation of it, all too revealing in its gaucherie, which he gave as an adolescent, when he declared that if he could not be a *good* painter, he would rather be an apothecary.

I will now return to a fuller examination of his work. The period from 1753 to 1768, though including much that I have objected to, was nevertheless one of rewarding efforts and undeniable progress. He was a strong-willed artist and one can admire the determination with which he approached each large picture as a total problem or a group of partial problems. And one notes the discriminating skill with which he took inspiration from his predecessors. While he has much to say of Michelangelo, Quentin Bell has also emphasized the influence on him of Jacopo Bassano. Others have pointed out all that he owes to Titian. His portraits of women are of at least three kinds. There are those, first of all, which present mother and child together and which, in addition to more or less precise reminiscences of Madonnas, multiply sentimental touches, outstretched arms, roving hands, sly airs of mutual understanding, or – lacking the Apollo Belvedere – nude putti fluttering about the worthy mother, almost covering her up in front, fluttering over her shoulder and moving awkwardly right out of the composition and the picture space (*Lady Cockburn and her Children*). Sometimes, admittedly, as in *Mrs Hoare and her Child* (Wallace Collection), all this comes together nicely enough and composes a scene of gracious geniality, taking its tone from fair or amber-coloured complexions. Pleasant enough, but hardly memorable. Yet one does remember Gainsborough's admiring imprecation: 'Damn him, how varied he is.' And, as if to compensate for the sham of these mother-and-child pictures, there is a painting like *Georgiana, Countess Spencer, and her Daughter* (1761, Spencer Collection), which would have been more often proclaimed as the masterpiece it is, but for the lingering fear of being taken in by Reynolds. For this picture meets the standards of the best kind of painting. In terms of a rigorous selection, everything here shares, not in a false exterior vitality, but in an intrinsic, self-contained life. It is only a woman holding up a child on a console table, with a small dog sitting up on his hind paws beside the little girl who, charming in her gravity, balances, almost symmetrically (*pace* Hogarth), the vaporous sleeve of the mother, whose face maintains the same expression. How is it that this painter of so many disingenuous children succeeded in creating one of the few absolute masterpieces of children's portraiture, the *Lady Elizabeth Hamilton* (1758, National Gallery, Washington), with its naïve, self-absorbed face, with the exquisitely painted, exquisitely tremulous robe of faded red silk? For some reason, the Spencer Collection seems to contain some of the finest and subtlest of Reynolds' canvases. The Wallace Collection seems to contain some of the most elegant, most worldly and, on occasion, most vulgar: *Lady Bamfylde*, in white with her frothy scarf and a great lily, or *Mrs Braddyll*, a golden-hued, pearly-hued beauty. In the Wallace Collection, too, are the two small bust-length portraits of *Lady Elizabeth*

Sir Joshua Reynolds (1723-92)
Portrait of Nelly O'Brien, 1763. Oil on canvas. (50¼ × 40″). Wallace Collection, London.

Seymour-Conway and *Frances Seymour-Conway, Countess of Lincoln*. The portrait of Elizabeth is uninteresting but that of Frances is a different matter; in the simple perfection of her attitude, her head slightly bowed and turned, her shapely hand brushing her cheek, she is a figure wholly in keeping this time with the precepts of Hogarth. The *Portrait of a Woman* (Victoria and Albert Museum), with an evanescent blue ribbon in her hair, with a dusky gravity in her features mellowing into a faint smile, touches a secret chord of sympathy; and that chord is touched again by the *Sketch of a Girl* (Dulwich), an indistinct and poetic head, again slightly bowed, the flesh emerging like a glow from the mauve stuffs and the blue background.

A woman's beauty is an element of prestige for Reynolds, because his senses do not seem to have been touched by it. Hence the distant, purely external manner in which he paints women. An exceptional element of grace or frailty can, however, draw him out, and then the work gains a certain depth. He seems to feel most at ease when the beauty before him stands outside the context of class; and his best portraits of young women are those of the courtesans *Kitty Fisher* and above all *Nelly O'Brien* (1763, Wallace Collection). Private cares or a lack of self-confidence or fears for the future make them more subtly alive than the great ladies in their complacency or self-command. *Kitty Fisher* is rather spoilt by her dove (presumably symbolizing Venus) but *Nelly O'Brien*, on the other hand, is one of Reynolds' masterpieces. Wearing a blue-striped gown, she is seated in front view, slightly hunched up, as if in a melancholy mood, holding a fluffy little dog in her lap on a pink quilt: the weight of humanity which she seems to bear faintly recalls that of Carpaccio's more famous courtesans. Her face, shaded by the hat, is illuminated from below by a reflected light whose mildness suits her perfectly. The very same lighting is to be found in certain portraits by Rembrandt; a self-portrait in the Frick Collection, New York, comes to mind in particular. Reynolds is adept at stealing from the Old Masters.

In the case of a great lady, something else seems to enter into his reaction: her age. With grey hair before him, the factor of sexual intimidation ceases to operate, as for example in the portrait of *Lady Anne Lennox, Countess of Albemarle* (Tate Gallery), the mother of Admiral Keppel. The hall-mark of this fine picture is a true and deep-seated distinction, which might be analysed as dignity with just a touch of melancholy, kindliness with perhaps a touch of condescension, and reserve. As often when his colouring is not governed by set notions of the grand manner, the harmonies, which one is tempted to describe as facile, are developed in an attenuated, almost muffled lighting of silvery greens and reddish tints. Light is focused on the face, hands and lap, while the bust is left in shadow. As a decorous attribute of her age, a ball of wool lies in her lap, suggesting the domestic virtues of a Roman matron. The excessive paleness of the sitter, carried to the point of discolouration, which detracts from *Susanna Beckford* (1756, Tate Gallery), happens in this case to suit her; but it is one of the more striking and sometimes deplorable alterations of Reynolds' pictures.

Another parallel between Reynolds and Gainsborough is suggested by the portrait of *Sir Watkin Williams Wynn and his Mother*. They are just setting out for a walk, with the solid vertical masonry of their house on the left, some overhanging leafage in the centre setting off their heads, and a rocky landscape opening on the right. The sweeping gesture, with the three-cornered hat in the outstretched hand, and the subtle lighting mark this work in the same way that the couple in Gainsborough's *Morning Walk* are marked by a diffident grace set off by a gentle radiance.

But the fact is that this almost sexless painter (such is Nicolson's reading of Angelica Kauffmann's portrait of him) is essentially a painter of men. In 1761 he showed at the exhibition of the Society of Artists an acute, disturbing, intense portrait of *Sterne*, psychologically penetrating, curiously perverse, and one might almost say diabolical, were it not that the humanity of the man is cruelly hinted at in this emaciated figure. There can have been little sympathy between Reynolds and Sterne, the artist deprecating the writer's moral laxity. Of *Dr Johnson*, however, Reynolds did two portraits (Tate Gallery and National Portrait Gallery) which may flatter him a little but nevertheless convey the essential character of the man. The second, a pale head on a massive body, pregnant with thought, catches him at a moment of mild-mannered intentness, with the delicate left hand resting on the table against his paper (1772).

Boswell figures in turn (National Portrait Gallery) in a landscape which is no more than an intimation. It is scarcely more than a face against a black coat, but it is a marvel of expressive presence in which the whole man is summed up, alert, self-important, bizarre. Reynolds was not on good terms with the great architect *Sir William Chambers*, who is supposed to have behaved badly towards him. But he painted a portrait of him (Royal Academy), with one hand raised towards his face, his brow taking all the light, his red coat almost wholly in shadow, which does full justice to this man of thought.

These sitters were intellectuals, men of his own kind. Military men were more of a problem because he was not on the same footing with them, and his concern, it is pretty clear, was with an explicit art in which each man should have his mark and symbol. In military matters the question of greatness inevitably arose. Here it was imperative for the picture to smell of powder and danger. Hence the temptation of the epic and equestrian, resulting in such a picture as *Lord Ligonier on Horseback* (1760, Tate Gallery), supposedly at the battle of Dettingen, with a mêlée of horses and soldiers in the middle distance and clouds of smoke rising into the sky. But it fails to carry conviction. Another is *Colonel Tarleton*, with all the drama of battle written in the crazed eyes of the horses, while the colonel himself maintains a calm, martial pose; unfortunately one fails to grasp the situation of the horses in relation to the cannon, whose open mouth untowardly touches the warrior's behind. Horses, in fact, raise almost insoluble problems, even in the quieter scenes (e.g. *Captain Robert Orme*): they were bulky, disproportionate and cumbersome for an artist who knew little about them. When all is said and done, only two of his military portraits linger in the memory. First, *Admiral Keppel* (1780, Tate Gallery), who since 1753 had risen in rank and put on weight. This later portrait in dark red is manly and powerful; the face stands out against an almost black sky, whose light passes underneath the cloud cover. A reddish blue sunset can be glimpsed just above the sea. The handling is broad and sober and, for Reynolds, sparing of modelling. More unusual and more memorable is the portrait of *Lord Heathfield, Governor of Gibraltar* (1787, National Gallery). Here again the symbolic attribute was called for: the huge key of the fortress which he holds in his hand. Its size is in keeping with the imposing figure of the old soldier, whose tanned, blotchy face and large nose verge on the grotesque. Both sitter and painter triumph over that thanks to the resoluteness and energy written in this face. A faint note of sham creeps in with the echoes of the Keppel portrait, in the sky almost black with clouds and smoke beyond the rampart. I fancy it was such a portrait as this that Ruskin had in mind when he hailed Reynolds as one of the world's seven great colourists. One is often reminded in the *Discourses* of his theories on colour, the lesser, picturesque, broken colouring of the Venetians and the grander colouring: 'The distinct blue, red, and yellow colours which are seen in the draperies of the Roman and Florentine schools, though they have not that kind of harmony which is produced by a variety of broken and transparent colours, have that effect of grandeur which was intended. Perhaps these distinct colours strike the mind more forcibly, from there not being any great union between them; as martial music... has its effect from the sudden and strongly marked transitions from one note to another.' There was, however, no question of laying in a raw red like that of the milk woman's dress in Hogarth's *Distressed Poet*, but rather of setting the very strong red of this officer's tunic in a sonorous relation with the whole dark area surrounding it, and it is here that Reynolds' aesthetic meditations bore fruit.

In the case of Reynolds there is something else besides the normal progression of a creative artist through his successive lines of research; something else which coincides with the cultural movement of the period. Hogarth, it will be remembered, was strongly opposed to any academic institution because he feared that living art would be stifled by the weight and pressure of a tradition imposed by an academy. Nevertheless, in 1768, the Society of Artists was superseded by the Royal Academy of Painting, and, as Hogarth had foreseen, the annual exhibitions changed their nature and became official shows, Salons like their French counterparts, representing at once a manner of cultural promotion and the maintenance of certain principles. They afforded painters the opportunity of displaying their talent and doing their best. Reynolds, it is true, did not wait until 1768 to transform the portrait into a subject picture, and even into a subject picture in the grand manner. In 1762 he had exhibited *Garrick Between Comedy and Tragedy*, in which he seemed to have in mind such pictures as *The Poet's Inspiration* by Nicolas Poussin, though he was incapable of Poussin's characteristic restraint and produced a blatantly theatrical group. For want of that vital concentration and unity, everything here lapses into a naïve pantomime, at once grandiloquent and frivolous. The living portrait of the actor in action is thereby spoilt. This was a sign of what was to come: from 1768, the practice became common with him and awkwardly emphatic.

There is a fatal lack of sincerity here, so that the procedure employed results in sheer duplicity. Yet it was not a new procedure. After all, Filippo Lippi painted his mistress and called her the Madonna. But in the act of doing so, the dual nature of the subject underwent a transmutation, the mistress fading away and Madonna emerging. Everything depends on the vision. Reynolds remained by vocation a Society painter, and instead of the picture alone becoming an object of commerce, its subject and motif became so as well. Hogarth painted Garrick 'as Richard III', and that was in the normal course of things; his sitter being an actor, there can be no objection to the artist identifying him with a famous

Sir Joshua Reynolds (1723-92)

Lord Heathfield, Governor of Gibraltar, 1787. Oil on canvas. (56 × 44¾″). National Gallery, London.

role. Equally Reynolds painted *Sarah Siddons as the Tragic Muse* (1784, Huntington Foundation, San Marino, California, replica at Dulwich). And since the purpose here was to present the sitter in mythological guise, the gesture of Michelangelo's Isaiah in the Sistine Chapel suited the actress as well as any theatrical gesture. But the painter failed to find the simple and profound sonorities associated with great painting. Hence the bituminous and tawdry ornamentation and the hollowness of presence, regrettable and – the artist's mentality being what it was – doubtless inevitable. It was not in itself reprehensible to portray *Mrs Sheridan as St Cecilia*; she had been born a Miss Linley, and it was a very musical family. So there was some justification for her promotion to that status, however excessive it may seem. But between Reynolds' first manner or period and the one beginning, roughly, after 1768, one observes a complete difference in his way of applying this symbolic increment to a particular portrait. Commodore Keppel was not turned into Apollo, he was not portrayed 'as Apollo'; he was simply an unwitting reminiscence of Apollo. But what is one to say of *Miss Emily Pott as Thaïs, Mrs Musters as Hebe*, or *The Duchess of Hamilton as Venus? Lady Sarah Bunbury Sacrificing to the Graces*, it is true, dates from 1765 and so she did not wait for the creation of the Royal Academy to appear beside a smoking tripod, while *The Montgomery Sisters* take their pompous place in 1773 as *The Graces Adorning a Term of Hymen*. Their gestures are not even those of an actress, but rather of a raw pupil at a provincial conservatoire; the rhythms thus generated are extraneous to painting and the proper functions of the eye, and indeed nothing is lacking that might serve to heighten one's annoyance. Everyday dress would not have been appropriate to the mythological theme; so these ladies are necessarily clad in draperies of a classical, vaguely Roman cut, like unfortunate premonitions of 'empire' costume. As such sitters are never satisfied, some of them complained of having been portrayed in their night-gowns. No, this mythological charade is not good painting. One turns with relief to a sitter so perfectly real in her artifices as *Mrs Carnac* (Wallace Collection), with her high, plumed chevelure, coming forward like a great lady through the landscape of Watteauesque trees, thoroughly familiar with the art of holding her arms in their voluminous sleeves and stepping forward without allowing her legs to be divined beneath the sweeping drapery of her gown. One cannot help regretting that, with what may be termed his sense of glory, he was not more often the painter of such fine aristocratic insolence as is found in *The Ladies Waldegrave* (1780-81, Edinburgh, National Gallery of Scotland), too proud to be humane, too self-assured to have any contact even amongst themselves, sitting in their fine stylish gowns, of a texture as creamy as their own complexion, their heads set off by a drapery whose deep red is like an emanation of their scornful hauteur.

Handsome society ladies deified are a saleable commodity. Reynolds aimed higher: he felt in duty bound to rise to the level of subject painting, to symbolic subjects by then somewhat corrupted, such as the *Snake in the Grass* (National Gallery), in which Cupid pulls at the sash of the nymph's flimsy dress, while with a coquettish hand in front of her face and a sly glance at the spectator, she seems to say, as her dress slips down: 'Look what he's doing to me!' Gleaming ominously in the grass, the snake glides towards her. This is Reynolds à la Greuze. Mythological subjects (*Ariadne, Wood Nymph, Young Bacchus, The Infant Hercules, Cimon and Iphigenia*), legendary and historical subjects (*Death of Dido, Death of Cleopatra*), and biblical subjects (*Moses in the Bulrushes, Holy Family, Flight into*

Egypt) – all this art in the 'grand manner' came to him much more naturally than to Hogarth, but there was no future in it. Some points of novelty, if not of originality, nevertheless mark the impact on Reynolds of the pre-Romantic spirit of the time. Hogarth had kept to the history plays of Shakespeare; Reynolds ventured into the tragedies, with *King Lear*, much in favour around 1770, and *Macbeth and the Witches*. Realism was superseded by sentimentalism: *Mother with her Sick Child* (1768, Dulwich). All the phantoms of anguish, balanced by divine aid, swarm round her; this is the first of the 'nightmares', which were soon to be legion. Boydell's Shakespeare Gallery was launched and painters were called upon to contribute to it.

Does all this mark the end of Reynolds' evolution? Or, on the contrary, should the last word be left to Ellis K. Waterhouse, according to whom 'in later life, in the 1780s, he came to see that the Grand Style should be used in portraiture only with considerable discretion and on a character who could bear it'? If only one could believe it. But was he lucid enough to realize that he was going astray in following the academic tradition of Guido Reni and Francesco Albani, in giving painting the equivalent of that 'poetic diction' which poetry was about to break away from? Actually, would it not be truer to say that he remained something of a double-dealer and that with him one never quite knows whether it is calculated sincerity or innocent insincerity which has the upper hand? After turning his Italian experiences to account in the best and the worst ways he could, he made a journey to Flanders in 1781 and there studied Rubens in particular, and the influence of his richly textured pigments, his vivid and truthful rendering, is apparent in both smaller and greater subjects. *Lord Heathfield*, after all, may owe something to Rubens, and certainly this final period is rich in admirable portraits, especially of men.

Reynolds was the son, grandson and nephew of clergymen, and he must have been an early connoisseur of Sunday sermons. From 1768 to 1790, as president of the Royal Academy, he delivered fifteen *Discourses*, in an unsteady, unpleasing and at times high-pitched voice. These have come down, not as they were spoken but as he rewrote them. They did for painting what Dr Johnson at the same time was doing for literature: they set forth a comprehensive body of classical doctrine. The least one can say is that his cerebral painting squares perfectly with this set of propositions designed to promote it. There is no place here for spontaneity and inspiration. Everything that intelligence, study, memory, judgment and reflection can do for a painter is summed up by Reynolds and reduced to recipes. No one could have done much more in this line, without confusing the domain of sensibility and that of thought. As against inspiration, he proposes an intellectual art in which preconceptions and the choice of the subject determine the invention and govern composition, colouring and lighting, in the interests of what in literary classicism was known as decorum, a set of converging proprieties.

As in classical literary theory, everything here is based on a correspondence between man and the world, a correspondence marked by the pre-eminence of man, of what was held to be specifically human in him, i.e. reason. Nature is thus rational in its essence, possessing an eternal, universal, rational quiddity sifted out by abstraction from the accidental and contingent, from the temporal, particular and subjective, from passion and all that disturbs order, idea and intention. Bernini's David bites his lip; he thereby becomes a boy armed with a sling, intent on not missing the mark, and thus loses his status in the hierarchy of the Fine Arts. Just as intention and idea are opposed to the disorder of passion, so they are also opposed to irrational beauty based on habit. Any aesthetic specificness, any 'line of beauty', would be irrational, and would be undesirable. Beauty lies in the correspondence of a reality with an intention: for each species or category there is a 'central form' whose approximation must be sought out.[6] To nature, the artist on the strength of his training adds culture, the element of temporal permanence embodying the past creations of man's genius and constituting history, from which so many lessons are to be learnt. Masters and models record and confirm what has been discovered about the forms of beauty and set forth its laws. Thus is prepared the formulation of rules, the aggregate of these lessons, which is the proper task of Academies. Those rules serve to mark out limits and confirm the dependence of individual genius on the principles of human creation. They are meant to guide the student of any age and the practitioner of the present time, towards the observation of particular lessons which may be drawn from the masters and which Reynolds considered of more value than the copying of whole pictures (and here Hogarth would have agreed with him). These lessons, then, all concerned specific points, and the recipient of them was expected to preserve his creative freedom. It is clear that the result of drawing 'freely' on this or that artist cannot be anything more than an eclectic art; but, with inspiration ruled out, the reasoning mind was prepared to make the best of this. What mattered was to promote and preserve a graded order of general forms, which meant a hierarchy of genres. Inevitably, from this point of view, history painting was held to be far superior to portraiture, in which the most universal principles had to be brought down to earth and applied to the most particular of motifs. Equally particular was landscape; indeed, in this view of things, it was even more so, having lost that element of generality which is still represented in human dignity. There was also, within each genre, a scale of degrees: Rubens localized everything, whereas Claude generalized and idealized.

One sees from all this how small a place the pictorial occupied in this view of painting. Van de Velde and Claude stood pretty far down in the scale, but what was that to the lowly position of genre painting in which Reynolds included the *scènes galantes* of Watteau? Lowlier yet, indeed right at the bottom, was still life. It was thought, in its manifold associations, which in Reynolds' opinion fed and stimulated the imagination – but which in such a hierarchy seems singularly lacking. This inequality of genres was doubtless part and parcel of the cultural scheme of things at that time, and it was destined to last as long as the external touchstones of representational art. It took abstract art to abolish it completely.

Dignity and decorum on one side stood opposed to everyday life on the other. History painting was the painting of the non-present; hence its prestige, as with Reynolds himself when he aimed at the grand manner. It took a small revolution to give history the visual aspect of the contemporary world.

George Romney (1734-1802)
Portrait of Mrs Verelst, 1773. Oil on canvas. (92 ½ × 57″).
Private Collection, on loan to the City Museum and Art Gallery, Birmingham.

In art, each technique has its due place and specific use; here Reynolds is in agreement with Diderot. Visual art must meet the requirements of the eye, and the visual form, unlike the literary image, cannot function effectively on several levels of suggestion. The symbolism must be one and coherent: a hero in painting must look the part, and it is no good for St Sebastian, as in Titian's picture of him, to have a spindly pair of legs. The unexpected parallel with Diderot is borne out: 'As the painter cannot make his hero speak like a great man, he must make him look like one.' To do that, he must have a flair for the analysis of those circumstances which, in real life, go to make up the dignity of a man's appearance.

Reynolds, who did not scruple to borrow from Ramsay, influenced him in turn, even though Ramsay was ten years his senior. Given the calculated prestige of his own painting and the didactic intent of his fifteen *Discourses*, it may be said of him, as it cannot be said of any English painter before him, that he was the leader of a school. Though he did not rank portraiture very high, ironically, it was the portrait painters in particular, down to and including Lawrence, who followed his example and manner. One of the most curious and interesting artists of that day was George Romney (1734-1802), an excitable, capricious, over-sensitive introvert, whose career reflects his temperament. Highly appreciated by the public, and with good reason, he yet never became a member of the Royal Academy. One wonders whether his humble origins may not have had something to do with his exclusion, for he was the son of a cabinet-maker at Dalton-in-Furness in the north of Lancashire and began as his father's apprentice. While it was Jonathan Richardson who opened Reynolds' eyes to his vocation, it was Leonardo da Vinci's treatise on painting that did the same for Romney. An itinerant portraitist whose pupil he became taught him to grind and prepare his own colours. With the result that, unlike those of Reynolds, Romney's have remained unaltered and very beautiful.

During his formative years he lived at Kendal in the Lake District. There he fell ill and was nursed through a fever by his landlady's daughter. He then married her, but at the end of six years, in 1762, left her to set up as a painter in London. In 1798, with his health irremediably shattered, completing the cycle of a bizarre destiny, he returned to the north to Kendal, where his faithful wife tended him until his death in 1802.

After two years in London he went to Paris (1764) where he admired Le Sueur and possibly came under the influence of Greuze. In 1772 he went to Italy. In Rome he copied Raphael and Michelangelo, which was by no means unusual; but he was more particularly responsive to antique sculpture, and henceforth he saw and painted the human body with something of a sculptor's sensibility. Returning to London in 1775, Romney established himself in Cavendish Square and became the favourite painter of the Society of Arts, the rival of the Royal Academy. The next four or five years were a fruitful and prosperous period for him. He had a natural sense for the elegance of line, and it is probably for this reason, because of the clarity, firmness and emphasis of his outlines, that he was esteemed by Blake, in opposition to Reynolds and Gainsborough. With the nice tilt of her head, his *Perdita* in the Wallace Collection, where she vies with the 'Perditas' of Reynolds and Gainsborough, retains all her charm. Romney was not ambitious, and as a painter he contented himself with the superficial nature of things, being perhaps only too intent on making his works graceful and appealing. He made the most of the visible prestige of handsome bodies, and the draperies with which he adorned them reveal more than they conceal. He had an eye, too much of an eye, for the decorative motif, and his chief defect is to neglect the whole in the interest of the parts. This is most apparent in a picture like *The Beaumont Family* (1778, National Gallery), grouping six people; but while it may lack Hogarth's easy assurance in composing a large figure group or Reynolds' authority, it does have attractive features of its own: the naturalness of the poses, the sensual grace of the seated young woman whose light dress so well brings out her figure, the vivid colouring, brighter than in Reynolds, more broadly handled than in Gainsborough, and the shaded reds of the two military men enhancing a discreet and delicate harmony. At the beginning of Romney's career the portrait of *Mr Morland* (1763) is still almost naïve in its freshness, but already appealingly bright. At the end, the portrait of *Sir Christopher and Lady Sykes* (1786, Sledmere, Yorks) inevitably invites comparison with Gainsborough's *Morning*

Sir Henry Raeburn (1756-1823)

Sir John and Lady Clerk, c. 1790. Oil on canvas. (57 × 81″). Collection Sir Alfred Beit.

Walk, whose magic it may lack, while yet showing a singular grasp of human reality and tangible presence. On occasion, the decorative prevails to the point of audacity, as in *Mrs Booth* (National Gallery of Scotland, Edinburgh) where the human presence is wholly absorbed in the amusing and aggressive pattern formed by the edges of fur and muff. Such lack of balance is symptomatic.

In 1781 he met Emma Hart, the future Lady Hamilton, famous for her connection with Nelson. Not even Bonnard was more obsessed with his model. Emma portrayed from life, Emma spinning, Emma as a bacchante (as she was also for Reynolds), Emma as a nun and so on, as Romney pursues her with his brush. He took to Emma as one takes to drink; she bewitched and intoxicated him.

Though already broken in health, or for that very reason, he painted in 1795 what is no doubt his finest portrait, the most searching and most sombre – *Warren Hastings*, acquitted in that year after standing trial on charges of corruption in his rule of British India.

In the deeper nature of this artist torn between two classes, there remained something morbid, confused and unaccountable. 'Fear has ever been my enemy,' he told his friend Hayley. In a state of mental depression and failing health, he returned to the north of England to die.

Sir Henry Raeburn (1756-1823) scarcely left his native Edinburgh, apart from two years spent in Italy (1785-87). Apprenticed at first to a goldsmith, he then became a miniaturist. In his pictures he seems to have retained a bright, enamel-like colouring, insufficiently adapted to oils; its curious crudeness, admitting of no gradations, was not often attenuated. Seldom can a stay in Italy have left so little trace. Before these large bodies, painted with broad strokes, hardly drawn at all, as if line had no further currency on this scale, one has a sense of being amongst Scandinavians. Large, with him, does not mean monumental and this painting lacks tension. One is not surprised, in view of their size, to see that Raeburn places himself on a lower level than his sitters and thus builds up the image more strongly. Like his fellow Scot, Ramsay, he was no painter of women, though he liked a low-cut dress and a full bosom; his women usually have the stance of a grenadier. His men are more interesting. *Professor John Wilson*, with his cheerful face and fine horse, reflects honour on a respectable profession, but Raeburn is at his best with the picturesque soldiers of the North: *Major Wilson Clunes*, man and horse merging into a rhythmic group more successfully than with Reynolds; or *Sir John Sinclair* (National Gallery of Scotland, Edinburgh), in which the greens of plaid and trousers, the red of the tunic and the whites of sporran and baldrick stand out beautifully against the sky. He did not shrink from painting black shadows, on occasion he coloured them, and always remained intent on contrasts, as in the fine and already very Romantic portrait of *Sir Duncan Campbell* (San Francisco, De Young Museum). One may hesitate to choose between this work and the *Portrait of Colonel Alastair Macdonell of Glengarry* (National Gallery of Scotland, Edinburgh), with its subtler lighting, better absorbed contrasts and softer harmonies between the greenish browns of the

Sir Henry Raeburn (1756-1823)

Portrait of Colonel Alastair Macdonell of Glengarry. Oil on canvas. (95 × 59″).

National Gallery of Scotland, Edinburgh.

John Opie (1761-1807)
The Peasant's Family, c. 1783-85.
Oil on canvas. (60½ × 72¼″). Tate Gallery, London.

background and the pinkish brown of the tartan; but the exceptional delicacy of this picture makes up for its lesser vitality. Intelligent and resourceful, he varies his approach and sometimes comes up with an inventive composition like that of *Sir John and Lady Clerk* (*c.* 1790, Collection Sir Alfred Beit), who occupy only the right side of the picture. There is an unusual suggestion of space emphasized by Sir John's outstretched arm, and with an ambiguous sunset glow bathing the two faces and the light-coloured dress, the picture is reminiscent perhaps of Aelbert Cuyp.

A very deliberate and wilful painter, Raeburn had his mannerisms: he emphasizes the line of the mouth and often the ridges of the brow. This was his way of conveying the touch of life. Hence the effect of fleeting actuality and immediacy in his portraits, so different from the would-be permanence of Reynolds' figures. Those of Raeburn, caught in the present moment and heedless of the past, look towards the future with all the assurance of ruddy health and comfortable prosperity.

This school of portraiture is so rich that there can be no question of treating it in detail here. Suffice it to mention some of the more representative figures. Of James Northcote (1746-1831), the pupil and biographer of Reynolds, there is a fresh, frank and charming *Portrait of a Child* in the Victoria and Albert Museum, but much of his large output is distressingly tasteless and insincere.

John Opie (1761-1807) was much more gifted. A carpenter's son, largely untrained, the 'Cornish Wonder' created a sensation with the instinctive vigour of his execution and the powerful working of his chiaroscuro. But Opie was only really at home in subjects drawn from his own experience and walk of life. A picture like *The Peasant's Family* (*c.* 1783-85, Tate Gallery) accordingly shows him at his best. The lighting is a little forced, as almost always with him, to make the scene more intense. But the attitude of the figures thus thrown into relief is all the more striking: the mother tilts a large jug so that the younger of the little girls can drink from it directly, while the dog (the only false note of sentimentality which dates the picture) paws her arm and begs for his share. The other little girl carries a pitcher in one hand, which she balances by extending the other arm. The background landscape, setting off faces and arms, is dark and schematic. The painters of this period, like Opie here, seem to have been fond of heavy impastoes.

A new generation is represented by Sir Thomas Lawrence (1769-1830), born at Bristol. The son of an innkeeper, he exercised his gifts on the customers of the Black Boar, in the form of pastel portraits which gave him a taste for light tonalities. An infant prodigy, he had his own studio at Bath before he was twelve, and sitters flocked to him. At fourteen he took up oil painting and came to London at eighteen to study at the Royal Academy schools. He quickly assimilated all that could be learned there, Reynolds remarking that he had obviously studied the Old Masters but that now he must study nature. An Academician at twenty-five, he succeeded Reynolds as principal painter to the King. In 1792 he made portraits of the King and Queen for the Emperor of China – a sure sign of modern times. With the return of peace in 1815, he set off on a tour of Europe and painted portraits of the people who mattered, the Pope, the Duke of Reichstadt, Lady Blessington. He was knighted at forty-two and elected president of the Royal Academy when still under fifty. All this suggests another Reynolds, and it is easy to condemn him as the epitome of the worldly, fashionable type of painter. Of his own portrait the poet Campbell said: 'This is the merit of

Lawrence's painting: he makes one seem to have got into a drawing room in the mansion of the blest and to be looking at oneself in the mirror.' His insincerity is often patent and his glittering technique does not mend matters. Working too fast, he counted on this brio for a superficial brilliance. He was the last exponent of the Van Dyck tradition, with something indeed of the latter's temperament – his overwrought sensibility, his restlessness, his eagerness to press on, in life as in painting. In his quest for prestige, he often reverted to the facile symbolism which associates the human figure with the dignity of a column. But with him the old immobility gives place to a dashing, spirited treatment of the sitter, and this vivacity becomes more important than the truthful rendering of character. But did he really flatter the sitter all that much? One may judge of this from the admirable portrait of *Queen Charlotte* (1789-90, National Gallery), a luminous painting with a particularly attractive colour scheme of blue and silvery pink.

Tastes fluctuate, and painters and schools are condemned at one time only to be rehabilitated at another. True, Lawrence was neither a Reynolds nor a Gainsborough, and the improvisations of too hasty an art, too eager for immediate effect, are often unworthy of his gifts. But is it certain that he did not have a vision of his own, and perhaps a new sincerity behind his apparent insincerity? Ultimately he is a Romantic, with the primacy he gives to expression. The portrait of *Arthur Atherley* (1782?), shown at the bi-centenary of the Royal Academy in 1968, is striking in its intensity. There is a Byronic flamboyance of character in this young man in a white waistcoat and red coat, seen against a dramatic sky and dark landscape.

Reynolds failed in his efforts at self-promotion, for no one today takes his subject painting seriously or the little of what might be called his history painting. But his theorizings coincided with a growing awareness of what a national art meant. In 1757, in his famous *Philosophical Enquiry into the Origin of our Ideas of the Sublime and Beautiful*, Edmund Burke began promoting the Sublime. The sense of history was taking shape. The heroic was associated with certain phases in the march of humanity, the Hellenic phase in particular (alternatively, the Hebraic), but it was also brought nearer the present by picturing the exploits and dramas of the nation.

The first painter to do so was a Scots laird, Gavin Hamilton (1723-98), a contemporary of Reynolds himself. He spent a few years in Italy in the 1740s and practised for a while as a portrait painter in London. Then, obsessed with history, he returned to Italy for good. He soon acquired a European reputation, and there seems to be no doubt that the fashion in painting for Greek and Roman history, which led to David, began in a British context with Hamilton, for example with *Hector's Farewell to Andromache* (Holyrood Palace, Edinburgh).

Several painters were both portraitists and history painters, like the American John Singleton Copley (1738-1815) of Boston. He was in Italy in 1774 and settled in London in 1775. A good example of his portraiture is *Mrs Michael Gill*, a study of an old woman which takes its place between that of Giorgione and that of Géricault. In 1778 at the Royal Academy he exhibited *Watson and the Shark* (Boston), an unusual genre scene or adventure

Sir Thomas Lawrence (1769-1830)

Queen Charlotte, 1789-90. Oil on canvas. (94½ × 58″). National Gallery, London.

Benjamin West (1738-1820)

The Death of General Wolfe, 1770. Oil on canvas. (59½ × 84″). The National Gallery of Canada, Ottawa, Ontario. Gift of the Duke of Westminster, 1918.

Sir Thomas Lawrence (1769-1830)

◁ *John Lord Mountstuart,* 1795. Oil on canvas. (92 × 57½″). Collection the Marquess of Bute.

picture, anecdotal rather than historical, but treated broadly with dramatic intensity. From the gestures of this heroic male nude Géricault was to learn something. Among the best of Copley's history paintings are the *Siege of Gibraltar* (1791, Tate Gallery) and *The Death of Major Pierson* (1782-84, Tate Gallery). The latter records a recent event. On 8 January 1781 the French had invaded Jersey and nearly taken the island. The attack was only repulsed thanks to the spirited leadership of a young British officer, Major Francis Pierson, who rallied the local militia and saved the day. At the moment of victory, Major Pierson was slain. The picture accurately represents the street fighting in the town square of St Helier and the baroque sway of the composition is strongly expressive. A skilful contrast is made between the military men in the centre and the fleeing civilians on the right.

James Barry (1741-1806)
King Lear Weeping Over the Dead Body of Cordelia, 1786-88. Oil on canvas. (106 × 144 ½"). Tate Gallery, London.

Benjamin West (1738-1820), also an American, came of Pennsylvania Quaker stock. After studying in Italy from 1760 to 1763, he set himself up in London. History painting being all the fashion, the young artist was commissioned to paint an *Agrippina Landing at Brindisi with the Ashes of Germanicus* (1768) and the following year, for the King, he painted *The Final Departure of Regulus from Rome*. In 1770 he passed on to contemporary history with *The Death of General Wolfe* (National Gallery of Canada, Ottawa), which must be considered as a pictorial turning-point. His biographer described Reynolds' dismay on learning that West had decided to dress his general and soldiers in modern uniforms instead of Roman tunics, an impropriety which Reynolds allegedly warned him not to commit. West persisted and Reynolds in the end was won over and conceded the value and revolutionary import of the innovation.

West, for whom posterity has been severe, had a most successful career and became president of the Royal Academy. With his conspicuous but faltering gifts he had an open-minded eagerness for experience and novelty and he is, therefore, not without interest. A canvas such as *The Golden Age* (Tate Gallery), for example, with its bright tonality may one day take its place, with the canvases of Mulready, in the ancestry of the Pre-Raphaelites. In the end he might have rested on his laurels. But with his restless temperament he proceeded to paint his *Death on a Pale Horse* (1817) in a strain of Romantic violence.

An Irishman, too, ranks high among these history painters: James Barry (1741-1806), born in Cork of humble parents and self-trained. He exhibited his first historical pictures in Dublin in 1763. Burke was impressed and took him to London in 1764. Out of his own purse Burke provided him with the means to go to Italy, where Barry lived from 1766 to 1771, studying the antique and the work of Michelangelo.

On his return to England Barry enjoyed great success, becoming a member of the Academy in 1773. But in his enthusiasm for the grand style, he had nothing but scorn for those who did not share his views, and he poured ridicule on the idea of doing a history picture in its modern setting. He had the art of making enemies – many of them. He decorated the Great Room of the Society of Arts with some huge canvases illustrating *The Progress of Human Culture*. After finishing this in 1783, he became professor of painting at the Royal Academy. He availed himself of his position to attack and abuse his antagonists and was finally turned out of the Academy in 1799. He died in poverty and neglect. But his pictorial vision moved and influenced Blake, who could not but contrast the solitary, forsaken Barry with the worldly prosperity of Reynolds and Gainsborough. Barry painted a *King Lear Weeping Over the Dead Body of Cordelia* (1786-88, Tate Gallery), conjuring up a noble, vague, monumental antiquity in a colour scheme prevailingly brown and faintly classical. King Lear himself is a fine, very Blakean figure.

3

Art in Quest of Reality. Portraiture and Nature.
The Rise of Landscape: Gainsborough, Wilson, Jones, Hodges.

HOGARTH was a Londoner, of northern stock. Reynolds was a native of southern England, whose tepidness seems its essence. Thomas Gainsborough (1727-88), born at Sudbury, in Suffolk, was a man of East Anglia. In the inwardness and secrecy of this landscape, dotted with windmills, criss-crossed by rivers, canals and mill-races, there is already something Flemish. The landowners filled their fine houses as a matter of course with the genre scenes and landscapes of their Dutch and Flemish cousins across the sea, for those pictures fitted perfectly into the setting.

Gainsborough's father was a clothier. The atmosphere at home was thoroughly cheerful. His father was gay, whimsical, generous and usually short of money. As a boy he was allowed to develop freely and found his vocation early; at about thirteen he began a landscape and as a result secured his father's consent to study in London. It may be the one he referred to at the end of his life, in 1788, as having been finished in 1748.

Chronologically, he belongs to the same generation as Reynolds. In sensibility and emotional responsiveness, he belongs rather to the next generation: he is a pre-Romantic. Nothing is more characteristic than his attachment to his childhood and to the revelation of reality then granted him. It was, as he evokes it, a visual revelation: 'There was not a picturesque clump of trees nor even a single tree of any beauty, no, not hedgerow, stem or post in or around my native town that I did not treasure in my memory from earliest years.' He painted not so much what he saw as what he retrieved of that world through the eye and the play of the brush.

Arriving in London in 1740, he was apprenticed first to a goldsmith, then to the engraver Gravelot, a well-known book illustrator, whose work re-echoes Watteau and who transmitted to the young student the tradition of a slightly affected feminine grace. He seems to have studied subsequently under Hayman, who influenced the style of his early portraits. The meagreness and inadequacy of this technical training, one cannot call it an academic training, meant that he was always to lack a firm basis for conscious and critical self-scrutiny.

In 1745, at eighteen, he set himself up as portraitist and landscapist. He was too young, too eager to enjoy the good things of life; he did not have Hogarth's knack of turning his pleasures to account in art. Thirty years later he wrote to a young actor: 'Don't run about London streets, fancying you are catching strokes of nature, at the hazard of your constitution. It was my first school, and deeply read in petticoats as I am, therefore you may allow me to caution you.'

Thomas Gainsborough (1727-88)

Mary, Countess Howe, c. 1760. Oil on canvas. (96×60"). The Greater London Council as Trustees of the Iveagh Bequest.

By 1746 he was back at Sudbury. He fell in love with the natural daughter of the Duke of Beaufort, a young lady of many charms, including an annuity of £200. He married her but soon realized that they had very little in common. With his usual frankness he wrote: 'My wife is weak but good, and never much formed to humour my happiness.' He was not the man to give up the pursuit of happiness, however, and sought it in frequent escapades – what he called 'wagging the dog's tail out of the straight road.' He led a loose life. Though gay and optimistic, he had those sudden shifts of mood and temper which today would be called neurotic.[7] As is often the case with neurotics, he was extremely receptive. The gift of mimicry that Hogarth had had since childhood became with Gainsborough almost an infirmity. After spending an evening with Dr Johnson, himself a neuropath afflicted with incessant tics and twitchings, Gainsborough instinctively mimicked them and then found that he could hardly get rid of them. He was not so much worldly as irrepressibly sociable, for in fact he cared nothing for fine ladies, their tea parties, balls, marriageable daughters and polite conversation; they robbed him of 'ten good years'. He detested banal, stilted or would-be intellectual conversation; he liked good talk with its give and take, its unexpected turns, following the leap of the imagination. William Jackson, a young musician with whom he corresponded, says that his own talk was lively and ribald. Wine stimulated and inspired him. He loved music and if ever there was a musical painter it was Gainsborough. 'My comfort is I have five viols-da-gamba.' No matter whether or not he was a virtuoso performer. He was no enemy to conviviality, after which it might be two or three days before he could get back to work again. His easy-going ways were interpreted as indolence.

The catalogue of his œuvre varies as scholars add to or subtract from it,[8] but he left about 700 portraits, 125 of them full length, between 200 and 300 landscapes, and a very large and very valuable body of drawings, watercolours and gouaches. He never made the journey to Italy and he lacked that knowledge of the Old Masters which Reynolds of course overrated. A landscapist by instinct and taste, he knew little or nothing of the Continental schools beyond the Flemings, whose landscape paintings reminded him of the land of his childhood. To understand Gainsborough's development, it is worth looking at the often second-rate works which he might have seen in the England of his day. The first group would include the common run of Dutch and Flemish artists, such as Hobbema and Wynants. In the Dulwich Gallery is a landscape by Jan Wynants called the *Edge of a Wood*. In the road winding to the left, the passing horse and the fallen tree-trunk used as a focus of light, one readily recognizes a prototype for the realistic construction of *Cornard Wood* (1748, National Gallery), or *Gainsborough's Forest*, as it is sometimes called. It is a landscape of everyday occurrence, marked by the human presence that gives it movement, life, appeal: two little donkeys, a village on the horizon, a winding road, a horse at the far turn, its rump alone still visible, with a peasant and his dog plodding homewards – that is enough for the landscape to break away from that immobility which irked Hogarth. Gainsborough himself said of it: 'Though there is very little idea of composition in the picture, the touch and closeness to nature in the study of the parts and minutiae are equal to any of my latter productions.' The stormy lighting, diffused in the large clouds, is at once successful and facile; it produces those greens discreetly, iridescently merged with blues which remind one of the tonality and colouring of Rubens. There is a little pond with reflections, the first of those sheets of water which seem to form an indispensable part of his landscapes.

This is good work, but there are no surprises in it. That comes with another landscape offered that same year to the Foundling Hospital dear to Hogarth: *The Charterhouse*. It is here, in this pure landscape, the work of a twenty-year-old youth, that one finds something similar to the composite works or landscape-portraits like *Mr and Mrs Andrews*, painted shortly afterwards. True, there is something naïve in the schematic interpretation of the luminous clouds in the sky; moreover, this urban landscape, relieved only by a line of trees on the left whose trunks and leafage catch the light in vivid green touches, is reminiscent of Pieter de Hooch, particularly in the receding perspective of walls and brick buildings. Yet what force and individuality there is here, what skilful and instinctive equilibrium between the broad horizontals of the picture and the tall verticals on the right; what gaiety of lighting, resolved into the oblique band where the flagstones turn from reddish brown to bright yellow, like the top of the low wall above them – a gaiety which seems to be summed up in the two little boys playing marbles, apparently, on the borderline between light and shade.

Thomas Gainsborough (1727-88)
Mr and Mrs Andrews, c. 1748-50. Oil on canvas. (27½ × 47″).
National Gallery, London.

The conversation portrait of *Mr and Mrs Andrews* (National Gallery) dates from about 1748-50. It is not unique, but it is the young artist's most successful attempt at what was to become one of the hall-marks of his vision: the insertion of a portrait in a landscape, each setting off the other. Mrs Andrews is seated, rather stiffly, on a garden bench of green metal, whose curves are like a foretaste of Art Nouveau, her gleaming blue dress, on which lies the dead bird, spread out around her. Behind, the trunk of the oak receives its share of light. Standing beside her is Mr Andrews, in a beautiful light grey coat, his gun hanging down under his arm, his dog gazing up at him, his legs rather clumsily crossed in an attitude of would-be nonchalance which Gainsborough never quite mastered. No matter; the picture glows with greens and mauves whose finesse was scarcely matched by Constable. The fields recede from the lighter green of the sheaves of corn in the foreground towards the horizon, first obliquely, then in cross-strips, one with sheep, another with copses. Certain elements may be schematic and clumsy; the over-simplified modelling of the faces may be closer to biscuit-ware than flesh; and this scene in which the shadows are almost as bright as the lights has something of a naïve painting. No matter; its gaucherie is part and parcel of its beauty. To illustrate the pattern of equilibrium he had devised, he did not of course content himself with a single picture. The tree, the man standing on the left, the lady sitting on the right with outspread hoop-skirt, with the landscape beside her receding to the horizon – these same elements appear in *A Lady and a Gentleman* (Dulwich). But in the latter the tonality is less airy, the impression less luminous, the colouring less intense, the keynote being set by the red waistcoat and the bluish-black colour beside it. Mineral greens replace the pale greens around the Andrews couple. It is less radiant, but nonetheless interesting.

Round about 1750 Gainsborough moved from Sudbury to Ipswich in search of a more lively and attractive milieu. There he met his first patron and critic, Philip Thicknesse, who noted the gaucherie of his early work and helped him to complete his training.

To about 1751 may be dated the group of *The Artist, his Wife and Child*, in an idealized and lightly handled landscape, a group which recalls that of Rubens and his family in their garden. It may be, as Ellis Waterhouse conjectures, that he learned to treat the human figure more freely by painting his own family. It is certain that his spontaneity and youthfulness gave him a true insight into childhood, which he felt and, unlike Reynolds, respected. His instinctive sympathy with its attitudes and movements is plain from *The Painter's Daughters* (in half length, National Gallery), *Miss Gainsborough Gleaning*, *The Painter's Daughters Chasing a Butterfly* (National Gallery), or the same teasing a cat (National Gallery). There is nothing in common here with the lingering artifice of Hogarth's children (the *Graham Children*, for example). Gainsborough portrays children for their own sake, with no thought of the spectator, and with him their high spirits and innocence coalesce perfectly. Late in 1759, at the urging of Philip Thicknesse, who spent the winters there, he moved to Bath. This was his first large city, his first extensive contact with people of fashion, and there he met with instant success. More than that: the great houses thereabouts, like Wilton, had large private collections and there Gainsborough discovered the work of Van Dyck and Rubens. He must have felt affinities with Van Dyck, with his blend of nervous intensity and languor, and he relished the beauty of this light, supple painting, its restless transparencies, its subtle and effective scumblings. He painted his *Blue Boy* in a Van Dyck costume. Rubens, with whom he had less in common, may have taught him still more, not in the way of figure painting but of landscape. It was not just a matter of rendering with the brush what the eye sees; it was a matter of style, of suiting the interpretation to the intention, keeping or eliminating detail, going beyond the 'thing seen' and taking up afresh in each canvas the old quarrel between the general and the particular. According to Turner, his first efforts in landscape were in imitation of Hobbema (though one is inclined to think rather of Wynants). This influence was followed by that of Ruisdael. The change that comes over Gainsborough's landscape painting during the Bath period owes nothing to nature, which it now resembles less, not more; it owes everything, or anyhow much, to the Rubenses at Wilton.

At Bath, in 1760, he was asked to do a portrait of *Miss Ford* (Cincinnati), soon to become Mrs Thicknesse. It is a curious picture. She sits with her elbow on a table, over which flows the lace of her sleeve, her legs bent one way, her ample gown thrown back the other way, so that the gown forms with the head a straight line cutting across two-thirds of the picture in a broad diagonal; the figure as a whole forms a large triangle. A bass-viol, apparently, hangs on the wall. Seeing it in that year, a Mrs Delany commented: 'A most extraordinary figure, handsome and bold; but I should be very sorry to have anyone I loved set forth in such a manner.' What she probably disapproved of was the informal, unstudied pose and the crossed legs – a thing no longer done perhaps in 1760. Reynolds would never have laid himself open to such blame. Gainsborough, even when he had solved the difficulties caused him by men's legs, never sought an academic pose.

In 1764 he painted *General Honeywood* (Sarasota, Florida) in the equestrian style, which still shows signs of Van Dyck's influence. It is rare to find him departing so far from his own vein. With his increasingly successful portrait practice, he moved in 1766 to the fine 'Circus' recently built by John Wood. Among his musical friends in Bath were the composer Thomas Linley and his children, Tom and Elizabeth, who became Sheridan's wife. He portrayed the Linleys several times, in different phases. He became friendly with Garrick. He was happy and prosperous. In 1768 he became a foundation member of the Royal Academy. This was his great period. He too, for different reasons than Reynolds, was not at his best in painting beautiful women. Their beauty checked that direct, straightforward gaze which was so naturally his, and to which his equally direct, straightforward touch answered. The portrait of a mature lady, *Mrs Portman* (lent to the Tate Gallery by Viscount Portman), seems to me one of the finest he ever painted, the figure broadly posed in an armchair set against the wall, radiates a milder humanity than Reynolds had been able to impart to *Lady Anne Lennox, Countess of Albemarle*. She holds a rose instead of a ball of wool, and her half-smile is well in keeping with the gracious benignity of her pose. The sea-green satin of her gown, the reddish wall and the grey door go to form a discreet harmony well suited to the subject and to Gainsborough himself. More decorative but less interesting is the portrait of the young *Mary, Countess Howe* (c. 1760, Iveagh Bequest), all in shimmering pinks and greys, against an undefined landscape. At Bath, surrounded by such elegant representatives of the English aristocracy, he may have failed to realize that it was still a ruling class, that it had reserves of energy and will, that these bodies were made for action. Is not a certain languor in Gainsborough himself reflected in his interpretation of his subjects? Of the portrait of *Ralph Schomberg* (1772), it has been pointed out that what the sitter shows is not *self*-awareness, but awareness of having Gainsborough in front of him; he shows an artificial liveliness, which is felt to be so from the inertia of the pose. So it is that, as a means of expressing a period and its social relations, Gainsborough's art does not quite have the scope of Reynolds' – though as art it is superior. The Schomberg portrait is very subtle; instead of standing out, the man emerges softly from the sketchy landscape, a subdued light playing on his face and the bleached shoulders of his faintly red coat. From the same period dates the still more delicate and more lyrical portrait of *Elizabeth and Mary Linley* (Dulwich), in some ways the most modern he ever painted. The faces of these two musical ladies (who are not particularly pretty), with a strange intensity in their gaze, which seems to draw them towards the forefront of the picture, have a singular timelessness and immediacy. One is standing, the other sitting, quite firmly and naturally, with no thought for effect. The eye is attracted by these two blue and ochre presences in a landscape – or, better, outside it. The leafage is brushed in with light streakings in the manner of Watteau, but the two figures are still dominant.

In 1774 he made his last move, leaving Bath for London. Some risk was involved, for relations with Reynolds were never easy. And since 1772 he had been out of temper with the Royal Academy, which did not hang his exhibition pictures as he wished; his lighting requirements were probably difficult to satisfy. He did not meet in London with the immediate success he had enjoyed at Bath. Possibly for this reason he turned more to landscape painting. Already in 1767 he had painted an unusually animated landscape scene, the *Harvest Wagon* (Barber Institute, Birmingham), a subject he took up again seventeen years later. This *Harvest Wagon* has been likened to a *fête galante* converted into a *fête rustique*. Gainsborough's affinities with Watteau are unmistakable, though the French painter, in almost every work, leaves his figures in a state of suspense – a way of creating a mood of reverie. The scene is not wholly convincing: it pictures the moment when a girl – who betrays the distinctive profile of Margaret Gainsborough – is trying to climb on to the wagon, which a boy has brought to a halt with some difficulty, by seizing the bridle of the lead horse; she has already placed one leg on the spoke of a wheel (a risky step, one would think), while another boy leans down to help her up. Is this the best chosen moment for two other boys, standing in the wagon, to struggle for possession of a small cask, from which one of them is drinking straight from the bung-hole? Practically, the answer is no, but pictorially it is yes. What Gainsborough wanted was a perfect pyramidal design, such as the baroque aesthetic would call for, with the continuous, rising line of three bodies on one side and three on the other, accompanying less strenuously a like movement, this actual vertical thrust being curiously balanced by the virtual forward thrust of the three horses barely held in check. In no other landscape by Gainsborough is there this intensity of movement. The clump of trees on the left and the tree on the right seem to share in it, as they bend towards each other. Vivid, romantic high-lights heighten this momentum while the strongest lights and brightest colours are concentrated round a red cloth hanging down from the wagon. But as pointed out by Ellis Waterhouse, Gainsborough had seen and even copied a small *Descent from the Cross* by Rubens whose design is based on the very same movement, the English master simply turning a downward into an upward thrust. Here then, in landscape, was a mutation similar to that which portraiture had undergone with Ramsay, then with Reynolds: an infusion of culture leaving a substratum which changes the order of dignity of the works which avail themselves of it.

Thomas Gainsborough (1727-88)

The Harvest Wagon, 1767. Oil on canvas. (47⅜ × 56⅞″). The Barber Institute of Fine Arts, University of Birmingham.

In 1775 Gainsborough painted the *Watering Place*. He was familiar with Rubens' painting on the same theme and had already drawn inspiration from its design and style. But in this case he does not seem to owe any great debt to Rubens: his picture is highly original. Horace Walpole said of it that this 'landscape in the style of Rubens is the most beautiful which has ever been painted in England.' And one sees why he said it, for it is very English indeed, lightly touching a deep and intimate chord of lyricism. There is a hint perhaps of Claude – always the favourite 'Italian' landscapist in England – in the choice of lighting, the dusky golden light of the close of day irradiating the whole landscape, in a way seldom seen in the Flemish masters, and imparting a new transparency to the clumps of trees. Emanating from the sky and the fleecy, gold-flecked clouds, the light gleams in the hollow, on the water that throws a bluish cast around it, on the backs of the cows, which were as dear to Gainsborough the landscapist as they were to Constable. Gainsborough had already tried his hand, more clumsily but in a sense more romantically, at this same subject round about 1760 with his *Sunset: Carthorses Drinking at a Stream* (Tate Gallery). The landscape dips down towards the water-hole where two horses are already drinking, with intense high-lights on a white rump, then rises again along a curve, as if about to form a circle rimmed by one of those dead trees for which the painter also had a predilection. The light is conveyed this time by large pinkish clouds, interwoven with blue and the pale gold that glows on the trees with bright green glints. Though without much form, the picture is sharp and sonorous, with a slightly showy charm. The *Market Cart* of 1786-87 (Tate Gallery), one of the painter's very last works, is of course more subtle and intriguing. The cart moves (as one might expect) towards a water-hole, against a luminous curtain of trees, while in a small green clearing on the right a man is gathering wood. The cart seems to issue directly from the bluish reaches of the horizon, with its load of carrots and little girls. A dog moves along beside the horse with the same brisk step, bathed in the same light. Gladness and movement are the characteristics of this picture, which makes play with very few colours, the reddish glow of a tree-trunk answering to the red of the carrots.

The landscapist in Gainsborough was a Romantic at heart, and to excess (like every true Romantic). One of his most fascinating landscapes is one of the last, and in fact he did not have time to finish it: the *Mountain Landscape with Peasants Crossing a Bridge* (National Gallery, Washington). Its tonality, so far as I know, is the most high-pitched of all his works, with a mauve sky, greenery combining forthright greens with pure blues, and a minimum of tonal perspective, apart from a background of mountains, mauve like the sky. A multitude of small flat touches of pure yellow, brown, green and carmine-tinted pink make up an exotic landscape in which a horseman, glowing with pink light, crosses the bridge over a blue and brownish stream. A chalky cliff juts out over the scene, covered with greenery shot through with pinkish brown and pure blues. It may not be very soundly designed, it may not be quite real, but it shows how far Gainsborough could go as a painter. He sketched out of doors but he was not an open-air painter; he often painted his landscapes by candlelight after coming in from a walk. He was not the only one to work out his perspective in a camera obscura. Reynolds in his fourteenth *Discourse*, in which on the whole he judges Gainsborough very fairly, describes some of his methods: 'From the fields he brought into his painting-room stumps of trees, weeds, and animals of various kinds; and designed them, not from memory, but immediately from the objects. He even framed a kind of model of landscapes on his table; composed of broken stones, dried herbs, and pieces of looking-glass, which he magnified and improved into rocks, trees, and water.' As compared with Reynolds' intellectualism, all this points to a salutary dependence on material reality, the necessary starting point for the creative imagination. Edward Edwards, in his *Anecdotes of Painting* (1808), prefers the earlier to the later landscapes, whose subjects he describes as unduly Romantic and indefinite.

It is difficult to make a choice among the many fine portraits of his London period. One of the more Van Dyckian among them is that of *Mrs Graham* (1775-77, National

Thomas Gainsborough (1727-88)

Sunset: Carthorses Drinking at a Stream, c. 1760. Oil on canvas. (56½ × 60½″). Tate Gallery, London.

Gallery of Scotland, Edinburgh), a haughty beauty leaning against the base of a column, the delicate colours of her elaborate gown standing out in contrast against the dark background. When Thoré-Bürger saw the portrait of *Mrs Siddons* (1783-85, National Gallery) just over a century ago, he was so dazzled that he read into it all the genius of the great tragic actress. But what if one did not know that this is Mrs Siddons? Would the large plumed hat against the vast red backdrop suffice to suggest the emotive power of a tragic actress? Would the averted face, staring eye and rather tight-lipped mouth confirm that suggestion? One may wonder. What is evident at once, however, is the quality of the painting as such, the choice of colours – the blue collar and ochre scarf – the play of half-tones, the intensity of the shadows. All this, even to the fur muff with the same red and the same yellow ochre, clearly denotes a strong personality.

There are, of course, at least two Gainsboroughs. When he paints his family for his own satisfaction, he works on a higher level of open-mindedness and penetration, as can be seen in *The Artist's Daughter Mary* (1777, Tate Gallery), who appears in the glow of another light, which shines upon the open lace collar and the bodice faintly sketched in and at once reabsorbed in the background.

Two Gainsboroughs? Yes and no. He was too much a man of his time not to know what had to be sacrificed to society; otherwise he would not have execrated fashionable people as he did. But in private he regained his freedom and his power to cast a spell. If he had to paint Mrs Robinson (1781-82), who for all her contemporaries was *Perdita*, after one of her acting roles, he could not forget that she was also the mistress of the Prince of Wales. In a conventional landscape, roughly brushed in, Perdita is as frail and silky as, and no more 'prominent' than, her little dog. With its discreet, low-pitched tonality, the painting is pearly and iridescent, with shimmering effects in the manner of Rubens.

The masterpiece of these years is the portrait of Squire Hallett and his wife, known as *The Morning Walk* (1785, National Gallery). Here again is that light and happy touch, that wizardry in the evocation of light, which shows him at his best. Grave and almost introspective, yet with quiet confidence, the young couple in this marriage portrait step lightly forward in the morning of life. As in Marvell's poem,

> Annihilating all that's made
> To a green thought in a green shade,

the light bathes her dress, bringing out its gossamer transparencies. The dog is there as usual, associated with the lady in her outing, just as the painter's first dogs had been associated with a hunter, sharing in the walk.

The Mall of 1783-84 (Frick Collection, New York) multiplies the movement of *The Morning Walk*, but by neatly and ingeniously combining nineteen moving or pausing figures and three little dogs, it somewhat vulgarizes that movement. Appearances notwithstanding, it is not so close to Watteau as it is to Debucourt and Rowlandson. Gravelot is said to have taught Gainsborough to use dolls as models in figure painting, as in his landscapes he used stones and dried herbs as mentioned above. In addition to dolls, he

Thomas Gainsborough (1727-88)
The Artist's Daughter Mary, 1777. Oil on canvas. (30 × 25½″). Tate Gallery, London.

made clay models of cows, whose exaggerated relief often appears to be perpetuated in his pastoral paintings. The value of such 'material aids' depends on the imagination of the artist using them. Gainsborough's imagination lets him down on occasion. As, for example, in the portrait of *Mrs Moodey and her Children* of the late 1770s, where the child held in her right arm has all the air of a doll; the painter failed to endow the picture either with vitality or the right scale.

Did Gainsborough, in the fatigue (rather than decline) of his last years, begin to lose interest in the contact with reality or anyhow in the reinvention of it as such? No explanation is ever quite simple, and the changing mood of the century itself must be allowed for. It had been realistic, with Hogarth, Fielding and Smollett; it had been rational and cultural, with Reynolds, Pope and Johnson; now it was becoming sentimental. Its novelist was Fanny Burney. One side of Gainsborough's nature found itself in agreement with the new mood, and the result was his fancy pictures. Unqualified admirers of Gainsborough rank them very high. Personally I do not care for them. The one called *Girl with Pigs* (1782) was purchased by Reynolds, understandably enough. He must have said to himself: 'At last Gainsborough is painting children as I do.' In the *Cottage Girl with Dog and Pitcher* (1785), the eyes are set in the shadow of deep sockets and the corners of the lips have that stock pucker of sadness which is all too familiar from the work of Reynolds. Her sleeve is in tatters. The puppy she holds in her arms looks as if its legs could hardly carry it and wears the same mournful expression. Even the pitcher has posed and betrays the intention that has brought it to be thus posed, following the mediocre Dutch and Flemish tradition from which, after all, these fancy pictures stem: Van Herp's *Sheep at the Pond* anticipates Gainsborough's *Cottage Door*. The painter's state of mind at that time being indivisible, one cannot help associating these fancy pictures with the letter which Gainsborough wrote to Reynolds a few days before his death: 'I am just to write what I fear you will not read, after lying in a dying state for six months. The extreme affection which I am informed of by a friend which Sir Joshua has expressed induces me to beg a last favour, which is to come once under my roof and look at my things, my woodman you never saw, if what I ask is not disagreeable to you, feeling that I may have the honour to speak to you. I can from a sincere heart say that I always admired and sincerely loved Sir Joshua Reynolds.'

One may prefer the spirit in which he wrote to the Earl of Hardwicke, who had asked him to paint a view of a particular spot: 'Mr Gainsborough presents his humble respects to Lord Hardwicke; and shall always think it an honour to be employ'd in anything for his Lordship; but with respect to real views from Nature in this country he has never seen any place that affords a subject equal to the poorest imitations of Gaspar or Claude. Paul Sandby is the only man of genius, he believes, who has employ'd his pencil that way...'

Gainsborough was averse to working in the topographical tradition of faithful and not aesthetically interpreted reproductions of a specific site. 'The subject', he insisted, 'must be of his own brain.' Actually, these last years were not entirely spent on mawkish fancy

Thomas Gainsborough (1727-88)

The Morning Walk, c. 1785. Oil on canvas. (93 × 70½"). National Gallery, London.

pictures, for he also turned to a particularly strong type of landscape painting: sea pictures. A high wind filling the sails and beating the waves against the rocks comes as a welcome change. Grey clouds, bluish-grey skies, greenish-grey water and grey rocks combine in one of these pictures to form a subtle tonality that delights the eye.

I have been reluctant to separate the portraitist from the landscapist. Yet they are quite distinct. Reynolds declared Gainsborough to be the first landscape painter in Europe, to which Wilson replied that he was the greatest portrait painter. Such statements do not mean very much. He has often been praised as an admirable draughtsman, as an artist with a much keener sense of life than Reynolds. But did he always make the most of those qualities? Did he have Hogarth's irresistible empathy? So full of life himself, did he feel the pulse of life in the bodies in front of him? If the answer is yes, then how is one to explain those awkward touches, those inert, dangling arms which occur in his women to the very end? His figures are charming images rather than substantial realities. In landscape, these problems did not arise.

In his fourteenth *Discourse*, Reynolds professed a preference for Gainsborough's 'humble attempts' in 'a lower rank of art' as against the decadent masters of the Italian school. Predicting an honourable place for him among the founders of an English School, he emphasizes 'the powerful impression of nature which Gainsborough exhibited in his portraits and in his landscapes, and the interesting simplicity and elegance of his little ordinary beggar-children.' He contrasts what Gainsborough had learned from nature with what he had not learned from the Academy or antiquity. Here one can only see the caution of a jealous man anxious to brush aside a dangerous rival. In praising him for the fact that 'he very judiciously applied himself to the Flemish School,' he tacitly blames him for knowing nothing of the Italians. But he lays stress on 'his manner of forming all the parts of his picture together; the whole going on at the same time, in the same manner as nature creates her works.' It is interesting to compare what Gainsborough himself says of his manner of composing: 'One part of a picture ought to be like the first part of a tune; that you can guess what follows, and that makes the second part of the tune.' Significantly enough, it is the musician who speaks and emphasizes the peculiar unity of the pictorial work of art as he sees it, an organic and not simply a spatial unity as Reynolds implies. The unity of a piece of music, of a tune, is of another sort. But if that unity appertains to time, time also appertains to it, and it is not just a matter of sequence. For a parallel to this conception of the making of a picture, one need not go so far as music, for it is found in the making of a poem. Unity, by which he no doubt meant tonal unity, seemed to Gainsborough a thing of primordial importance, on no account to be sacrificed; so that if the artist 'cannot master a number of objects so as to introduce them in friendship, let him do but a few.'

His daughter Margaret has left some account of his methods of work. He used long brushes (sometimes fixed on sticks as much as six feet long!) and colours as fluid and diluted as possible. Indeed, one is struck by the thinness of his paints and the rarity of impasto. But he worked with such ease and speed that, while allowing for all the demands of rhythmic movement and transparency, he was still able to make the picture surface vibrate with small, distinct, juxtaposed touches of pigment: such as in the background of the portrait of Miss Linley, for example. He seemed to be spurred on by an eagerness to overtake his vision, to achieve a promised freedom. Oil painting makes technical demands with which he could juggle but which he could not disregard. With gouache, watercolour, chalk drawing and various combinations of these media, he could let himself go. Here his arrowy speed was such as to convey what to Reynolds must have seemed the direct impression of nature. It results in an astonishing modernism of both interpretation and rendering. A contemporary lady referred disdainfully to his 'moppings'. His friends were amused to see him lay in his shadows with a sponge, his lights with a piece of chalk held with tongs. The traces that remain even in his oil paintings must have set Reynolds' teeth on edge, but he speaks of it understandingly:

> All those odd scratches and marks, which, on a close examination, are so observable in Gainsborough's pictures, and which even to experienced painters appear rather the effect of accident than design: this chaos, this uncouth and shapeless appearance, by a kind of magic, at a certain distance assumes form, and all the parts seem to drop into their proper places, so that we can hardly refuse acknowledging the full effect of diligence, under the appearance of chance and hasty negligence... It must be allowed that this hatching manner of Gainsborough did very much contribute to the lightness of effect which is so eminent a beauty in his pictures.

Reynolds' remarks are curiously pertinent and full of insight. Gainsborough's break-up of modelling was decisively anti-classical. So was his colouring. The luminous blues, the vivid pinks that so often set off the tonality, the ochres, the mauves, the bright and acid greens that make up the palette of this painter so skilled in getting the subtlest effects from a few forthright tones, all bring to mind another artist – Goya. A certain naïveté in the posing of the figure also points to the affinity between them.

When he died his house was full of unsold landscapes: 'They stood', says Sir William Beechey, 'ranged in long lines from his hall to his painting-room.' It took over half a century for them to become acceptable and enter national museums. But Constable championed his cause. Opposing and preferring him to the Italians, he admired his early pictures for their fidelity to nature and the tradition of the North. *Cornard Wood* belonged to his uncle. 'The landscape of Gainsborough', said Constable, 'is soothing, tender, and affecting. The stillness of noon, the depths of twilight, and the dews and pearls of the morning, are all to be found on the canvases of this most benevolent and kind-hearted man. On looking at them we find tears in our eyes and know not what brought them.'

English landscape art in Gainsborough's day inevitably followed the Dutch and Flemish example, and for seascape painting the arrival of the Van de Veldes in England in 1673 may be regarded as decisive. Fighting on land was seldom represented, but naval battles, with two or three ships skilfully laid out in the picture space and firing broadsides in clouds of smoke, were a favourite subject; Samuel Scott (1702-72) made variations on this theme with some originality. Of landscape properly so called, George Lambert (1700-65) is considered the father, at least as regards oil painting in England. It is also generally conceded that he is not very original and owes much to the manner of Gaspard Dughet. He is noted for those country-house views which are so characteristic of the period. Classical influence had at long last been assimilated and Lambert seems to respond to the peculiarly English atmosphere.

But the presence of Canaletto in England from 1746 to 1755 exerted a perhaps decisive influence on this still unsettled type of painting. Venice had accustomed him to urban prospects, and London seems to have further stimulated his taste for broad panoramic views. A picture like *Whitehall from Richmond House* (Goodwood Collection) conveys, at first sight, the sense of this almost panoramic sweep; then, looking more closely, one is made aware of countless details rendered with skilful illusion. The scene teems with human figures; but each consists simply of tiny dabs of pigment deftly laid in. Canaletto is the father of view-painting in London, and with the vision of Venice behind him it was only natural that he should return again and again to the river and its bridges (*Old London Bridge with its Houses, Construction of Westminster Bridge* or the blue and golden *View from the Thames of Westminster Abbey and Bridge*). His influence lasted down till Constable. Sometimes he also painted the river without the city, as in his amazing *Old Walton Bridge* (Dulwich), in which the exaggerated high-lights give an almost stereoscopic effect to the layout of bridge and figures.

Canaletto influenced Samuel Scott so that he changed from marine painting to views of London. Scott also depicted *Westminster Bridge* and the *Entrance to the Fleet River* (Guildhall) with a sharpness of detail reminiscent of Canaletto's views of the Grand Canal. But he gradually anglicized his work and the atmospheric haze of the North hangs over his noble, sweeping but simple view of the *Tower of London* (1753, Hambleden Collection) and his *Arch of Westminster Bridge* (Tate Gallery).

Apart from Gainsborough, the dominant figure in eighteenth-century English landscape painting is Richard Wilson (1714-82). He illustrates the renewal of English art as it went from one source to another, from the North to the Mediterranean. His career also shows how rash it would be to overstate the affinity of the English genius with nature. The son of a Welsh clergyman, he came to London to study painting, portraiture in particular. He practised portrait painting with some success, but comparing his *Admiral Thomas Smith* (Greenwich Hospital) with exactly contemporary portraits by Hogarth and Ramsay or even Highmore and Hayman, one is struck by the inadequacy of the modelling and an insensitive response to the human figure generally.

An important thing to note is that in 1746, well before the vogue for landscape painting, he was already painting small landscapes (Foundling Hospital) and in 1747 produced a view of Dover, full of light even in the shadows. He was a painter who had still not yet found himself when at the age of thirty-four, already a late stage in an artist's life, he left for France and Italy. In November 1750 he reached Venice and remained there till the end of 1751. There he met and became friendly with Francesco Zuccarelli, a Tuscan landscapist who, at a time when Wilson was still doing portraits, encouraged him to take up landscape. He was still undecided when in January 1752 he went on to Rome, where he lived until 1756. There he found his true vocation. Venice perhaps had already made him vaguely aware of the importance of this type of painting; he may have seen something of what Titian and Giorgione had done, but Rome for a century past had been the European centre of landscape. Thither had come Frenchmen after Claude and Poussin, Germans after Elsheimer, Dutchmen, Italians themselves with and after Salvator Rosa, and each nation, group and individual had contributed something to an increasingly complex tradition, in which classical, picturesque and by now even Romantic influences were interwoven, though the dominant form of this art was a broad, embracing, formal, idealizing vision which for a man of the north must have been a revelation. Nowhere else perhaps were nature and art so closely and movingly related. The Roman Campagna was still a place of unspoilt beauty with its unmatched combination of natural sites, tombs and ruins – a beauty which could not help being mainly architectural, imbued with a sense of time and a mood of melancholy.

Among other painters in Rome, Wilson saw much of the French landscapist Joseph Vernet, and it was apparently Vernet who did most to make him take up the same career. By the time he left Rome in 1756 he had a store of subjects sufficient to last out his life. Descending the Rhine and passing through Holland, he added Aelbert Cuyp to the

Richard Wilson (1714-82)

Croome Court, Worcestershire, 1758. Oil on canvas. (48×66″). By kind permission of The Croome Estate Trustees.

influences shaping his work. By 1757 he was back in England and in 1760 exhibited at the Society of Artists; but the prize for landscape was awarded to a certain George Smith of Chichester. A *View of Sion House* aroused the interest of George III, who sent Lord Bute to negotiate the purchase. But the price was too high for him – sixty guineas. Wilson's comment was that the King might pay by instalments. Like Whistler later, he had the art of making enemies. He became more and more blunt, bitter, aggressive. The public was alienated and sarcasm became more pointed. He drank (though only beer) and was nicknamed 'red-nosed Wilson'. As commissions dwindled, he sank into poverty and loneliness. In 1776 a few loyal friends procured him the post of librarian of the Academy. It was a humiliation to him to accept it but he had no alternative. In 1781 he retired to his native Wales where he died the following year.

He has given his references: 'Claude for air and Gaspard for composition and sentiment... But there are two painters whose merit the world does not yet know, who will not fail hereafter to be highly valued, Cuyp and Mompers.'

It is not easy to date his Italian landscapes, for after his return to England he continued to paint the same subjects. Wilson was not an open-air painter, he worked from memory; so it hardly matters whether he painted his subject after an interval of six hours or six years. It is important to remember that landscape painting at that time was what it has always been in China and Japan: a vigorously autonomous creation, a series of variations on set formulas, depending on the particular aspect of reality under consideration. Here the problem of style depends on the degree of idealization and what might be called the function of the landscape. Reynolds understood this, though he perversely overstated it. In that same fourteenth *Discourse*, in which he pays tribute to Gainsborough, he puts Wilson in his place, blaming him for introducing gods and goddesses into landscapes which are too close to common nature: 'In a very admirable picture of a storm which I have seen of his hand, many figures are introduced in the foreground, some in apparent distress, and some struck dead, as a spectator would naturally suppose, by the lightning; had not the painter injudiciously (as I think) rather chosen that their death should be imputed to a little Apollo, who appears in the sky, with his bent bow, and that those figures should be considered as the children of Niobe.' This was the grave problem of decorum. This affair of Wilson's *Niobe* reminds me of Bruegel's *Fall of Icarus* (Brussels), which actually represents a Flemish peasant ploughing his field; but at the foot of the cliff bordering that field, one catches sight of two little legs kicking in the sea, which is Icarus.

From his own academic point of view, then, Reynolds was right, and it must be admitted, too, that he puts his finger on a deep-seated contradiction between the painter's mythical sense and his feeling for external nature. It calls for a well-disposed imagination to carry through effectively a transposition which results in a change of tone, adapting the landscape to a poetic, historical or legendary subject. No, Wilson is not Poussin and when he paints *Apollo and the Seasons*, the result is a poor imitation of Claude. But his landscapes of the Roman Campagna mark the start of a vision, not of course mythico-poetic, but simply Romantic, whose next stage would be Cozens and the next after that Turner. Tivoli, Nemi, Albano, Castel Gandolfo, a gleam of afternoon light over Castel Gandolfo behind the lake, a spirited play of shadows in the foreground – that is what Wilson has to offer. These are specific, modern landscapes. *Lake Nemi with Two Monks* is modulated like a Constable from blue to russet – light, lustreless blues. The *Bridge at Rimini* (Fitzwilliam Museum, Cambridge) has the lurid lighting of a stormy day. The bay of Naples provides him with Cape Misenum, the Lucrine lake, the lake of Agnano, Lake Avernus and the bay of Baiae. His usual time of day is, like Claude's, when the sun is on the far horizon, glowing on hills, sea or lake. Such is the view of the *Lake of Agnano* in the Ashmolean Museum in Oxford, all in pale gold. As he continued Wilson tended towards a later hour and a cooler landscape. Take the *Italian River Scene with Figures* (Victoria and Albert Museum): the sun has set and a melancholy coolness invades the air. Another *Lake of Agnano* (Victoria and Albert Museum) shows the wan greenish-blue of twilight, with a dark foreground. His *Rome and the Ponte Molle* (National Museum of Wales, Cardiff) is unusual at that time for its poetic simplifications of structure, its apt evocation of all Rome with a pink strip from which the dome of St Peter's emerges, its forcible rendering and the prominence of the trees in the foreground; yet, in a general design obviously close to Claude, the green keynote owes nothing to him.

Richard Wilson (1714-82)

Ariccia: Fallen Tree. Oil on canvas. (18¾ × 28¾'').

Collection Earl of Pembroke, Wilton House, Salisbury.

Richard Wilson (1714-82)
Snowdon from Llyn Nantlle, c. 1766. Oil on canvas. (39½ × 50"). Walker Art Gallery, Liverpool.

After his return home, a process of interchange began between the Italian landscape, with its traditional movements and the tonal translation of them, and the English landscape (not yet catalogued as such), whose movements are rarely dramatic and whose subtler tonalities call for closer observation and a finer appreciation of mood. Already in Italy Wilson showed a predilection for mysterious and solitary places, crater lakes for example. *Solitude* is the name and theme of an Anglo-Italian picture of 1762 in which the human presence (shepherd? hermit?) is confronted with a rather stifling landscape of stagnant water and dense trees. He read this solitude and mystery into the landscapes of his own country, whence the familiar presence and ubiquity of man would seem to banish them. In Italy the tradition of painting was one of idealization and generalization. In England he was led to dwell on revealing particularities of sky and water. First, the neighbourhood of London called for a more secret, more silent or simply less resonant light, caught on the wane. So it is found in *The Thames at Twickenham* (c. 1760-62, City of Norwich Museums), which keeps the traditional glow of sunset in the sky and on the foliage, but gives it a new quality with the bather who has taken off his shirt. A coolness has come over the tones, whose key – though of course there is not the slightest hint of pointillism in the execution – is actually closer to Seurat than to Claude. The sailing-boat with its reflection in the water, the misty blue and the lad leaning against a tree in this subdued, faintly melancholy light make this a most attractive picture.

Constable, in painting his *Malvern Hall*, must have remembered Wilson's *Croome Court* (1758, Croome Estate Trustees). The classical landscape, with the architectural enhancement of the fine country house reflected in the stream, is admirably balanced between a lighter and a darker zone in which the light gleams fitfully on the figures and a drinking cow. Comparing *Croome Court* with *Rome and the Ponte Molle*, one can measure the fresh strength which Wilson's genius had gained from renewed contact with native realities. But in this pre-Romantic age Wilson may well have guessed that his own country would provide a more introspective, more 'interesting' light for the great silent shapes whose fascination had been revealed to him in Italy.

The *View on the Wye* (Tate Gallery) completes the peaceful foreground of river and ochre-coloured hills with a very schematic background of blue-grey mountains, under a sky in which small bright clouds float lazily – a placid, summer-evening landscape, with a hint of oncoming night. Here, at last, he was on his native ground, among those sites which the Romantics were to call Snowdonia. Of Mount Snowdon Wilson painted several versions (c. 1766). The best known are those in the Walker Art Gallery, Liverpool, and the Castle Museum, Nottingham. These two pictures are almost replicas; only the time of day is a little later in the Liverpool version, and the steeps on the other side of the water are already in shadow. Through a gap in those steeps rises Snowdon, remote and aloof, in a tone of blue whose paleness contrasts with the dark reflections in the lake. Once again the foreground figures, isolated in and by the light, stand in solitude.

The peak on the right of the picture reappears in the *View of Cader Ydris* (Tate Gallery), a composition full of emphatic rhythms set up by bold forms, the most prominent one being the dark blue mountain lake under a bluff of the same tone. The blue and greenish-blue of the shadows take on ochre tints in the light, where small figures move about. The design is less attractive and the mood less certain, less convincing, than in the case of the Snowdon pictures, but he continued to find his most congenial themes in wild and rugged scenery, though they met with little response from the public.

Years later, in 1823, at a time when Constable, disregarded by his countrymen, was about to be discovered by the French, an exhibition was held in London at which Wilson, forty years after his death, was at last given due recognition. Constable commented: 'I recollect nothing so much as a large, solemn, bright, warm, fresh landscape by Wilson which still swims in my brain like a delicious dream.' And in a letter he referred to Wilson as a martyr and 'one of the great men who show to the world what exists in nature but

Richard Wilson (1714-82)

The Thames at Twickenham, c. 1760-62. Oil on canvas. (23 ½ × 36″). By courtesy of the City of Norwich Museums.

Thomas Jones (1742-1803)

Penkerigg, 1772. Oil on paper. (9 × 12″). By courtesy of the City Museum and Art Gallery, Birmingham.

which was not known before his time.' Ruskin expressed his belief that 'with the name of Richard Wilson, the history of sincere landscape art founded on a meditative love of nature begins in England.' Girtin, Cotman and Turner did not forget him.

Another Welshman, Thomas Jones (1742-1803), was Wilson's pupil from 1763 to 1765 and like him went in search of inspiration to Italy, where he lived from 1776 to 1783. His work is very uneven and it would be tempting to dismiss him as a mere copyist of his master. For many the sight of his *Buildings in Naples* (1782, National Museum of Wales, Cardiff), shown in two recent exhibitions, came as a surprise and revelation. Here was a more serious Utrillo who had lived two centuries ago. A wall and its windows, a door, the line of a roof, right angles fitted together with a sure hand, the odd balance of two unequal black rectangles in the foreground door and window, the almost naïve straightforwardness

Thomas Jones (1742-1803)
Buildings in Naples, 1782. Oil on paper. (5 ½ × 8 ½″). National Museum of Wales, Cardiff.

William Hodges (1744-97)

A Crater in the Pacific, 1772-75. Oil on canvas. (40 × 50″). The Art Gallery and Museum, Brighton.

of this construction which conveys an intense feeling of reality with two or three colours, for under the whitish tone of the house one divines the brownish ochre of the door which, mixed with the blue of the sky, forms the greenish tone of the buildings in shadow in the middle distance – all this goes to make up a strangely successful and arresting picture.

This half-amateur painter has a seductive and singular talent, an eye of his own. In his *Penkerigg* (1772, City Museum and Art Gallery, Birmingham), leaving aside the rather tamely dramatic sky (notable, however, for an unusual mauve pink), it is the actual terrain of this hill that holds the eye; the grainy texture wrought in successive patches and criss-crossed by the dark hedgerows, and the greenish tint that seems to ignore problems of tonality and, one is tempted to say, triumphs over them. In another landscape of *Cascades at Tivoli* (1777, Fitzwilliam Museum, Cambridge) he uses a curious blue, almost like Nattier, to mark out all the hills to the left of the cascades and the trees to the right, a blue with undercurrents of pink streaking the landscape.

William Hodges (1744-97) was also a pupil of Wilson's in the years 1763-66, when the latter's importance was still recognized. None of his early work is of particular interest, but in 1772 he was engaged as draughtsman for Captain Cook's second expedition to the South Seas, and those exotic landscapes were revealed to him before any conventions attached to them. His views of Tahiti gain a notable airiness from the thin trunks of the coconut palms, while the mountainous scenery looms up spectrally in the background. His *A Crater in the Pacific* (1772-75, The Art Gallery and Museum, Brighton), may have been situated somewhere in New Zealand where, before engineers discovered a source of energy in them, such volcanoes with their bursts of weirdly coloured smoke must have been one of the most spectacular sights in the world. Hodges felt this and expressed it. With the support of Warren Hastings he worked in India from 1780 to 1784, rendering the strange yellowish plains with admirable sobriety. Hodges and Jones stand outside the confines of official art, with them landscape was an adventure.

4

Art and Its Social Involvement.
Middle-Class Society, the World of Fashion and the New Classes.
Joseph Wright of Derby, Zoffany, Stubbs and Morland.
The Evolution of Caricature:
From Expressive Realism to Expressionism: Rowlandson and Gillray.

JOSEPH WRIGHT OF DERBY (1734-97) is one of those artists who, rediscovered after several generations of oblivion or disdain, is seen to represent something characteristic in the English past. Belonging by birth and background to the middle class, he rose above its conventions in his eager attachment to the spirit of the new age. He studied under Thomas Hudson, who was also Reynolds' teacher. After painting portraits, he went on to genre scenes associated with scientific investigations, and from there passed on to industrial themes. He quarrelled with the Academy but had an immediate success with the public. Making the journey to Italy in 1773, he remained there until 1775, chiefly in Rome, with an excursion to Naples. Returning to Derby for good in 1777, he devoted himself to portraiture and landscape, Derbyshire having a great reputation for its picturesque sites. He built up a new clientele among the middle class and intellectuals of the region, together with his old patrons, the industrialists.

He seems to have been quite unaware of the academic and critical taboos attaching to familiar, serviceable, everyday things. He lived in that part of the country where industrial development made use of scientific inventions, but where the spirit of the century, the spirit of experiment, was not confined to practical applications but became a passion for discovery. Why was that spirit associated with candlelight in his pictures? Perhaps because the use of artificial light for study had a symbolic value. He linked up of course with a long tradition of vehement chiaroscuro painting. When Northcote, the pupil of Reynolds, called Wright the most famous painter of his time for candlelight scenes, he implicitly recognized that it was a genre with tricks and rules of its own to focus light, from an invisible source, more dramatically on figures and, above all, faces. Wright's *Experiment with the Air Pump* (1768, Tate Gallery) is admirably grouped and superbly painted. Never did he express with such variously posed heads so delicate a play of emotions reflected in young and beautiful faces – wonder, surprise, perplexity, anguish – for the bird is 'dead' , pending the return of the air that will revive it.

The *Academy by Candlelight* of 1769 marks the end of a phase. After 1770 the focus of his art shifted from science and the fine arts to work. The ruddy glow of *The Iron Forge* (1772, Broadlands Collection) associates work with light, and the white-hot metal illuminates faces and muscular arms. The painter knew his business and it was not only by lighting effects in the manner of Honthorst and Caravaggio (it is unlikely that he knew anything of Georges de La Tour) that he showed it. The figure grouping is at once superb and artful, though the baby in the arms of the over-elegant blacksmith's wife is not much more natural than a child by Reynolds; it is too conscious of being on display, as is the young girl who completes the trio. But the back of the workman placing the metal on the anvil is a fine piece of foreshortening. Most reminiscent perhaps of the earlier masters of chiaroscuro are the left-hand figure and the little girl leaning drowsily against his knee, the light playing over them with such delicacy and precision, the shadows lying on them so broad and warm. Most unusual is the architecture of another forge (not reproduced here), which looks like an imposing ruin with its heavy beams, but also with pilasters and semicircular arches, one adorned with angel reliefs. Was ever such a forge seen in England or, in introducing it into painting, did Wright intend it to recall Christ's crib?

Everything in the way of candlelight and lamplight effects had already been done by the Tenebrists; there was little left for Wright to invent. But nonetheless what is novel, illustrating a new age and a new vision, is an outdoor night-piece like *Arkwright's Cotton Mill by Night* (*c.* 1783, Booth Collection). Though there is a faint infusion of moonlight, it is

Joseph Wright of Derby (1734-97)

Eruption of Vesuvius, 1774. Gouache on paper. (12⅝ × 18½"). Derby Museum and Art Gallery.

Joseph Wright of Derby (1734-97)

A Cavern, Evening, 1774. Oil on canvas. (40 × 50″). Smith College Museum of Art, Northampton, Mass.

not the moon that gives this strange pinkish flush to the night, but the man-made light by which men are working and which, through all the windows of these buildings typical of the following century, sheds its glow over the landscape. For all his diligence Wright does not seem to have learned much in Italy, but it must have been Italy that opened his eyes to the fascinations of fire, his favourite element. His *Fireworks at the Castel Sant'Angelo,* with flaring rockets lighting up the sky and the serene alignment of buildings from which St Peter's emerges, with its umbrella pines in the foreground, is almost like Wilson's *Rome and the Ponte Molle* in reverse. But his *Eruption of Vesuvius* (Derby Museum and Art Gallery) in

Joseph Wright of Derby (1734-97)
The Iron Forge, 1772. Oil on canvas. (48 × 52″). From the Broadlands Collection.

broad daylight, probably painted on the spot in 1774 when he had the good luck to see that glorious sight, is certainly one of the most extraordinary works ever done in the gouache technique. Hokusai never did a finer picture of Fujiyama. Overhung with mighty columns of smoke and flame that broaden into clouds covering the whole width of the picture, the volcano pours out zigzagging streams of lava which also broaden out to left and right, spanning the whole landscape. What is puzzling about Wright is the fantastic disparity between his sense of tonality and his control of colour. Everything here is perfect and seems to have been obtained by apt combinations of the three primary colours and white. Elsewhere one is put off by a pinkish-brown keynote very much in vogue in colour lithographs of the late nineteenth century, and often combined with yellowish greens (*Sir Brooke Boothby*, 1781; *The Coke Family*; *Stephen Jones*, 1785). Apart from that, his portraits must be recognized as an important record of an age of varied endeavour and momentous changes. Wright's realism is no longer that of Hogarth. *Sir Richard Arkwright*, with a model machine beside him, is not meant, as *Captain Coram* was, to evoke, transpose and parody a nobler style. Sir Richard Arkwright is what he is, and he only spreads his sturdy legs to allow his fat manufacturer's belly to settle more comfortably into position. Sir Brooke Boothby was one of the last friends to enjoy Rousseau's confidence; in 1776 the latter gave him the manuscript of *Rousseau juge de Jean-Jacques*, which he published at Lichfield in 1780. Wright's portrait of him, lying reading the book in a woody glade, shows the genuine nature lover, despite the gloved hands, one of them supporting the delicate face.

It has been said of him, what cannot be said of Romney, Gainsborough and Reynolds, that he posed his figures as little as possible, or not at all. He portrayed them as they lived, under a sunshade with a pencil and portfolio by way of symbolic attributes, as with the *Gisbornes*, or chatting familiarly as they ride out on horseback, like the *Coltmans*.

Wright is an intimist, and like the intimists of that period he was torn between two claims; in other words, he was also a Romantic, and night-pieces of one kind or another are the only constant feature of his work. The *Lighthouse on the Coast of Tuscany* (c. 1790, Tate Gallery) may be described by art historians as 'painted in the manner of Joseph Vernet'; yet it has the main characteristics of Wright's night-scenes – the interplay of the bluish light of the full moon and the faintly pinkish light of the beacon with the clouds and waves. More literary, but with a similar bluish cast, is *The Lady in Milton's 'Comus'*, looking up as a large, reassuring moon appears above a 'sable cloud'.

One could hardly imagine a greater contrast than that between Wright of Derby and Johann Zoffany (1734/5-1810). Born in Frankfurt, probably of a Bohemian family, he studied in Rome, apparently for some time, before coming to London about 1760. His name is usually associated with a type of genre painting which he contributed to create: theatrical scenes. He was no doubt encouraged to pursue this line of work by Garrick who, as an actor portrayed in his roles, only stood to gain by it. Garrick even put him up in his own house, encouraging and orienting him in his early days in England. The century was veering towards sentiment and England saw its theatre as Diderot wished to see the theatre in France, as a readily understood language of gestures expressive of strong or touching sentiments. Zoffany's stage pictures hesitate between a pure, almost photographic illustration of the scene and a more or less free interpretation of his text, such as Highmore had already given in his *Pamela* series.

Johann Zoffany (1734/5-1810)

Portrait of Mrs Oswald, c. 1760-65. Oil on canvas. (89¼ × 62½″). National Gallery, London. ▷

Sir Lawrence Dundas and his Grandson Lawrence, c. 1769. Oil on canvas. Collection Marquess of Zetland.

After 1770 Zoffany turned from the theatre to conversation pieces executed to order, family groups usually with several children. He passed easily from the family of Lord Bute to the royal family and portrayed *Queen Charlotte and her Two Elder Sons* (Windsor Castle). Here one sees at once that Highmore, with his naïve and clumsy touches, has been left far behind. This is a small masterpiece in the European style of the day, with its sound design, the force of the verticals which, though perfectly simple (this could be a middle-class home), sustain the dignity of the royal personage, the play of clear-cut relief effects in direct or indirect lighting, the easy familiarity of the poses (the Queen's hand is resting on the head of a big friendly dog) and the charm of the light colouring which first appeared in interiors before being taken up in other forms of painting. Comparing Zoffany's interiors with Hogarth's, one notes a transition from baroque envelopment to the linear clarity of neo-classicism, from the measured, concentrated, dramatized light of Hogarth, like the glow of a candlelight scene, to the broad diffusion and perhaps excessive luminism of *Sir Lawrence Dundas and his Grandson Lawrence* (*c.* 1769, Collection Marquess of Zetland), in which the seascape over the mantelpiece looks as if it were illuminated by a projector, as do in fact all the other pictures, ornaments and objects in the room.

Zoffany's qualities are those of acquired skill rather than genius. Witness the (again) almost photographic precision of his *Life Class at the Royal Academy* (Windsor), in which the academicians, each a perfect likeness, are brought together in a large, admirably organized group. Impressed by this performance, Queen Charlotte commissioned Zoffany to go to Florence and paint the *Tribuna of the Uffizi* (Windsor). It took him four years to finish this exacting piece of work. He did not simply reproduce what he saw there, a room crowded with paintings, statuary and *cognoscenti*, but composed his picture by omitting this or that work, changing the size or position of another, and solving the problem of the patterned floor tiles by masking them with a host of objects which had no place there.

His *Portrait of Mrs Oswald* (*c.* 1770, National Gallery) is a work of exquisite refinement showing an elderly lady sitting at the foot of a tree, her pensive face standing out against the trunk, her hands crossed in her lap, a large, pale yellow hat hanging on her arm and setting off her black shawl and blue gown – a blue of which the painter was very fond. Zoffany's gifts were varied and, though he may have had a touch of genius, it is masked by opportunism.

Zoffany enjoyed a full share of honours and prosperity but George Stubbs (1724-1806) was never more than an Associate of the Royal Academy and fame and fortune eluded him. Both his training and his specialization were unusual and gave him a useful, appreciated, but inferior position in a society ordered on the hierarchical system. An eager, lifelong student of both human and animal anatomy, he painted portraits for a livelihood. For several years, until 1760, he lived in an isolated Lincolnshire farmhouse, dissecting horses and doing the drawings which went to illustrate his classic *Anatomy of the Horse*, published in 1766. He had gone to Italy in the 1750s, travelling as far as Rome, in order to assure himself that nature was superior to art. Hogarth in his youth had come to the same conclusion; but he stated it with a touch of humour that, somehow, one does not expect to find in Stubbs. He is said to have returned home by way of Morocco, where, according to his biographer, he saw a lion attack and devour a horse, and the sight haunted his mind for the rest of his life. He settled in London about 1760 and exhibited in 1761 at the Society of

Artists. During the 1760s he produced a series of pictures of *Mares and Foals*, with a variety of closely observed expressions, even including that glint of terror peculiar to a horse's eyes. Then, too, he painted his dramatic animal pictures, like the *Lion Attacking a Horse* (1765, National Gallery of Victoria, Melbourne) and the *White Horse Frightened by a Lion* (1770, Walker Art Gallery, Liverpool). The former seems to me one of his finest, with a kind of savanna dotted with trees rolling away into the dimness of the distant background.[9] The *White Horse Frightened by a Lion* offers the superb contrast of its white coat against the dark brown rocks where the lion is lurking. But the head of that lion rather

George Stubbs (1724-1806)

White Horse Frightened by a Lion, 1770. Oil on canvas. (40 × 50½″). Walker Art Gallery, Liverpool.

reminds one of Lewis Carroll's Cheshire cat, and the landscape is more like cardboard than reality. All his life Stubbs was attracted by wild-animal subjects and seems to have been torn between the Classical vision of an ordered nature and the Romantic vision of a cruel, disordered world. One hardly knows where to classify his last project for a book on the *Comparative Anatomy of Man, Tiger and Fowl*; perhaps in a special category on Science and Humour. While his lions are not always very convincing, one cannot help admiring the truthfulness and compelling presence of his *Cheetah with Two Indian Attendants and a Stag* (1765, City Art Galleries, Manchester). The highlights on the white fur are more intense than the white tunics of the Indian attendants against their dark skin. The stag, possibly a stuffed animal, was only added to fill out the picture and motivate the cheetah.

The strange picture of a *Baboon and Albino Macaque Monkey* is informed by the same enthusiasm for unusually white or eerily lurking animal figures, very much in a romantic vein. This depiction of a 'freak of nature', though based on careful observation, takes on an

George Stubbs (1724-1806)

Lion Attacking a Horse, 1765. Oil on canvas. (26 × 38¼"). National Gallery of Victoria, Melbourne.

George Stubbs (1724-1806)
A Lady and Gentleman in a Phaeton, 1787. Oil on canvas. (32½ × 40″).
National Gallery, London.

almost Surrealist quality. With his dark face and white belly, the baboon is a personage, while the macaque monkey is an object. Holding a staff in its right hand, like a chimpanzee in a circus, and raising its left hand with a pointing index finger, this baboon has the memorable pose of a preacher.

The association of man and horse appears repeatedly in Stubbs's work. The picture in the Tate Gallery, oddly entitled *Landscape with Portrait of a Gentleman Holding a Horse* exemplifies both his qualities and his defects. The light is conventional. The landscape is a picturesque construction of water and rocks, without any gradations of colour, against which the white coat of the horse shines resplendently. A graceful curve that would have pleased Hogarth runs from the horse's nostrils and muzzle over its arching back to the tail of the dog, which is also white. The rhythm is sustained and the picture filled out by the gentleman in a riding coat of intense, enamel-like blue with a red collar and red braid, standing to best effect between horse and dog.

The most fascinating of his open-air conversation pieces is *A Lady and Gentleman in a Phaeton* (1787, National Gallery). As far as the landscape is concerned, he did what he could: a tree, presumably an oak, in the middle distance to maintain the figures; several trees, presumably poplars, in the background; more trees, ill-defined, on the left. The gentleman holding the reins and the lady beside him are smiling, gracious and attentive, but are still barely lifelike. The lady's huge, white, plumed hat and neckerchief give a bright note and contrast with the intensely black coats of the two horses, who belong to a world of which this lady and gentleman know nothing, but of which one is made aware by the taut arc of the animals' necks and their bending heads.

Although British art historians insist that Stubbs is an artist like any other, unjustly treated merely because his subjects were considered inferior, I think it must in all fairness

George Stubbs (1724-1806)
Mares and Foals Disturbed by Approaching Storm, 1764-65. Oil on canvas. (39 × 74″).
Collection Viscountess Ward of Witley, London.

George Stubbs (1724-1806)
Gimcrack with a Groom on Newmarket Heath, c. 1765. Oil on canvas. (38 × 73 ½″).
Reproduced by kind permission of the Stewards of the Jockey Club.

be said that he was a painter who had to meet that dual claim, scientific and artistic, which has already been noted in Wright of Derby, and that in the result he was too much interested in the nature of things to sacrifice it to the impression and the rendering. Those who dislike the smell of painting may let Stubbs be. The others had better bring a magnifying glass. Thus equipped, they can count the buckles of the harness and even the number of studs and eyelets, and then observe the phaeton, which is so carefully rendered down to the last detail of the springs and traps. To all intents and purposes, this is naïve painting. This depiction of objects, however, goes beyond their individuality, embracing even their disposition. Nothing mentioned up to now can be described as a sporting picture, but a fine example of that genre is *Gimcrack with a Groom on Newmarket Heath* (c. 1765, Jockey Club). Gimcrack, a superb thoroughbred, is very much the hero of the scene, standing in the foreground between a groom and jockey, with a stable lad underneath inspecting his feet. But, in the characteristic manner of naïve art, Gimcrack also appears in the background, outrunning three other horses. One side of a nearly isosceles triangle runs from the rooftop of the building in the foreground and meets the horizon line just at the second building towards which Gimcrack is galloping. The eye is satisfied with the run it is induced to make, and this is a prime requirement of sporting prints.

Though he seems to have worked very little out of doors, Stubbs is a superb painter of open-air scenes. One such represents *Lord and Lady Melbourne, Sir Ralph Milbanke and John Milbanke* (1770, Desborough Collection), with three horses, the one on the left forming with the two others a sharp angle that is emphasized by the curve of the second horse's bending neck. This is unquestionably one of his finest works, with the neat play of light on the left-hand couple and a perfect ease and balance in the layout of the human figures and horses under the great oak spreading out above them.

What about the Morlands? I use the plural because it is clear that George (1763-1804) owed his technique, if not his gifts, to the strict training which he received from his father Henry Robert Morland (1716-97); and also because the latter already shows the dual characteristic that was to distinguish his son, an unusual manual skill and an acute sensitivity to visual appearances, which were rendered with a certain lightness and freedom of touch. As much may be said no doubt of many little masters of genre painting. Though few works of any note by Henry Robert Morland are known, it must be said that no Dutch or Flemish work can match the charming nocturnal effect of *A Girl Singing Ballads by a Paper Lanthorn* in the Tate Gallery, where it is set off by the surprising *Laundry Maid* with an iron, a pattern of whites arranged as if with symbolic intent.

Henry Walton (1746-1816), who had much the same gifts, showed more care and thought in organizing similar subjects, as in the *Girl Buying a Ballad* (1778). Instead of merely presenting a touching or attractive figure, he builds up a setting and a scene, and in the same direct and forthright lighting he contrasts two presences, the darker figure of the poor ballad vendor, seen against his sheets pinned to the wall, and the bright figure of a pretty maid standing between the sharp edges of a pilaster.

George Morland is disappointing. He is like those pupils of whom the master says: 'Amateurish, could do better.' He simply takes what comes his way, and does so little with it. He is the painter of a sturdy, rustic, very Flemish, very countrified England, due to pass away with the industrial revolution. An 'English Teniers', he painted the delights of rural life and the charm of cattle. His work is too literal to be anything like Gainsborough's fancy pictures: Morland's donkeys and goats (*On the Farm*, Ashmolean Museum, Oxford) have no need of charming little girls. Their existence is purely material and the brushwork sensual: Morland's luminous painting followed the abundant aesthetic speculation of that day, which was of the opinion that the rougher an animal's coat, the more picturesque it is. His drinkers and peasants are, needless to say, equally picturesque, when they are not emotively appealing, as in those 'cottage doors' that alternate with 'alehouse doors' (*Outside the Alehouse Door*, 1792, Tate Gallery). The handling is always interesting: it is good painting with a broad treatment of light. But the perception of things is insensitive. In England, where criticism is traditionally based on moral considerations, this caused no surprise. After all, Morland drank and lived wildly; how could his painting be serious? But one cannot help noting the morbid character of that dissipated and often hunted life. Whether by temperament or from his father's over-strict discipline, he was unbalanced from the start and did not gradually become so. The relative indigence of his work must be seen in that context.[10]

Morland was a friend of Thomas Rowlandson (1756-1827): is this another case of a mismanaged career? If pictorial art is regarded as an objective hierarchy rather than a manifestation of individual genius, Rowlandson's career was something of a disaster. Yet all witnesses agree that he could do anything and that, for example, 'he painted the nude better than Mortimer.' Only one or two (mediocre) oil paintings by his hand are known. Some may say, perhaps, that there are all too many watercolours.

George Moore made no secret of his contempt for English art. Someone countered: 'Yet you esteem Rowlandson?' 'Yes', was the reply, 'so long as I don't think of Goya.' The Goya, presumably, of the *Caprichos*. Perhaps the problem should be stated this way: is Rowlandson inferior within his own way of seeing? It must first be defined.

The scope of his work is enormous and so rich in lessons that it may be described as inexhaustible. Geography, topography, ports, cities, landscapes, fairs, occupations, entertainments, shows and more besides, are portrayed, all with powerful individuality. His

George Morland (1763-1804)

Outside the Alehouse Door, 1792. Oil on canvas. (13¾ × 10¾"). Tate Gallery, London.

hand was equally skilful with pen or brush, despite gaming, lechery and all-night orgies. He seems to have had connections with the underworld of vice and cruelty, for at one time, having been robbed, he went looking for the thief in his haunts, and failing to find him, observed and drew another criminal, who by this means was recognized, taken and hanged. In 1785 he watched and drew an amputation, done of course without anaesthesia. He shows the surgeon leering horribly at the wretched patient, as he holds down the leg with his knee and saws away at it like a butcher while the blood pours down. But, as an English commentator notes, there is so much humour in the figure of the surgeon, and so subtle a play of interweaving lines, that the horror written on the patient's face and the insensitivity to pain pass almost unnoticed.

Handsome, a fine figure of a man, he revelled with insolent gusto in the pleasures of life. His realism is that of the cynic, based on those attitudes which are most commonly shared – contempt for the weak and the ugly. The ugliness he sneers at is often that of the old and wealthy, placed in an unfairly advantageous position. Hogarth must have been familiar enough with the disreputable haunts of Covent Garden, but he did not think it anything to boast about. In a powerful composition of 1787, *Sharpers in Smithfield*, Rowlandson pictured himself among the tricksters, with a disquieting cast of features. Sitting round the table, cards in hand, are a victim and villains, their common villainy pointed up with a wonderful variety of expression – an eye regarding the prey, a faintly leering face, the tension of the game marked in the hand holding cards, pipe or glass of punch. All this distinguishes individuals united by a purpose. These are physiognomies after the heart of Lavater or Fuseli: the foxy rogue, the apish rogue, the good-natured rogue, whose highlighted belly dominates the card table; also the wolfish rogue, hard-featured and keen-eyed as a wild beast. He is Rowlandson, aged thirty-one.

Caricature is instinctively levelled *against* something. It does not need to be strongly motivated, because aggressiveness is in its very nature and in that of its practitioners. Rowlandson was indifferent, especially where politics was concerned. If Georgiana, the beautiful Duchess of Devonshire, in the course of a notorious election campaign, bought votes for her party with kisses, it provided a first-rate 'subject', amusing and alluring. And that was all that mattered.

Rowlandson's England was neither politically nor socially structured. It consisted only of individuals, individually associated or opposed in positions of strength or weakness. Hogarth in 1740 prefigured the England of 1840 and anticipated the importance of the class that was to make itself master of production; with him, a century in advance, one finds the 'morality' of Dickens. Rowlandson, in his reckless irresponsibility, seems to antedate 1700. His œuvre seems to embrace a whole nation which, though even then in course of being proletarianized, had not yet noticed it and went its way freely in all directions. Though his men and women are dominated by lusty humour, it cannot be said that that is all there is to them, nor that, with or without a class context, Rowlandson has much respect for people; he is neither awed by fine clothes nor condescending with humble folk. That is the wonderful thing about him: he gets right inside the part of his brazen, pipe-smoking *Fishwives* (or *Billingsgate Market*, 1784), taking stock of the customer with a shrewd glance. His grimy, tattered rag-pickers sort out their wretched pickings; if they are young, like the couple in *Love and Dust*, they can always fall back on the pleasures of love.

Pleasure runs riot here, and there is a Flemish gusto about these carousals, banquets and love-makings, for the girls are willing enough and more often bare-breasted than not. But he handles his cast more discriminatingly than Hogarth, for while the girls are often good-looking, with a rounded beauty, his men are not spared and are usually turned into comic lovers. He likes to group a schematic crowd around a fair, a cock fight, or a bull and dog, or bear and dog fight, a boxing or wrestling match, fencers, jugglers, tight-rope walkers or dancers, with the inevitable pickpockets. It is unusual for him to record so refined a scene as *Christie's Auction Rooms* (British Museum): it gives further proof of his virtuosity, for even here the expressive variety and force of his darting line succeeds triumphantly.

Life in Rowlandson's England seems to have been lived almost wholly out of doors. It was only under Victoria that the rain and fog kept people at home. This is a world of active bodies, giving rein to their vitality in games, somersaults, embraces, enjoying the delights

Thomas Rowlandson (1756-1827)

Christie's Auction Rooms. Watercolour. British Museum, London.

and bearing with the mishaps of physical activity. The moral of it all? *Gaudeamus igitur, juvenes dum sumus...*, for age is hideous and the old man's appetites are ridiculous. It is brief and apt to be nasty, like the human condition; and then in the end, it conveys the moral lessons of experience. For age is what youth has made it: fat, gouty, helpless, from over-drinking and over-eating. And the pox plays its part. *A Bawd on her Last Legs* is not nice to look at. If decay is the price that must be paid for life, decay with a vengeance is the price paid for a life lived to the full, and vice quickens the pace. The stereotype of the healthy life harks back to Hogarth: *The Town Beau and the Country Beau* are, in the one case, ridiculous, in the other provocative. Finally, such an artist could hardly have so strong a grasp of individuals without also being disgusted at certain gross iniquities in their relations: the parson, already gouty, receiving a tithe pig from a starving peasant; overfed officers giving alms to a pregnant beggar woman with a child on her back. In the final analysis, then, the mob is seen to be rich in lusty young fellows and blooming girls begging to be embraced, while the leisured classes gave full scope to Rowlandson's genius for the grotesque.

Where exactly, in this more or less satirical delineation of the times, does the artist come in? How far does this caricaturist deserve to be ranked among the painters? Unlike Gillray, for example, who usually had his print in mind, so that his working instrument was the burin, Rowlandson is essentially a watercolourist, and for him the first stage of creation is the watercolour, often three or four of them, before the print was made. I cannot say whether an inventory of them has ever been attempted. The holdings of the British Museum, the Victoria and Albert Museum and the Cabinet des Estampes in Paris represent only a fraction of these works, while private collections are inexhaustibly rich in them.

He is a watercolourist, but not primarily a colourist, though one of his working methods, giving further proof of his fantastic virtuosity, consisted in applying the colours first, then the outlines. He is a calligrapher, perhaps one of the most fabulously gifted that the West has ever produced. His calligraphy outlines objects and plots the movements and intended movements of figures. It manifests his immediate and seemingly instinctive grasp of that baroque design which Hogarth so assiduously pursued. His line darts forward, surrounding and catching a body, tying up with both internal lines and contours, enveloping, coiling and breaking into arabesques. His hand is incredibly supple, it seems to draw faster than the eye can see. The full curves and spirals have the smoothness of a caress or the flutters of passion. But while the libido underlies it all, its manifestations are very various and an independent life seems to quicken the lines holding individual forms together, merging in one dancing whole the just and the unjust, the beautiful, the ugly and the grotesque.

Rowlandson's work is seen at once to fall into two classes, one of picturesque delineation, the other of expressive or over-expressive design. Pictures like *Vauxhall Gardens* (1789), whatever their charm, are of much the same order as those of Debucourt in France. An almost equally broad and collective scene like *Landing at Greenwich* differs from it in the unity of rhythm and movement: a human movement strongly built up and running counter to the courses of the river and the steady recession of houses beside it, like a kind of joyful forward sweep storming the steps that mount up between two inns. The *Fencing Match* (1788) is more strongly marked by an overall movement and the design is balanced with almost flawless symmetry; the two fencers with the two onlookers standing in the centre and the two seated forming a triangle repeated by the remaining onlookers. The most famous of these expressive designs is *The Exhibition Starecase* of 1811. As usual, it is a combination of contradictory movements which are nevertheless locked together in a unique and eye-catching effect. Taking the strongly ascending curve of the stairway, he fills it with a cascade of bare-legged and bare-breasted girls tumbling headlong down; this provides the momentum, and it is combined with the slow and peaceful movement of other figures mounting the stairs. The principle of analogical parallelism, so often exemplified in Hogarth, is represented here by the movement of the nude figures in the frieze, and in particular the Callipygian Venus turning round in her niche with a play of serpentine curves.

Hogarth's concern in his figures was with the expression of character. Rowlandson's imagination functioned on different lines, and his concern was rather with expression suggestive of a situation. This means, on the one hand, that he distorts his figures much more; and, on the other, that the forces brought into play, often in the full stress of violence, are handled in a vein bordering on expressionism.

Rowlandson is an artist of extraordinary powers, but he is not a great artist. He did not take his art seriously and the consequences were fatal. Fine draughtsmanship and effective design were virtues which he could not help having. To lend solidity to his grace, colour was needed. But his palette of watercolours in light washes is essentially decorative; it varies greatly but usually consists of cobalt blue, pure or more or less carmine-coloured pinks, light-yellow ochres, and Veronese greens extending to the palest. And all that fails to create space. Space for him was like a stage property, a limited mould in which he installed his action. Movements of terrain had no interest for him. He preferred a shapely leg. Because he is so much admired, a few of his landscapes have been rescued from oblivion. They cannot match the crowded figure scenes which I have referred to, but even these are apt to fail in their attempts to convey distance. This is, ultimately, because with him space is so associated with time that he admits it only in its immediacy. Except when he is dealing with the sea: to that liquid space he seems more responsive. He has a keen feeling for water, its flat expanse relieved by the pure, thin, straight lines of masts and yard-arms or the curves of rounded hulls. And these lines, linked up with those of wharfs and near-by places (*Coast Scene, Deptford*), go to create the overall unity of a landscape. His *English Dance of Death*, on the other hand, is quite devoid of any imaginative grasp of what death means. Klingender was right, however, in emphasizing the importance of the 1799 composition, *Distress*. But he would seem to go too far in carrying its influence down to Delacroix's *Christ on the Sea of Gennesareth* of 1853 (unless there is some reference to Rowlandson by Delacroix which has escaped me); it may not even extend as far as the *Raft of the Medusa*, for in the interval there had been Turner's *Shipwreck* of 1805. I have no doubt whatever that Turner had Rowlandson in mind, taking up where the latter left off. *Distress* represents the castaways in an open boat, as a dead body is being tipped overboard; one bowed, broad-backed figure seen from behind grips the gunwale with an outstretched arm; the sea is powerfully drawn, with the black sail merging into the dark sky, while the crest of the waves looms darkly in the comparative whiteness of the left quarter of the picture. *Distress* is the product either of a singular effort of imagination or, quite possibly, of supreme skill.

James Gillray (1757-1815) was unquestionably more profound than Rowlandson, and if he had been more of a painter, even of a watercolourist, he would deserve a prominent place here. But his drawings do not often show the same power that informs his prints. Like Hogarth, he came of a poor family and received little or no schooling in the formal sense. Like Hogarth again, he was apprenticed to an engraver before being able to devote himself to graphic art. After wandering about with a company of strolling players, he was admitted as a student to the Royal Academy schools. There he learnt to compose his inventions and to parody those of others (West's *Death of Wolfe*). To this regular course of training was probably due in part the allegorical and emblematic character of his early caricatures. It may have stemmed in part, too, from the peculiar stamp of his imagination, which veered away from observed realities.

He was a heavy drinker and this may have heightened the hallucinatory quality of so much of his work. By about 1809 his hand had lost its sure touch, his imagination was flagging and in 1810 he went mad. In the space of thirty years he had produced nearly a thousand caricatures.

This is not the place to examine the political significance of his art. Satire, of which caricature is one variety, depends on its public, and the public, like Shakespeare's ground-lings, is a weathercock. The caricaturist sometimes follows and sometimes leads; as Gillray cynically remarked, he must go where the money is. He had an exuberant sense of the grotesque and ludicrous and a love of the spacious and noisy. There is an epic grandeur in some of his parodies. In his mock-heroic and burlesque veins he produced travesties of the Apocalypse, Shakespeare and Milton, turned of course in such a way as to touch contemporary events. The satire diverges in two directions, for it is usually 'in the manner of' and ridicules both model and subject.

Among his chief targets were Revolutionary France and Napoleon and, at home, Fox. It has been well said that the *Apotheosis of Hoche* concentrates the excesses of the French Revolution in a single vision. Gillray's anti-French conservatism is found again in *Voltaire Instructing the Infant Jacobinism* (c. 1798, New York Public Library).

To these two obsessions must be added the long series of caricatures of George III, the Queen and the Prince of Wales, almost unbelievable in the impudence and audacity with which they lampoon the King's miserly habits and his prodigal son with his succession of mistresses. They are full of erotic innuendoes. While Rowlandson is the man of calligraphic draughtsmanship, Gillray is the man of gesture, of expressive line and mass, sharply defining and distributing forms to surprising effect. He is also the man of distortion and excess, monstrously exaggerating any motif, hat, hair, back of a chair, belly, bed or pool of shadow, that becomes the centre of gravity of the picture and supports all the rest. The interrelations of the figures and the unanimity of the gestures parodied from Fuseli (or Blake) denote the interplay of moods and govern an organic, rhythmically organized composition which never calls for many protagonists in the foreground group (though behind there may be a profusion of hallucinating figures) and balances them with baroque accents round a neatly placed central figure. Glancing eyes play a remarkable part throughout his work; noting the intensity of the connections they set up between certain groups, one is reminded of Permeke.

Strenuous movement, swarming crowds, figure groups in which individual faces stand out memorably distinct, the precision of Hogarth and the calligraphy of Rowlandson, superseded by a violently overwrought expressionism which distorts and exaggerates prominent features and points of interest – such is the aggressive art of Gillray.

James Gillray (1757-1815)
Voltaire Instructing the Infant Jacobinism, c. 1798.
Brush drawing in brown ink with white wash on brown tracing paper. (10¹³⁄₁₆ × 8″).
The New York Public Library.

5

The Watercolourists.
A Landscape is a State of Mind. From Seeing to Vision:
Sandby, Alexander Cozens, John Robert Cozens, Towne,
Girtin, Cotman, Cox, Bonington.

THE importance of watercolour painting in eighteenth-century English art needs no
emphasizing. But it may be worth while to situate it on two main axes, one of
which, broadly speaking, may be called ideological, the other aesthetic.

Coming after a phase of rational-minded cosmopolitanism which produced both Reynolds and Pope, the movement that led England to Romanticism was, first of all, a return
to national sources, to memories of the past and the sentiments connected with it. Hogarth,
as has been seen, was hostile to Palladian architecture, which originating in Italy was taken
up by an aristocracy unmindful of national frontiers. How, on the other hand, could he
object to the landscape garden which on the Continent was to be known as the 'English
garden' and which made such lavish use of the serpentine line? The reason was that these
gardens and parks, often of great size and remodelled at great expense, were not based on
the English landscape but on those painted by Claude and his followers – those 'Italian
landscapes', as they were known to all, which still floated before the eyes of Richard Wilson
when he painted the Thames, the Wye and the mountains of Wales.[11] Gainsborough, no
cosmopolitan, took another road and the dogmatic Horace Walpole settled the matter
when, in 1761, he expressed surprise that a country 'so profusely beautified with the ameni-
ties of nature as England had produced so few good painters of landscape... Our ever
verdant lawns, rich vales, fields of haycocks and hopgrounds are neglected as homely
subjects whilst our painters draw rocks and precipices and castellated mountains because
Virgil gasped for breath at Naples.'

Walpole thus proposed a new picturesque which, he felt, should appeal more deeply to
his countrymen, but which had to be sanctified by art before it could be consciously
perceived. This the watercolourists were to accomplish. Artistically speaking, the important
thing about watercolour was that it was not a fixed and settled thing, it was not controlled
by any academy and had no set rules, only habits, and these continually changed in the
course of an evolution that was speeded up by the very liberty it enjoyed. It is characteristic that an amateur like William Taverner (1703-72) should have discovered things which
his contemporaries had not even attempted; his tonal experiments were only to be followed
up by Sandby. It is characteristic that a regular painter like Gainsborough should have felt
so free outside the field of oil painting. The movement gained such impetus and its practitioners were so numerous from 1750 to 1860 that the ordinary Englishman naturally
imagined that watercolour was an English creation. It may have been at least a simul-
taneous creation, both there and on the Continent, but it happens that its very appearance

in England, and not its creation, took place with the arrival of the Bohemian artist Wenceslaus Hollar in the time of Charles I. Already in this early stage it was realized that watercolour was well suited to landscape, as a means of accurately rendering its lines, structure and atmosphere. When the marine painter Peter Monamy (*c.* 1690-1749), of Jersey, was preparing his picture of the *Old East India Wharf* (Victoria and Albert Museum), he made a preliminary sketch 'in watercolour'; it is only a grey and brown wash drawing.

Samuel Scott (1702-72), who has already been mentioned as a follower in oils of Canaletto, provides a good example of watercolour practice at that time in the technique of his *St Paul's from the River* and *Westminster Abbey and Hall from the River*. He began by laying in his shadows in neutral grey, then added notes of local colour, a red and also a green fairly bright on occasion but usually very restrained. One may speak of a generally prevailing monochrome stage in English watercolour painting, due at least in part to a concern for atmospheric unity, and certainly facilitating the practice of this art.

But something new was stirring the imagination of artists and it found expression in painting a generation earlier than in poetry. In painting there was already something of the spirit of Wordsworth, that spirit which felt

> . . .a sense sublime
> Of something far more deeply interfused,
> Whose dwelling is the light of setting suns,
> And the round ocean and the living air,
> And the blue sky. . . [12]

This poetry and this painting were two forms of the same intimist art, springing from an emotional realization of a secret mystery underlying solitude and an awed perceptional realization of the infinite, both conveyed through a sense impression. A moment of being was thus identified with the essence of a landscape:

> I wandered lonely as a cloud. . . [13]

> Once again
> Do I behold these steep and lofty cliffs,
> Which on a wild secluded scene impress
> Thoughts of more deep seclusion; and connect
> The landscape with the quiet of the sky. . . [14]

> The sounding cataract
> Haunted me like a passion. . . [14]

These parallels are particularly apt when considering the work of Paul Sandby (1725-1809), who was born in Nottingham, moved to London in 1741 and became a topographical draughtsman employed by the Crown. As such he was sent to the Highlands of Scotland to work on the Ordnance Survey carried out after the 1745 rising. Laurence Binyon pointed out in this connection that landscape painting in China had been an integral part of military mapping and surveying. Sandby is peculiar in being an official topographer, for many young artists down to and including Turner, nearly half a century later, began as topographers in private employ. By then it was no longer a matter of topographical surveys, but of a different application of the term. The artist was simply employed to do what documentary photography does today: to record the appearance of a place, generally a country house or a site, in as accurate a line drawing as possible. If greater precision was called for, some tinting was permissible – just as in a photograph of this kind, today, some attempt may be made to bring out the play of light and shadow. The point was to convey something of the charm of a place, and by that means an element of choice and self-expression entered into the picture: the topographer, if he was to charm, had to become an artist. It was not always the owner, moreover, who called in his services. The taste for 'national antiquities' was growing, and to the picturesque appeal of ruins was added an architectural interest in them. So it was that pencil and brush were set to work on Tintern Abbey, Kirkstall Abbey and countless other historic buildings and ruins. Such were the external motivations.

But Sandby did not yet specialize in such watercolour landscapes. At first, both in Scotland and then in London, he seems to have been attracted to figures and scenes, for he produced a series of *Cries of London* (1760), which are full of interest and 'picturesque' notations. They amuse, but do not invite one to follow the artist in his moods and thoughts. His brother Thomas was Deputy Ranger of Windsor Forest, and Paul Sandby's decision to join him there seems to have been a decisive step in his career. Windsor Forest, with all its charming features, such as Virginia Water, then but recently formed by the Duke of Cumberland, was much less 'picturesque' than the Highlands. His extreme precision of design subsisted here but changed its import. A revelation took place, but scarcely on the conscious level, between the artist and his 'motif', which assumed its full import in the spectator's imagination. A watercolour by Dürer, with a sheet of water reflecting a boat or a hut, may produce a magical effect on a deeper level; that is, it takes the imagination in hand and makes it share in a separate, self-contained reality. One cannot credit Sandby with this; he was neither Dürer nor Lucas van Leyden. He was a realist, and his son emphasized his concern for realism when he indicated that what Sandby aimed at giving his 'drawings' – such works long being known as 'water-colour drawings', with the stress on the latter word – was an appearance similar to what one sees in a camera obscura. A certain degree of illusionism was therefore necessary and as long as a painting was meant to represent something, this device contributed to indicate and express the third dimension.

With Rowlandson, a calligraphic scribble signifying leaves and branches is tinted with greens and that suffices as a backdrop (for example, *The Ferry*, Victoria and Albert Museum). It was Sandby's understanding of trees, of what their presence means, that enabled him to make the decisive transition from seeing to what already, if on a modest level, was vision. For that, it was no longer necessary for the trees to be individualized, for one to be an oak and another a beech. As with all the poets who have ever rhapsodized over a forest, it was only necessary for the trees to occupy space in a fairly monumental way, to open up sufficiently to allow a play of light, and to close together sufficiently to form masses of shadow. A painter discovers these things only if he looks for them; Rowlandson never looked for them, but Sandby did. He preferred the slighter trees, like the ash and willow, and did full justice to their elegance of outline. In *Windsor Park from Snow Hill* (British Museum, Print Room[15]), for example, the eye is caught first by the might of those trees in the foreground, before moving, by way of the delicate play of light gilding the grass in the middle distance, to the modulations of the horizon. Looking towards the horizon, the eye, as if shortsighted, can only make out the blurred white shapes of buildings. By way of Samuel Scott, Paul Sandby is the heir of Canaletto and the view painters, and *Windsor:*

East View from Crown Corner (British Museum) is very much in this tradition, even to the insertion of the river between two clumps of trees and two groups of buildings in order to guide the eye towards the point where, from the wide-open angle in the foreground, the lines link up. Canaletto is certainly there, but his southern tradition is overlaid with a northern influence, represented at its best by Vermeer's *View of Delft*.

Sandby did not long remain a topographer. He quickly won recognition as an artist and in 1768 was invited to become one of the foundation members of the Royal Academy. The two great landscape artists already discussed, Wilson and Gainsborough, contributed to set him free. As a draughtsman first of all, Sandby retained from Samuel Scott and his own topographical training a concern for the accurate, almost architectural rendering of buildings; but from Gainsborough and Wilson he learnt to situate them at the right distance, in the right climate, by means of an atmospheric tonality. By degrees he learned that reality is not a matter of objects in themselves, but of objects in a situation; and, accuracy being inveterate and innate with him, he made a point of rendering a precise aspect in a certain lighting, keeping firmly in their place the indications of local colour, which went to form the tonality.

He remained attached to human interest, meaning in this case the eternal northern genre scene with its keen enjoyment of active life in town and country, but especially country. Peasants in their waggons or with a rake on their shoulder, with wife, children and animals, thus continue to enliven these landscapes, though the landscape element became predominant.

The topographers were knights-errant of watercolour landscape painting and Sandby was one of the most active of all, travelling over the length and breadth of Great Britain. After 1770 he became the second artist, after Wilson, to discover Wales, but while the latter was inclined by temperament towards the sublime, Sandby in accordance with his own kept largely to the picturesque. In 1775 he reproduced twelve of his Welsh watercolours in aquatint (he was the first to use this medium in England), and in these aquatints there is a tendency to dramatize landscape by an emphasis, indeed an over-emphasis, of contrasts. For example, in *The Iron Forge between Dolgelli and Barmouth*, published by the artist in 1776, one finds, in broad daylight, the violent contrasts of light and shadow that are so prominent a feature of Wright's night-pieces. The light bathing the landscape, including the waterfall and the old mill, is wholly framed by strong, dark horizontals; the tall chimney pours forth black smoke that floats away horizontally. By way of a new art, Sandby seems to have entered a new world.

His countrymen were not prepared to follow him. To them it seemed that it was for each man to know his place and keep to it. It was for Sandby to discern the objective poetry – as in those lines by Wordsworth – of reality and to render it in discreetly subjective and personal terms. For that he had a perfect medium: transparent watercolours conveying not so much the solidity of forms as the essence of light, allowing the white paper to show through or to stand intact as the highest lights and obtaining gradations of colour and tone by washes laid in one over another.

But however unadventurous he was (and he was not so steady a person as all that, for he led a spiteful, hard-hitting campaign against Hogarth's *Analysis of Beauty*), he did not feel obliged to keep to tradition. Indeed, he was one of the first to draw with the brush.

Sandby began exhibiting his work in 1760, the year of the first exhibition of the Society of Artists. From 1769 he exhibited at the Royal Academy. These early exhibitions were governed by rules that may seem surprising today. For one thing, no rooms were set aside for watercolours nor was any particular allowance made for their presentation. The general rule was that every picture should be exhibited in a gilt frame. One can imagine its crushing impact on the aerial lightness and delicate washes of a watercolour.

If Sandby aimed at exhibiting his watercolours, how could he help changing his manner? Attenuating circumstances are the utmost that may be granted the criminal. His crime lay in resorting to gouache.

A. J. Finberg, in an old but revealing book on watercolours, starts from the point of view of artistic rightness.

In the transparent drawings the whiteness of the paper plays an important part in producing the general luminous effect. The washes of pure colour with which it is covered merely temper or colour its lightness; they never destroy it. But the gouache or distemper, though still strictly speaking water colour, is essentially an opaque medium. It is simply ordinary water colour material mixed with gum and water and with a certain quantity of white pigment to give it 'body' or opacity. So that in a distemper drawing the surface of the paper counts for nothing; all that is seen is the 'mat' or dead surface of the paint.[16]

Finberg cites the case of Sandby's *Carrick Ferry* (British Museum), noting that 'the poverty of the distemper medium is most conspicuous in the darker parts, the rocks, trees and castle standing dark against the sunset. There is no illusion of reality.'

All this is partly obvious and partly untrue. What is obvious is the opacity of body colour or gouache. But it is not true that that opacity must necessarily extinguish the light of a picture; one need only look at Joseph Wright's *Eruption of Vesuvius* to convince oneself of that. But in the particular case of Sandby what is one to think of his use of gouache? Perhaps he simply came to see that its effect is variable, so much so that in considering, for example, his *Welsh Bridge, Shrewsbury* (British Museum) one is tempted to side with his detractors. The straining after intensity is all too evident; the large oak is given too great a prominence and here, it is true, the heavy colour does away with tonality. On the other hand, *Windsor Castle, the North Terrace, looking West at Sunset* (Victoria and Albert Museum) is an unusually fine piece of work. The way in which the horizontal light glints from figure to figure and the way the bars of shadow are disposed are reminiscent of Canaletto. Hitherto Sandby had only delineated or expressed states of light, which evidently corresponded to a precise or precisely observed moment but which one was not called upon to identify. Now, in this *Windsor Castle, the North Terrace*, it corresponds to a sunset effect very marked in its singleness of impact.

Other watercolourists, like Thomas Hearne (1744-1817) and Michael Angelo Rooker (1743-1801), followed in Sandby's steps without adding anything essential to what had been done by the artist, whom Gainsborough described as the only man of genius who had painted real views of *English* landscapes. For I shall now deal with the two Cozenses, father and son, whose most significant works are as far removed as possible from the characteristically British landscapes of Sandby.

Paul Sandby (1725-1809)

Windsor Castle, the North Terrace, Looking West at Sunset. Watercolour on panel. (18¼ × 24¼″).

Victoria and Albert Museum, London.

The first is Alexander Cozens, who in older books is often presented in romantic colours as the natural son of Peter the Great and an Englishwoman from Deptford. This fable has now been superseded by a more sober version of such facts as are known. His father was an English shipbuilder who went to Petersburg to work for the Tsar when he was creating a navy. Alexander was born there, in 1716 or 1717 (the exact date is not known), and grew up in Russia. From there he was sent to Italy to study painting. In 1746 he settled in London. But he seems to have worked more as a teacher than as a practising artist and published a series of books. One of them is entitled *Principles of Beauty Relative to the Human Head*; it is of no great concern here, not dealing specifically with painting. Quite extraordinary, however, is *A New Method of Assisting the Invention in Drawing Original Compositions of Landscape*, which he published in 1785. It is full of the most unexpected inventiveness and ingenuity.

It is in this essay that he sets forth his method of 'blot-drawing', for which he was dubbed 'Blotmaster General' or 'Blotmaster to the Town.' The idea was that a blot of sepia or indian ink would provide the stimulus and starting point for the creative imagination. But what kind of blot? He conceded it to be somewhat artificial: 'An artificial blot is a production of chance, with a small degree of design; for in making it, the attention of the performer must be employed on the whole, or the general form of the composition, and upon this only, whilst the subordinate parts are left to the casual motion of the hand and the brush.'

The creation of a blot drawing, then, is not far removed from the automatic writing of the Surrealists. Cozens is rather vague and does not say whether he intended at the start to represent something in particular, or whether the intention and design only gradually became clear as he proceeded.

'A true blot', he goes on, 'is an assemblage of dark shapes or masses made with ink upon a piece of paper, and likewise of light ones produced by the paper being left blank. All the shapes are rude and unmeaning, as they are formed with the swiftest hand. But at the same time there appears a general disposition of these masses, producing one comprehensive form, which may be conceived and purposely intended before the blot is begun. This general form will exhibit some kind of subject, and this is all that should be done designedly.'

This rather confused text never clearly states whether the artist starts with a definite plan or simply depends on chance. But the general idea behind the method is significant. Cozens, moreover, never claimed that it originated with him, for he quotes Leonardo da Vinci: 'If you look upon an old wall covered with dirt, or the odd appearance of some streaked stones, you may discover several things like landscapes, battles, clouds, uncommon attitudes, humorous faces, draperies, etc. Out of this confused mass of objects, the mind will be furnished with abundance of designs and subjects perfectly new.'[17]

The first subject represented here, *Landscape with Distant Mountains* (British Museum) is illustrated in two forms, if 'form' is the right word. The first is very close to the blot technique. With the pen or brush dipped in Indian ink he made swift strokes over the paper, so that intention and chance were combined; coming and going over the whole width of the sheet and thus causing space to emerge between what perforce became the foreground and the background. With the same thick strokes of ink, he laid in recognizable lines of trees in the shape of small vertical blobs. When he had almost run out of ink, he swept the brush lightly over it all, pressing down a little more here, a little less there. The resulting outline of a hill beneath the sky has a curiously Japanese effect.

From these 'blots' turned into a landscape, the artist went on to the idea of a landscape in which chance, having played its part in the initial invention, ceased to intervene. From this moment on the artist's mind set to work, developing every possibility. The same movement brought forward a hill and extended it to the left by a small overlap, while on the right a second line or modulation to the rear repeated the first. The foreground, which in the first *Landscape with Distant Mountains* consisted mostly of the unpainted white paper, consists in the second of a heavy grounding of sepia (one being like a photographic negative, the other like a positive); and, with very little alteration, the initial pattern of black lines becomes the surface of a sheet of water, and where it is reduced to a bare hatching becomes a slightly luminous surface. From there begins a skilful tonal modulation, and the scribbles which become rows of trees are here and there notched with glints of light. And so the combination of chance, of a very personal kind, with an intellectual and self-willed artistry gives rise to the picture.

Alexander Cozens (*c.* 1717-86)

Landscape with Distant Mountains. Black ink. (6³⁄₁₆ × 7⅝″).

British Museum, London.

The *Landscape with a Dark Hill* in the Fitzwilliam Museum is the result of the same method applied to an initial but much more complicated play of the brush. It successfully overcomes the difficulties involved in creating *imaginary* landscapes, for such, it must be remembered, was the artist's purpose. The play of lines, the alternation of darker and lighter streaks running lengthwise, the avoidance of anything anecdotal (a house would have been anecdotal), of any recipe for the foreground (no tree nor anything vertical which would have given the illusion of rising above the slowly ascending levels of ground), all this shows an inflexible rigour and single-minded attention to structure.

The trouble here is that the details of the landscape are isomorphic at nearly all points, until the lighter streaks fade away and the hill stands forth as a much more homogeneous mass – and a dark mass, despite its position on the horizon. In a second kind of imaginary landscape, Cozens showed himself less disdainful of the habits acquired by the human eye in the course of so many generations of landscape invention. Those habits involve a certain emotive notion that things change their nature when transposed into the unreal blue of the horizon, and the whole point is to put the mind in the mood of self-communion which must be induced if it is to surrender to this meditation on space. Cozens achieved this admirably

Alexander Cozens (*c.* 1717-86)

Landscape with Distant Mountains. Sepia. (6⁵⁄₁₆ × 7¹¹⁄₁₆″).

British Museum, London.

in his *Classical Landscape* (Tate Gallery), whose importance seems to me at once intrinsic and seminal, for, though masquerading under the title 'classical', it is the perfect prototype of the Romantic landscape. A broad handling builds up, in a few dark and jagged masses, the coast line of what seems to be an arm of the sea. A tiny boat draws the eye towards a receding landscape which bars a headland, the latter treated in a comparatively realistic manner, with clumps and dipping lines of trees and, at the top, a large house. Behind extend distant hills, in pale reverie, against the sky. Such a landscape must have been seminal for Alexander's son, John Robert Cozens, who made good use of the principle behind it.

Can Alexander Cozens have had any knowledge of Chinese or Japanese landscape painting? Neither Paul Oppé nor Henri Lemaitre has adduced any proofs that he did. If one takes the trouble to look for it, Orientalism can be detected in the *Liber Veritatis* of Claude, and from painter to painter one finds many variations in the way of executing a landscape, of looking at it from above or below, of deliberately distorting its lines, vertical upsurge and recession. Likewise, the use of a brush dipped in ink, or a reed pen, or other instruments, is open to endless variations and offers many possibilities of chance concurrence and coincidence. But the 'chinoiserie' of Alexander Cozens is, nonetheless, more particular; it consists precisely in the idea of an *invented* landscape (as implied by the title of his book), in contradistinction to the practice of his time, when the sketch made in front of the motif and worked up afterwards in the studio was being superseded by the watercolour, painted in the open air. No invention is totally free of memory, for a man who had never seen a landscape would be incapable of inventing one; conversely, as a result of his long visual discipline, the artist, as Hogarth had seen, is at work when his eye is taking in the elements of reality. A Chinese painter might spend months or years contemplating what he wished to paint; then, turning away from it, he would take up his brush. No 'external' reality was any longer involved, but a form of memory, obeying the laws not of nature but of creative art.

John Robert Cozens, the son of Alexander, was born in 1752. His mind gave way in 1791 and he died in 1797. The shadow of his father hung over him. He was precocious, exhibiting for the first time in 1767 at the age of fifteen. Nine years later he presented at the Royal Academy his only known oil painting: *Hannibal Crossing the Alps Shows His Army the Fertile Plains of Italy*. This painting is lost but Turner knew and admired it; from it, he said, he had learnt more than from any other picture. It may have been painted during Cozens' first tour on the Continent, made in the company of the collector and critic Richard Payne Knight, who much appreciated his talent. Starting out in 1776, they first visited Switzerland where he was strongly impressed by the Alpine scenery, which filled him with Romantic emotions and a sense of the sublime. Burke had already analysed the element of terror that entered into it: between height and abyss the eye floats uncertainly and the mind is dizzied; the absolute, unrelenting otherness of mountains repels the ego and fills it with a sense of alienation. All this spelled solitude, and solitude predominates in the work of John Robert Cozens.

During this first tour he also visited Italy, staying there from 1777 to 1779, chiefly in Rome. He revisited Italy in 1782-83 and during this second stay he produced a fine group of watercolours and sketches.

Alexander Cozens (*c*. 1717-86)
Landscape with a Dark Hill.
Aquatint on paper, with brown wash and pencil in sky. (8¾ × 11⅝").
Fitzwilliam Museum, Cambridge.

Unlike his father, J. R. Cozens never proclaimed any intention of inventing landscapes. Or if he did invent them, he soon ceased to do so: the *Valley with Winding Streams* (Victoria and Albert Museum) dates from 1774. It is laid out on similar lines to Alexander's *Classical Landscape*, with a single, narrow, almost vertical flanking element on the left by way of foreground; the plane of the *Classical Landscape* is replaced by the recession of the flat floor of the valley marked by the streams winding away into the haze of the distant mountains. This, then, is a type-landscape, and one may appreciate the greater variety of its nature-patterning by comparing it with the *Pays du Valais* (Stourhead Collection). Here, in the same flat valley, the same stream winds away towards the same pale mountains; there is, however, a subtler balance between the threefold movement of the rugged crest on the right, while on the left a much lower and narrower projection of ground, with cottages amidst pines, is preceded by a paler and slighter pyramid, round which the valley turns before being lost to view.

Cozens was only moderately interested in architecture and his melancholy did not particularly incline him to ruins, though his *Tomb of the Horatii and the Curiatii* (Victoria and Albert Museum) is a work often mentioned. His *Paestum* is more interesting because here the architecture of the great temples seems to share in the sublimity of nature, being absorbed in an atmosphere of heavy clouds. The Roman Campagna, as a type of inspiration, puts Cozens between Wilson and Turner. With this theme he is far from 'views' and often near to vision. One must, however, emphasize the exceptional character of the *Lake of Albano and Castel Gandolfo (Sunset)* (Collection Mr and Mrs Tom Girtin). First of all, there is a strong contrast between the light lingering on the water and in the sky and the steep wooded shore already plunged into darkness. Along with the sombre reflection which it casts on the waters below, this stretch of wooded shore crosses the picture from corner to corner; though it is apparently opaque, the eye can just make out successive levels of trees separated by crests of a lighter hue. A faint line of purple marks the buildings of Castel Gandolfo. Beyond, the glow of sunset runs in a broad pinkish band across the sky, parallel to the shadow on the waters, while a patch of sky on the upper left, already night blue, corresponds to the patch of greenish-blue water on the lower right still in daylight. Clouds in which pink darkens into violet swirl dramatically over the castle. Indeed the whole landscape is unusually dramatic. The contrast is heightened by a narrow line of intenser light running between the zone of shadow and the zone of light, particularly towards Castel Gandolfo. It is a very fine landscape, but it is one of those (not being unrelated to Sandby's *Windsor Castle*) in which nothing remains of the hallowed transparency of watercolour. The pink of the sunset sky has the quality of gouache and the trees on the far left are painted in tiny touches individually applied, as they might be in oil paints. Much more characteristic, though still in the same vein is *Lake Nemi and the Town of Genzano* (Ashmolean Museum, Oxford). Here, except for a lingering hint of pink in the sky, everything is made up of blue and yellow, the fleecy effect of the delicately modulated trees being obtained by opaque touches of yellowish green over greenish blue. A human element is introduced into the meditation: a goatherd can be seen on the lower right driving his goats before him. Another *Lake Nemi* (Victoria and Albert Museum) draws the eye towards a gap in the pale, boundless horizons, beyond the broad surface of the lake which Mussolini had not yet drained in order to salvage some Roman galleys.

Contrast, in Cozens, is generally reduced to a strong modulation of tonality, which is most skilfully handled within a narrow range of colour. The earth is often interpreted in blues scarcely less aerial than the air itself, with equally light greens and greys and sometimes a long faint touch of pink marking the distant outline of a town, as in the *Mount Etna* in the Print Room of the British Museum. *The Valais Near the Lake of Geneva* in the Fitzwilliam Museum is a pattern of very pale blues traversed by even paler beams; the *View of the Isle of Elba* in the Victoria and Albert Museum treats the landscape in greenish grey. Henri Lemaitre thinks this is an imaginary landscape, and though I am not familiar with Elba I doubt if the island can show any such clear-cut mountains as these three peaks. One is all the more surprised by the precision of these rocky surfaces; but owing to the simplification of both form and colour, the work achieves a monumental quality.

His reluctance to imitate reality, or external appearances, is marked, except for certain touches of pink, by his reluctance to employ local colours and his determination to retain of

John Robert Cozens (1752-97)
Lake of Albano and Castel Gandolfo (Sunset). Watercolour. (17¼ × 24½″).
Collection Mr and Mrs Tom Girtin.

John Robert Cozens (1752-97)

Lake Nemi and the Town of Genzano. Watercolour over pencil. (19½ × 26¾'').

Ashmolean Museum, Oxford.

reality no more than its enchantments and its spatial references, often in the form of a plain where he merely indicates modifications of light. So it is that in his impressions of the *Lake of Lucerne*, while the trees are ideograms, the water is marked by delicate planes of light. The more one studies Cozens, the more one realizes that his Romantic essentialism was a justified choice. Certainly it was a revelation for Turner and Girtin when, at the house of Dr Monro, who looked after Cozens in his last sad years of insanity, they were shown his watercolours, many of which they copied. In view of what I have called Cozens's essentialism, i.e. his non-realism, Constable's famous tribute to him is all the more significant for them both: the 'greatest genius that ever touched landscape painting... Cozens is all poetry.' Clinging to the detailed manifestation of reality, Constable understood, in part at least through Cozens, that what counted was the self alone confronting space, awed by its amplitude and silence, and expressing that awe. With Alexander and John Robert Cozens, it is not enough to say that a landscape is a state of mind. The old formula needs to be completed by another: reality is an optical illusion.

The influence of the two Cozenses, either direct or indirect as transmitted by Girtin and Turner, was considerable and for this reason I have dealt with them at some length.

Francis Towne, a forgotten artist rediscovered in the twentieth century, is a different case. Born in Devon in 1739, he seems scarcely to have left the neighbourhood of Exeter until 1777. Then, in that year, he made a tour of Wales, and its mountains, waterfalls and torrents were a revelation to him. In 1780-81 he visited Switzerland and Italy (Rome and Naples). Finally, in 1786, he discovered the English Lakes. In the early 1800s he settled in London and at the age of nearly seventy married a young French dancer. Mrs Towne died in 1808 and he lived on until 1816.

Towne was not a watercolourist pure and simple, but his oil paintings never earned him membership in the Royal Academy, indeed they have no particular merit. With him the great Romantic dream of the Cozenses is left behind and one is confronted anew with the reality of things seen. A professed open-air painter, he drew and painted a definite spot at a definite moment, scrupulously recording not only the time of day but the direction of the lighting. It is not easy to pinpoint the change that came over him in 1777 or to say why he needed the external stimulus of picturesque scenery, for what he did with it depended so much on his own vision and so little on the scenery itself. It is true that before that change occurred he painted *Peamore Park near Exeter* (Fitzwilliam Museum, Cambridge), a perfectly familiar landscape in which, nevertheless, his private vision is already manifest at one point: the trees. For neither here nor elsewhere are Towne's trees actually trees. They are trees such as Rimbaud might have conceived them, turned into giant snakes, motionless and imperturbable. The leafage seems to be of no interest to him and he reduces it to a minimum. For the rest he was soon to do likewise. One may take as a starting point a watercolour like the *Salmon Leap from Pont Aberglaslyn* of 1777 (Scott-Elliot Collection). It is dated and, according to the inscription, was drawn on the spot, in the morning, with the light coming from the right. It is in pen and watercolour, and what a pen! With the finest, most astonishingly delicate and accurate lines, it records the texture of the stone and the structure of the rock face, as if the artist were intent on illustrating one of those fine old geography books of a former era. Every angle, cleft and pattern of the rock is there, linked up with the curious natural pavement on the valley floor; and it would seem that, having created a style of his own, whose sources are not apparent, he availed himself of its conventions to delineate the water cascading over the fall and swirling away in the stream: for a similar delineation, one would have to go to the art of the Far East, that of Hokusai, for example. One notes here the almost total absence of sky, thus one's gaze is forced to remain within the chasm.

The *Bridge and Waterfall near Llyn Cwellyn* (Laing Art Gallery, Newcastle) presents the same characteristics of a well-defined style, treating nature quite simply like a form of the visible. Now it is not the landscape that is a state of mind: instead of fusion, there is aloofness, and autonomy, with a sense almost of cruelty in the use of those thin, fibrous lines. The set waters of the *Bridge and Waterfall* seem to share in the structure and patterning of all that surrounds them, as also in the strong overall contrasts of light and shade.

Italy taught him the visual equivalence of ruin and rock. The seventy-four watercolours of Rome, Naples and the Roman Campagna show what now may be taken as the constant features of his work. The rocklike solidity of wall and mountain, their weight and force, go to create a Melvillean vision of landscape. As if petrified, these flat patterns of leafage will never again rustle in the wind, nor will these metamorphosed waters flow. He obtains his effect by simplified, abrupt, curiously broken lines.

As a landscapist, in unavoidable contact with the external world, Towne is not always successful, for his sense of colour is erratic and many of his Italian watercolours suffer from the all-pervasive presence of yellowish or washed-out greens. He fulfilled himself by painting mountain scenery, and the *Source of the Arveiron* is a picture that can have few if any rivals as a revelation of mountain scenery in painting.

Actually, he painted two pictures on this theme (Oppé Collection and Victoria and Albert Museum). It has been pointed out that, since the first is painted on two superimposed sheets of paper and the second on four sheets pasted together, they are unlikely to have been executed on the spot. And, though it would have been easy enough to paste the sheets together in advance, their size being quite manageable, the style would seem to bear out this assumption. There is too great a difference in the style of the two versions for them to correspond to natural variations in the light; and when one compares them, it seems impossible to decide whether either of the two styles adopted is nearer than the other to observed reality.

The Oppé version is rather more dated. It is even curious to note that it is roughly contemporary with John Robert Cozens's discovery of the Alps and that it has many points in common with his paintings. The blue keynote is similar, more modulated than contrasted, between the dark and the relatively light, showing the use of a pinkish-brown mixed with blue where the play of shadows, perhaps in the séracs of the glacier, calls for stronger emphasis. The blue then shifts to white, with just a few yellow accents to situate the glacier in the light, and with deeper blue transparencies in the under-levels. The foreground is not quite distinct, except on the right at the base of the brown boulder over which the ice has pushed its way down. The picture is marked by these four successive movements descending from right to left, which, beyond the invisible chasm, are countered by the enormous

Francis Towne (1739-1816)

The Source of the Arveiron, 1781. Watercolour on paper. (16¾ × 12⅛″). Victoria and Albert Museum, London.

d. Tourne. del
1781

Pl. 53

rounded slopes of mountains falling sharply from left to right, and blue with a few gleams of light. It is a sort of Cozens, only perhaps less confined. The other version of the *Source of the Arveiron* (1781, Victoria and Albert Museum) is much more personal in style, much nearer to what is found from the *Salmon Leap* on, despite the novelties that must have been assimilated. A curious thing about the Oppé version is that it shows no drawing in the formal sense; no lines can be made out apart from the always very distinct separation of the degrees of lighting. The Victoria and Albert version may not have any actual pen strokes, but the artist's Oriental brush builds up his rocks and séracs with short, squarish lines that are almost like a signature; and in the green mountain in the background one observes the brown tracery of his pen. The picture is divided in two by the high-pitched light of the mountains, which throws a pale yet intense gleam of pink over the ridge of ice. Everything on this side, the brown boulders on the right and the pink boulders in front, falls roughly into the same tonal group. Beyond, a broad slope of intense green precedes the paler green mass of the great peak rising skywards. The alternating pattern of broad parallels and broken angles is almost inspired, while the bright tonality is an integral part of this fine picture.

Ultimately, then, from Wales to the Alps and the Roman Campagna, from Italy to the Lake District, Towne, whether he knew it or not, was seeking not the picturesque, but through the picturesque something else – something new and strange, an alienating unrest. The reaffirmation of man through the subjectivity of the design is perhaps even more radical than it had been in the idealization of John Robert Cozens.

From now on, two traditions were pursued in English watercolour painting: that of the external world, deriving from Sandby, and that of the inner world tending towards vision, deriving from Cozens. As regards the first, there is nothing more to learn, and there would be no point in even naming Edward Dayes (1763-1804), were it not that he was the teacher of Thomas Girtin. His line is calligraphic and vigorous, his scenes are rendered with spirit, and the settings have at once a decorative value and a satisfying presence. One can hardly say much more than that.

Thomas Girtin (1775-1802) was born in Southwark, the son of a cordage maker. He was apprenticed to Edward Dayes, who was evidently a harsh disciplinarian, and an unverifiable tradition has it that he rebelled against his master who had him sent to prison as a refractory apprentice. Certain it is that they quarrelled and the legend at least reflects the fact that Girtin was a man of bold and wilful character.

From there Girtin went on to the mezzotint engraver John Raphael Smith, who employed him in documentary tasks and set him to colouring prints after Reynolds. A more important phase began when he met the antiquary and amateur draughtsman James Moore, who employed him on the illustrations for his *Monastic Remains and Ancient Castles in England and Wales* and may have taken Girtin with him on a journey to Scotland in 1792.

In 1795 he was welcomed at Dr Thomas Monro's house in Adelphi Terrace, among the group of young artists, including Turner, who were employed by the doctor to copy drawings by Cozens and others. Girtin was ambitious and applied himself with energy to copying other masters in order to perfect his technique, and among those he thus studied were Piranesi, Canaletto and Richard Wilson. His art may be said to have been influenced by a dual train of thought, one concerned with the study of his predecessors, the other inspired by nature itself. The interest he took in Canaletto is perhaps especially significant as regards the layout of space and the peculiar skill with which the Italian was able to combine extreme breadth in his landscapes with the illusion of great depth. It is not by chance that Girtin's panoramic views of the Thames have that same quality. But when he arrived at a style of his own, about 1800, one detects in a work like *Kirkstall Abbey, Evening* a series of calculations which owe nothing to any such predecessor and were designed to get the maximum expressive effect out of the subject. The time of day was chosen for the broad sweep of the lighting and the way in which the long glowing streak just above the horizon crosses the abbey tower and helps to mark its upsurge. It was a skilful touch to have pushed so far back towards the horizon the actual motif of the watercolour; the tiny figures and animals in the foreground and middle distance attract the eye without holding it, so that it returns easily to that bright streak of sky behind the abbey.

The debt to John Robert Cozens, and through him to Alexander, is deeper and more abiding than to anyone else. Girtin's *Hills and Stream*, however different in structure and tonal relations, stems from Cozens's *Landscape with a Dark Hill*, and the generality of the title, the reluctance to localize the scene, are also inspired by it. Here, as often, Girtin seems to work on a ground of light grey wash or, as is very often the case, on tinted paper. Blue, yellow, white, a bit of burnt sienna and a touch of pink suffice to brighten it up. There is no foreground, and the first curtain of trees to rise beyond the line of whitish water has already carried the eye far away and situated the chalky white hill at a greater distance still; while that hill throws far back into the picture the opaque blue mountain preceded by a curious series of dottings, very much in the manner of Cozens. The same is true of his *Denbigh*, done in an equally light watercolour technique, but less dry and more fluid. Here again all the little parallel lines patterning the plain with rows of trees and elongated ponds lead the eye to the hills standing before the sea; while the big hill on the left spanning half the picture and forming the usual interrupted foreground, with its ruins, shows the same small deft pattern of dotted lines. The composition, dominated by brownish, greenish or bluish greys, neutral greens and pinkish browns, is a bit austere. It does not have the enchantment of the two versions of *Above Bolton* (Print Room of the British Museum and Girtin Collection). The one in the British Museum is the earlier of the two, and in a lighter, more modulated, less contrasted tonality. A direct play of mild light illuminates practically the whole composition. The eye, checked only on the right by the pinkish-brown cliffs, ranges freely as far as the peaks looming on the horizon, where neutral violets and greens are softly blended. A series of barely continuous pools marks the course of the Wharfe. What may be a cornfield, far up on the heights, indicates the strongest point of light and it is not bright. The 'final' version of *Above Bolton* in the Girtin Collection is quite different in execution. The light falls beyond the third cliff on the right, which juts out from the other two and is treated as an element of strong contrast. The darker patches of water at the foot of the cliffs throw them into prominence. The picture is marked by a diagonal running from the upper right to the lower left corner; on the left are the strongest lights, mainly on the water, to a lesser extent on the foothills. Both versions bear the subtitle: *Stepping Stones on the Wharfe*. But the eye is attracted much more by two or three head of cattle, set along the river bank for scale and in order to give a sign of life. The painter seems to have placed himself at a fairly low viewpoint, nearly on a level with the cattle. In the first version, the viewpoint seems much higher.

In this restless, highly-strung artist, who died at twenty-seven of consumption (or possibly asthma), there was an obsessive passion for space, a vast sweep of space from which he skilfully elicited a principle of unity. With Girtin, the practice of contrasts seems to have been a matter of technique rather than instinctive movement. The contrasts are such as would tend to break up the unity of the picture space, were it not so well knit together by the convergent rhythms. With him, as a matter of fact, it is often a question of mood, which counts for a good deal in his manner. Thus *Bamburgh Castle, Northumberland* (*c*. 1797-99, Tate Gallery) suggests that the artist had just been reading M.G. Lewis's *The Monk* or some other gothic romance. It is a wayward romanticism here, all in stresses, clashes, contrasts and riddles (that singularly bright doorway, for example, with a figure coming through it: what does it open on to?). The sky against which this improbable mass of ruins stands is duly melodramatic. Sea birds wheel round the lower crags, well below the cows but far above the tiny sailing vessel. Girtin has come a long way from the time when he travelled over England drawing monuments for James Moore, and yet *Bamburgh Castle* has something in common with *Durham Cathedral and Bridge from the River Wear* (1799, Whitworth Art Gallery, Manchester) in that they are both magnificent, awe-inspiring piles. The latter, virtually in a stone-coloured monochrome, is the masterpiece of the topographical watercolour. The towers and pinnacles rise over roofs and chimneys like a vast set of organ pipes, and the warm amber tone of the whole is perfectly suited both to the minute precision of the architectural drawing and to the idealization of the site. The unreality of the two figures with a boat provides a welcome change for the eye; there is something fancifully Venetian about them, as if Girtin were mindful of his cultural background. The same aura of charming fancy clings to the washerwomen coming down towards the river.

In observing Girtin at work one suspects that the young artist put almost too much skill into his varied constructions of space, obviously aiming at effect. I would accordingly incline to approve the choice made by Turner in favour of something very pure, simple and unsophisticated. *The White House, Chelsea* (1800, Tate Gallery) is a landscape of profound and restful calm. A broad reach of the Thames fills the foreground. To the left is the bank on which stands the white house above its reflection. Running almost parallel to the picture plane, the line of land, a deep blue set off by the fainter blue of the sky, arches in a slight curve to carry the eye along. It must be remembered that at the same age Turner, too, had only begun to be at ease in terms of his own vision. The extraordinary promise of Girtin's work was not destined to be fulfilled, but thirty of his watercolours contributed to make a painter of Constable.

Several excellent books have done justice to Girtin, who as a matter of fact has never been neglected. Much remains to be done for John Sell Cotman who, like Richard Wilson before him, was something of an *artiste maudit*, despite his exceptional gifts and an œuvre of unique importance.

Cotman was born at Norwich on 16 May 1782 and died in London in 1842, completing in his father's house the cycle of creative work, solitude and discouragement through which he had passed. Coming to London while still an adolescent, he seems, like Girtin, to have

Thomas Girtin (1775-1802)

Bamburgh Castle, Northumberland, c. 1797-99. Watercolour on paper. (21⅝ × 17¾″). Tate Gallery, London.

Thomas Girtin (1775-1802)
Durham Cathedral and Bridge, from the Wear, 1799. Watercolour on paper. (16⅜ × 21⅛"). Whitworth Art Gallery,
University of Manchester.

Thomas Girtin (1775-1802)

The White House, Chelsea, 1800. Watercolour. (11¾ × 20¼"). Tate Gallery, London.

been largely self-taught, studying the work of his elders Girtin and Turner, whom he met at the house of Dr Monro in Adelphi Terrace. While all his life, especially in his seascapes, he remained under the influence of Turner, that influence took effect more on composition than atmosphere, for as regards his way of seeing there are few artists more personal, indeed more singular, than Cotman. Like Crome, he was a native of Norwich; like Gainsborough and Constable, who came from Suffolk, he was an East Anglian. One is therefore tempted to group them all together in an East Anglian school, characterized by a strong feeling for nature, tending rather to the intimate than to the sublime. Yet Cotman stands apart, for even familiar subjects are treated by him in a way which draws the intimacy from them. Like Crome, he painted nearly as much in oils as in watercolours, and if I treat him here rather in conjunction with the watercolourists, the reason is that, however interesting his canvases may be, they do not represent a decisive contribution; his use of the oil medium reveals nothing new. His use of watercolours does, so much so that it disconcerted the English public and was not understood in his time.

Like all the young artists of that day, he made sketching tours. Between 1800 and 1802 he explored the West Country and Wales, but it was in Yorkshire, which he visited several times between 1803 and 1805, that he found his major inspiration, just as Francis Towne had found it in Wales. He exhibited some of his works at the Royal Academy, but they failed to attract any notice. Discouraged, he returned to Norwich in 1806 and there married a farmer's daughter, as if he wished to cut himself off from the cultural world of London. He took part in the exhibitions of the Norwich Society of Artists, took pupils and experimented with different techniques. In 1812 he moved to Yarmouth, where he lived for the next twelve years, painting a great deal in oils, chiefly seascapes, and producing a series of etchings on architectural subjects. Thanks to his Yarmouth patron, the banker-antiquary Dawson Turner, he was able to make three sketching tours in Normandy in 1817, 1818 and 1820, which resulted in the etchings that went to illustrate the *Architectural Antiquities of Normandy*. In 1823 he moved back to Norwich, but suffered increasingly from neurosis and depression. He wrote, about this time: 'My views in life are so completely blasted, that I sink under the repeated and constant exertion of body and mind. Every effort has been tried, even without hope of success; hence that loss of spirits amounting almost to despair.' Cotman seems to have been something of a manic depressive, with alternating fits of hilarity and melancholia. All that is so singularly fine in his art may possibly stem, to some extent, from the morbid peculiarities of his perception and sensations. In 1834, through the agency of Dawson Turner and other friends, he was appointed Professor of Drawing at King's College, London, where Rossetti was one of his pupils.

All his life Cotman was obliged to do a large amount of antiquarian and topographical work, but it is not important to an assessment and appreciation of his art. It is easy to misjudge Cotman. At the sight of one of his seascapes with a dark swirling sky and surging waves (even so fine a one as the *Dismasted Brig* in the British Museum), one is apt to think: 'Turner'. Looking at a drawing like *St Mary Redcliffe, Bristol*, one is apt to think: 'Girtin'. An element of imitation does appear in his work, yet he has an unmistakable mark of his own. He was only twenty-one when he painted *Chirk Aqueduct* (c. 1804, Victoria and Albert Museum). Here already his personal vision can be seen at its purest. Treated as architecture, not as architectural drawing, these three arches are taken from the very angle where the sky overhead, a limpid patch of flat colour, is re-echoed by the patches of sky which they frame, while the reflection of the arches in the water is painted in yet another tone. The luminous surface of the aqueduct, the precisely delineated shadows under the arches, the schematized woods treated in a few flat tones, have nothing in common with anyone else, not even with Crome. The inspiration of the Yorkshire scenery resulted in studies of the Greta river and woods, such as the fine *Greta Bridge* (c. 1806, British Museum). The characteristics already noted appear here with even greater force and intensity. To begin with, the painting is more vivid. The unbroken line of the woods above the bridge is treated in masses modulated from reddish brown to dark green; they do not keep to any set formula of flat colouring and he gives them movement by the expressive surface texture. The whole is simplified in the extreme; through the straight lines and sharp angles a geometric pattern is carried from the bridge to the house and from the house to the mass of rock. With the almost excessive solidity of the lines and the intensity of the colours, the rich

John Sell Cotman (1782-1842)

Chirk Aqueduct, c. 1804. Watercolour. (12½ × 9⅛″). Victoria and Albert Museum, London.

browns and the pink grey, green grey, blue grey and brown grey of the water, this is, once again, non-atmospheric painting. Yet this solid, four-square work is a pure watercolour. A white patch left in reserve goes to form a cloud, for Cotman, unlike Girtin, who often used tinted paper, worked on white paper, only slightly primed with glue size, which at once absorbed the colours and did not allow the artist to make play with them. Here again Oriental art comes to mind, and while in Towne there was something of the solidity of Hokusai, Cotman suggests the decorative, linear elegance of Hiroshige.

The creamy whiteness of the water in the foreground of *Greta Bridge* should suggest the rush and swirl of the river over its rocky bed; but the solid shadows of the rocks are in flat contradiction to it. This landscape is spellbound, arrested for ever. It is characteristic of the artist that the picture of *Chirk Aqueduct* is spanned by the bar of the aqueduct and this one by the bridge. Unlike Girtin, Cotman cares nothing for luring the eye into the picture and leading it on in rapturous movement by way of landmarks suggesting distance and recession. The way space is built up and enclosed interests Cotman more than space in itself. It might almost be said that he composes by laying mass upon mass. Compared with other practitioners of the watercolour medium, Cotman applies his colours with violence, and while in *Greta Bridge* he also applies them with subtlety, this is not always the case. For example, in the *Landscape with River and Cattle* (c. 1810, Victoria and Albert Museum), the Prussian blue extends across the horizon in an uncompromising band, modelled on the slightly fainter blue in the sky, broken up by clouds. This blue has nothing of classic distances; it is duplicated with a blue-black line schematically representing trees, only a few of which stand out from the mass in any recognizable shape. They seem to have been grouped and laid out in a kind of frenzy. Again, as if taking a gamble, and doing what Girtin would have avoided at any price, Cotman bars his landscape (contrary to *Above Bolton*) with the high bank of the river. The movement of the water beyond the sharp curve in the middle distance is purely conjectural; the eye cannot follow it and is invited rather to linger over the amusing forms of the cattle at the water's edge; they are almost like the wooden cows that children play with, cut to a somewhat Cubist pattern.

But it would be unfair to confine him to any other formula but those which proceed from his impassioned geometry. He was too sensitive to grandeur to be unresponsive to that of a fine landscape. Lines and surfaces are simplified so as to convey the lie and sweep of the land. Instead of the single barred movement, as in the *Landscape with River and Cattle*, the *Dolgelly* in the Fitzwilliam Museum has a tiered recession of hills stretching to the horizon, above a zigzagging line of blue water, bringing out with singular effect the delicate shades of dark and light brown, of brownish and bluish grey. The bridge, with its reflection in the water on the right, has the delicacy of an embroidery; the town on the left displays its curious sequence of pink roofs and bluish tints; but nothing interferes with what seems to me to be one of the most complete meditations on space in the history of watercolour. Cotman has a wonderful knack of conveying the spiritual mood of a site, especially a dim or dismal one, rendering it with a fine sense of desolate yet decorative poetry. His *Yarmouth River* in the British Museum is almost the reverse of the prevailingly happy spatial modulation of *Dolgelly*. This river outlined to right and left with sombre earth colours is more like a cove, where a barge and a large boat, both in the same dark brown, ride placidly on the pale water, while in the middle distance, equally placid, a sailing vessel leans its frail rigging

John Sell Cotman (1782-1842)

Greta Bridge, c. 1806. Watercolour. (9 × 13″). British Museum, London.

John Sell Cotman (1782-1842)

Landscape with River and Cattle, c. 1810. Watercolour on paper. (8⅜ × 12⅜"). Victoria and Albert Museum, London.

over the shallows and the ascending smoke of a factory follows exactly the same broken rhythm as the clouds. The *Ploughed Field* (Leeds, City Art Galleries), apparently dating from his early period (*c.* 1807), had already shown a solid grasp and understanding of the main horizontal rhythms of a landscape and the parallel patterns of a tilled field.

Though his oil paintings are less novel and arresting, the fact remains that at that time they had few rivals apart from Turner. In themselves they have a remarkable vigour and manifold intensity, as in *Norwich Market Place* (Tate Gallery) with its thronging figures and profusion of ordered movements; for Cotman that was still a time of glad effort and cheerful assurance. One of his most poetic oils, doubtless on a par with his watercolours, is *The Drop Gate* (Tate Gallery), with the water treated in that mauve grey, a colour particularly his own, which he uses here for the gate and its reflections as well. The trees above, treated schematically much as in Constable's sketches, are strangely borne up by a network of pale, thin, skeletal trunks, which throw into still darker relief the neighbouring mass of shadow.

Because John Sell Cotman failed to appeal to Ruskin, his paintings, with their motionless waterfalls, pre-Cubist forms and modulated patches of flat colour, were consigned to oblivion and were not rediscovered until the end of the nineteenth century, thanks to the impact of Japanese prints. Even distinguished art writers of today sometimes state that he merely adapted the style of Girtin. He deserves to find a champion worthy of his own intensity and alive to the singular variety of his work, which few critics seem to have noticed but which may be seen by looking through any portfolio of his watercolours – *Mountain Farm*, with no farm in sight, but dominated by the blue violence of the mountain; *The Scotsman's Stone*, as conspicuously present as the farm was absent, a massive form round which colourless water streams and foams; *Fire at Vinegar Works*, an expressionistic blaze summed up by a few vertical streaks of red set off by a patch of yellow.[18]

He alone among the watercolourists had an imaginative sense of the fantastic, and no history of English Romantic art should fail to make mention of his *Weird Scene*, in pencil and grey wash, a night-piece centring on a black cross at the top of a knoll, set against a background of long, draped hills, with vivid gleams flashing through the broken, twisted clouds, and vague, baleful figures bending towards the cross.

Like every artist endowed with a sense of the fantastic, he also had a sense of the grotesque – the grotesque as a *way of seeing* and not as a thing seen. A *Norman Peasant*, seen by him from a fantastic angle of vision, becomes a Zen drawing. Cotman was born a century too soon.

David Cox (1783-1859), today at least, does not raise so many problems or stir up such violent passions. The son of a Birmingham blacksmith, he began as a scene painter in the local theatre and travelled with the company to various towns. In London he left the company and studied under a singular artist who had many pupils, John Varley, occultist, astrologer, one of the founders of the Water-Colour Society, and also a friend of Blake's. It is all too easy to say that Cox imitated Turner. It is more accurate to say that, more than any other watercolourist, not even excepting Girtin, he seized the sense of atmosphere and lighting as they vary with the time of day. With respect to the vision of a Girtin or a Cotman, he marks a regression towards the picturesque. One might describe him as a kind of fashionable Sandby, though that is perhaps unfair, for with him, as with Sandby, there is

David Cox (1783-1859)

Rhyl Sands, c. 1854. Oil on canvas. (18 × 25″). City of Manchester Art Galleries.

what one might call the 'pretty spot'. Such a pretty spot is his *Road in Wales* (British Museum), painted in those small, spirited touches which it is natural but not very illuminating to describe as pre-Impressionist. When all is said and done, there is something commonplace about Cox. Despite the light and 'poetic' tonality and the deft interchange of blues and pinks, his work fails to nourish the imagination. I have spoken of regression, but his brushwork is curiously modern. Like the topographers, he travalled far and wide on sketching tours in Wales and the North, as well as in Belgium and Holland. Like the open-air painters who were to mark the nineteenth century, he was 'on the motif' in all weathers. He was not a mere topographer; as proof one has only to look at his *Welsh Castle* (c. 1835, City Museum and Art Gallery, Birmingham). Here the rain pouring from the clouds does not only envelop the castle but tends to dissolve it into a semi-molten but still luminous state; the figures merge into strong shadows in the foreground of this dream world, which may be compared – though it lacks their tragic intimations – with Constable's *Hadleigh Castle*, then but recently painted, or with Turner's radiant and unreal *Norham Castle*.

Since the beginning of the nineteenth century, one notes a return to the city of all these artists who, like Wordsworth, had gone forth into the fields and mountains. Girtin had soundly built up his *Rue Saint-Denis* in a simple, forthright perspective, and his *Porte Saint-Denis* in an expansive play of outlines, with shifting light effects creating a lighter tonality. Now Cox in turn ventured on a *Street Scene in Paris* (1829 or 1832) and – though this is the work of an artist of lesser scope – one may measure the progress made in the space of a generation. In this vigorous attack of art on the stability and solidity of reality, he breaks up the tops of the shadow-girdled houses into serrated patterns gleaming in the sunlight. All the human stir and bustle of street life Cox boldly treats in a sketchy style, in broad, suggestive strokes, and this too is a novelty.

Like Bonington, Cox went to the sea for light effects, and it must be admitted that those he obtained owe much to Turner. This is apparent in *Shakespeare's Cliff, Dover* (British Museum), in the sky built up broadly in pale yellow merging into iridescent pinks, around the white disk of the setting sun, whose reflection flickers in the water, down to the small waves in the foreground. Cox, though a graceful and appealing artist, had no great success as a watercolourist. But he had none of Cotman's morbidity and suffered no depression of spirits. He earned a good livelihood as a drawing master and as early as 1814, moreover, published a *Treatise on Landscape Painting and Effect in Water-Colour*.

At fifty-six he took up oil painting and, unlike Cotman, showed a singular power. *Rhyl Sands* (c. 1854, City of Manchester Art Galleries) may of course be described as pre-Boudin, but 'pre' in this sense often suggests a successful stroke only half-consciously achieved. Cox was fully conscious of what could be done with oils, with fine pigments neatly applied and juxtaposed in touch upon touch of pure, bright colour. At first glance it gives the impression of being all in pink and blue, but it is then seen to darken slightly from the pure pink of a zone in full light where a skirt gleams out; but at the third glance one observes the way in which the picture tilts, and which, in the end, one hesitates to call odd or normal. For beaches tilt and dip, but in such a way that the sea replaces the land and the balance with the ever-peaceful horizon is restored. Cox proceeds like the old film-makers who tilted the camera, the better to render the swell of the sea. The seaside effect recorded here is delightfully successful.

Richard Parkes Bonington (1801-28)
François I and Marguerite de Navarre, 1827. Oil on canvas. (18⅛ × 13½″).
Wallace Collection, London.

Richard Parkes Bonington (1801-28), like Girtin, died prematurely, and however risky such comparative value-judgments may be, his work is equally important. But the way in which that importance took effect reflects his situation: it was in France that he was best known and recognized, and it was there that his sense of colour and light contributed, in however small a way, to change the course of art.

He was born at Arnold, near Nottingham. For reasons which are variously given by his biographers and do not matter in the story of his life, the family left Nottingham in 1817 and emigrated to Calais. His father, who drew and painted as an amateur, hoped to earn a living there by his painting. Fully alive to the gifts shown by his son at an early age, he set him to work under Louis Francia, a native of Calais, who had recently returned from England where he had been much impressed by the landscape art of Gainsborough and Girtin. From Francia, Bonington soon learned the watercolour technique and, if his *Port of Calais* really dates from 1817, as is supposed, it shows that even as a boy he was a proficient watercolourist and a master of those forthright seascapes deriving from the Dutch school. In 1820 he entered the Ecole des Beaux-Arts in Paris, becoming one of the four hundred pupils of Baron Gros. There he was caught up in the Romantic movement as it had then developed in France, and it was no doubt in Gros's studio that he fell under the influence of its characteristic medievalism. But his singular gifts are evident even in such romantic costume pieces as *Desdemona and Othello, Henry III and the English Ambassador, Henry IV and the Spanish Ambassador* (the famous scene with the King on all fours playing with his children) and the picture reproduced here of *François I and Marguerite de Navarre* (1827, Wallace Collection). The movement of the seated King, the baroque twist of his body as he

Richard Parkes Bonington (1801-28)
The Adriatic Coast. Oil on cardboard. (11¾ × 17″). Louvre, Paris.

Richard Parkes Bonington (1801-28)

View of the Norman Coast, 1823-24? Oil on canvas. (17¾ × 15″). Louvre, Paris.

turns towards the Princess, is emphasized by the strong reds of the costume and drapery, and the pronounced swelling of his sleeve. The whole scene is set off by highlights and vivid touches. To these brilliant, unpretentious history paintings, which might be described as historical genre pictures and often deal with French history but also include Shakespearean subjects, must be added some exotic Oriental scenes, represented above all by a number of odalisques; his two versions (at least) of the *Odalisque with a Red Parrot* are contemporary with, if not related to, Delacroix's *Reclining Odalisque*, also known as the *Woman with a Parrot*. Bonington remembered the genre painting properly so called which was a tradition in his country, and which was in accord with the intimist vein of Romanticism in contemporary France. He therefore had some success when he painted his *Invitation to Tea*, a watercolour of 1824 or 1825, which shows the artist himself about to offer tea.

Bonington branched out in several directions at once, including landscape and seascape – travel, observation and open-air work having followed his study in the Louvre of Dutch landscape painting, which began in 1818 when his family settled in Paris. In 1824, on his

Richard Parkes Bonington (1801-28)

A Sea Piece, 1827. Oil on canvas. (21 ½ × 33 ¼"). Wallace Collection, London.

return from a tour of Flanders, he exhibited several landscapes and marines at the Salon. This was the one in which the organizer, the Comte de Forbin, invited Constable to participate (with the *Hay Wain*, etc.), and the latter's work came like a revelation to Bonington, deepening and enriching his style. This influence was further extended by a trip to England in 1825. It is hardly possible to see his marines without being aware of the impact of Turner, in conjunction with the whole Dutch tradition which continued to haunt him.

A journey to Italy in 1826 took him to Venice, and he painted the landscapes of Italy and above all some views of the Adriatic coast. I am not so sure that his seascapes, however fresh, airy and spirited they may be, add much to that great tradition which Turner had been renewing for ten years or more and which Constable had just discovered. Bonington's colour and even the tonal texture of his clouds are full of echoes of them. He did not have, it would seem, the heroic stature required to extend the scope of landscape art. It has always seemed to me that coast scenes aroused a more personal inspiration in him than the sea itself, and the oil painting in the Louvre, *View of the Norman Coast* (1823-24?), bears this point out. True, it is only a sketch after the fashion of Constable, and the rainy sky with its swirl of luminous clouds is only painting as yet. A scumble of mat blue and a whitish impasto applied with the palette knife represent the thin and distant line of the sea under the enormous, disproportionate sweep of the sky. The *Adriatic Coast* (Louvre) is treated less boldly, breadthwise, with no foreground shore, only a series of posts sticking out of the water, and the low outline of a town on the horizon. However, the quantitative relation between the sky and the other elements, land or water, is roughly the same; and the tonal relation between this great mauve sky torn with dark and jagged clouds and the dark green sea which they overshadow, is exquisite.

Though he sometimes rashly combined watercolour and gouache, he recovers all his lightness of touch and gaiety of tone in a pure watercolour like the *Château of the Duchesse de Berry* (British Museum). Without overstressing it, he knows how to handle a fine reach of space, as in his Paris townscape, the *Institut Seen from the Embankments* (British Museum), with such perfect control of its architectural features that, surprisingly enough, instead of lapsing into the dryness of Girtin's *Durham Cathedral*, the buildings continue to bathe in an impalpable atmosphere. Among the talents which have not been sufficiently emphasized in Bonington, there is a calligraphic humour in the handling of figures as, for example, in *Norman Peasant Women* (British Museum), which is not unconnected with certain Oriental prints.

Corot has related how, when he was still a messenger boy, the sight of one of Bonington's watercolours in a shop fascinated him and inspired him to become a painter. His first picture at the Salon was hung between a Constable and a Bonington.

Yet Bonington was only a young artist. His skill is sometimes all too apparent. He is too free in his use of a red patch to situate a tonality. But that is not a very serious lapse. He was friendly with Delacroix whose studio he shared for a few months in 1825-26, and who spoke admiringly of his dextrous hand, 'so skilful that it outran his mind', and the 'deft execution which makes his works, in a certain sense, diamonds, by which the eye is enticed and charmed independently of the subject or of imitative appeal.'

6

*Landscape Painting and the East Anglian School Centred on John Crome.
Intimism and the Quest of Light.
John Constable in Search of his Childhood.
His Evolution, his Public Painting and his Private Vision.*

Any chapter division must to some extent be arbitrary, and I am only too well aware of it when, having placed John Sell Cotman of Norwich among the great water-colourists, I separate him from John Crome of Norwich, who is considered the central figure of one of the very few schools of painting in England with distinct regional characteristics.

The origins of John Crome (1768-1821), or Old Crome, as he is often called, again illustrate the essentially democratic character of English painting. The son of a journeyman weaver, he was born in a public house in Norwich. His father could give him only the scantiest education and he went to work early as a doctor's errand boy. At fifteen he was bound apprentice to a coach and sign painter. A few years later he tried his hand at land-scape painting and some of his early pictures came to the notice of a local collector, Thomas Harvey, whose house at Catton, two miles outside Norwich, contained some Gainsboroughs (*The Cottage Door*), some Wilsons and above all some works of the Dutch school, by Hobbema and Cuyp. Through Harvey, his eyes were opened to a tradition of painting. He meditated on Wilson and copied Hobbema. He was able to study a little in London in the studio of the portraitist William Beechey, whom he met at Harvey's house. He received advice from another self-made man, John Opie. Appointed drawing master at the local Grammar School, he became in 1803 one of the founders of the Norwich Society of Artists, which from 1805 on held annual exhibitions. In 1808 he became its president. He lived and worked in Norwich until 1814, when he went to Paris to see the Louvre. In France he painted his *Boulevard des Italiens, Paris* and *Fishmarket at Boulogne*. Devoted to his art, he began on the basis of familiar local scenery and a naïve emotional response to Dutch landscape and progressed steadily towards a freer, grander vision. If, as alleged, he died with Hobbema's name on his lips, it may be that he underestimated his own achievement.

His whole career unfolded in such purely local terms that a mere list of titles suggests a certain monotony: *View on the Solent, Moonrise on the Yare, Mousehold Heath, On the Yare, Boy Keeping Sheep, Yarmouth Beach*. He painted many scenes and buildings in Norwich itself, some variety being added with his one trip to the Continent, with such pictures as *Bruges River with Ostend in the Distance*.

These are not 'views', however. They are a further expression of Romantic, Wordsworthian wonder at the unfolding beauties of nature, a mystical union of a solitary soul with the solitude of a landscape. In effect, it is a series of small transfigurations that occurs in these unpretentious, enchanting insights into nature. They are always concerned with a

John Crome (1768-1821)

Poringland Oak, 1818. Oil on canvas. (49¼ × 39⅜″).

Tate Gallery, London.

state or flux of light, and it is very often moonlight, as if glimpsed through the floating haze of a dream. Crome's moonlight effects as well as the way he reduced his forms to essentials can be traced back to such Dutch masters as Aert van der Neer (for example, his *Scene on a Canal by Moonlight* in the Wallace Collection).

Crome tended to seek out an object calculated to catch, concentrate and express this light in all its singularity. The object then changes its import, its interest stemming not from its permanence but from its appearance in a single, irreversible movement. Just because his moonlight 'effects' *are* effects and thus imply a certain facility, the eye is more apt to linger over the most straightforwardly lyrical piece in his whole output, the *Poringland Oak* of 1818 (Tate Gallery). Comparing it with the far more complex landscapes of Gainsborough, for example, *Cornard Wood*, one realizes that in fact Gainsborough is nearer the Dutch masters, while Crome's *Poringland Oak* anticipates the best of the Barbizon School by more than a generation.

This tree was chosen because it is alone. Milton's words come to mind: 'the monumental oak'. Such is this tree. Indeed, it is not only monumental but mythological, its trunk and the reflection of it amidst the leafage having something of the erect majesty of a column. True, there is a receding road and a village on the horizon; but the road can barely be made out and it has no practicable continuity. The lightness of the trees alongside it is already that of the distances and the oak alone asserts its real presence. As compared with the lightness of Gainsborough's great trees, up to those of the *Market Cart*, one realizes that Crome's oak is much more conditioned by the light which it reflects, which bathes it and pervades it throughout, in every branch and leaf. And yet, as if to emphasize that the point of the picture lies not in the oak but in the light, Crome firmly divides the interest between the oak and the pond which does more than merely reflect it; for the pond is as rich in delicate refulgence as a rainbow, with the bare backs of the three bathers marking the point of highest luminosity. One notes that the small clouds have the same function of catching and radiating a little more light. One finds here none of the boldness and sweep, the almost headlong violence, of a Constable sketch, but it is a fine landscape and can stand up to even the best of Constable's finished and exhibited paintings.

Crome's few townscapes, such as the *Boulevard des Italiens, Paris*, contain a peculiar and quite distinctive vision of his own. The trees have all but blotted out the houses, and their tall, slender silhouettes dominate the construction and the openings through which light is let in. Neither here nor in the *Fishmarket at Boulogne* has he sufficiently resisted the temptation to multiply picturesque incidents. The oil sketch of *Yarmouth Water Frolic* (Private Collection), which has been reassigned to Old Crome after being attributed to his son John Bernay Crome, is probably his finest seascape. One can unreservedly admire not only the quality of the lighting and the beautifully intense forms of the sails, comparable to the elegance of his finest windmills, but also their harmonious layout which starts from left to right, culminating in the tall dark sail in the centre, then tapers off with increasing filminess to the horizon on the right. Behind this work is the influence of Cuyp, one of whose Dordrecht pictures is very similar in design. And what about Turner? All that need be recorded here is the statement made by one of Crome's patrons, the Norwich banker Dawson Turner (who was also Cotman's patron). According to him, Crome painted *The Wensum: Boys Bathing* 'immediately on his return from his midsummer journey to London, with his whole soul full of admiration at the effects of light and shade, and brilliant colour, and poetical feeling, and grandeur of conception, displayed in Turner's landscapes in the Exhibition.'

Judging by objective signs, Wilson's influence had been exerted earlier, more directly perhaps but less profitably. The spacious, luminous forms of his *Snowdon*, *Cader Idris* and *Valley of the Mawddach* had a marked effect on Crome's *Slate Quarries* (1802-05, Tate Gallery). This picture has been praised and criticized. Of all his landscapes so far mentioned, it is the most ambitious, in its expression of solitude and grandeur and the suggestion of atmospheric drama in the mist and cloud-rack hanging over the distant peaks. It is an impressive landscape, but it is by no means certain that it can stand up to an exacting scrutiny. Is the handling really so good? Are the colours, so pure in Wilson, not here a little murky? Are the tonal values sure, do they firmly set out the interlocking planes? One hesitates to go into the matter too closely, for fear of spoiling the pleasure of a picture which remains significant.

I have already referred to 'signs of the times'. Is there not one here in the fact that this artist, starting out from a naïve passion for local scenery, contained at first within narrow, almost topographical limits, should have arrived so soon at a conception of pure space significant in itself? In one of his few surviving letters, written to his pupil James Stark (one of the painters of that Norwich School which he had founded), he gives his opinion of a picture by Stark:

> I should have liked it better if you had made it more of a whole... Breadth must be attended to... making parts broad and of a good shape, that they may come in with your composition, forming one grand plan of light and shadow... Trifles in nature must be overlooked that we may have our feelings raised by seeing the whole picture at a glance...
>
> See that the masses retain their breadth... let the sky, which plays so important a part in any landscape and a decisive part in our landscapes with their low horizons, receive the prominence it deserves.

Corneille or Racine? Shelley or Keats? Wordsworth or Coleridge? From one country and generation to another, in art as well as in literature, this false problem of a meaningless choice seems to arise. Even today, in the scholarly and brilliant writings of Lord Clark, one reads: 'Fifty years ago English critics preferred Constable to Turner... Most lovers of English painting would agree today that Constable is not so great a painter as Turner.'[19]

But a good many previous issues would have to be settled before any such 'agreement' could be reached. One would have to ask: What is painting? What does the hand express in it and what does the eye seek in it? What are the stable and enduring qualities that one expects to find in it? Whatever progress criticism may have made in fifty years, no corresponding advance can be pointed out in the fine arts themselves. Has any definitive truth been revealed? Or should one simply say that the temperament of this generation is so much more Promethean and so much less evangelical, and Turner is so obviously Promethean and Constable so obviously evangelical, that present-day opinion has inevitably turned from the one to the other, though at the same time remaining intensely curious about Constable's rather sombre evangelicalism.

John Crome (1768-1821)

Slate Quarries, c. 1802-05. Oil on canvas. (48¾ × 62½″). Tate Gallery, London.

John Constable was born in 1776 at East Bergholt in Suffolk, a place (as its Saxon name indicates) of wooded hills, overlooking the valley of the Stour, which separates Suffolk from Essex. Uplands, meadow flats, woods, rivers, farms, flocks and villages – this was an ideal setting for pastoral art and Constable made the most of it.

He was the son of a well-to-do miller, Golding Constable, who owned two watermills and two windmills, thus seeming to have a direct link with the two elements which, for his son, were always the most moving. He lived in a solid, handsome, brick house which would easily have passed for a manor house; there was a fine view from it, often painted by his son.

As a boy, John was an undistinguished pupil in several different schools. His father wished to educate him for the Church, but his only scholarly attribute was his fine handwriting, and his father resigned himself to making a miller of him. Meanwhile he spent a happy childhood in the Suffolk countryside, on which he looked back with haunting nostalgia all his life. In 1800, having just settled in London as a student of the Academy schools, he wrote to his correspondent at home, John Dunthorne: 'This fine weather almost makes me melancholy; it recalls so forcibly every scene we have visited and drawn together. I even love every stile and stump, and every lane in the village, so deep-rooted are early impressions.' He was twenty-four. Gainsborough had expressed himself in much the same vein, thus showing that they were men of similar emotional responses. Gainsborough's paintings, moreover, became a key affording him access to nature, whose secrets his predecesssor had read and which this man of rare insights was to see and show even more clearly. In a letter of 18 August 1799, written from Ipswich to John Thomas Smith, one of the first to help and advise him, he said: 'It is a most delightful country for a painter. I fancy I see Gainsborough in every hedge and hollow tree.'

Years passed but the tone of his letters remained the same. In October 1821 he wrote to John Fisher of his regret at not having been with him on a fishing excursion in the New Forest. Fisher had described the river, 'with mills, roaring back-waters, withy beds', and Constable's mind was fired at once: 'The sound of water escaping from mill-dams, willows, old rotten planks, slimy posts, and brickwork, I love such things... As long as I do paint, I shall never cease to paint such places. They have always been my delight, and I should indeed have been delighted in seeing what you describe... Still I should paint my own places best; painting is with me but another word for feeling, and I associate "my careless boyhood" with all that lies on the banks of the Stour; those scenes made me a painter, and I am grateful; that is, I had often thought of pictures of them before I ever touched a pencil.'

Yet the idea of taking up pencil or brush had come to him early, from an enthusiastic amateur painter, John Dunthorne, a plumber and glazier at Bergholt, who was to become a lifelong friend. Dunthorne's son later became his pupil and assistant. Painting proved to be a vocation and in 1795 Golding Constable let his son go to London, where he studied under J. T. Smith, a draughtsman and engraver. The latter had published in 1797 his *Remarks on Rural Scenery* in which, among other discerning observations on nature, he called for a careful comparison of the whole range of greens and, more generally, of the innumerable tones that make up a patch of colour in nature. He observed that the colour of any natural object must be put in relation to that of the objects beside it. Constable scarcely needed his attention drawn to picturesque objects, ruined cottages and uneven surfaces such as shaggy thatch and broken plaster, whose rough texture catches and multiplies light, producing flickering light effects.

It is unusual – yet perhaps natural in the case of an introverted temperament – to find so fervent a vocation combined with such difficulty of expression and so uncertain a grasp of line and perspective. He never entirely overcame these failings. Indeed his genius, guided by his perseverance, lay in recognizing his limitations and not overstepping them. He nursed and exercised his gifts within a narrow field of vision, in this being fundamentally unlike the Cozenses, Girtin and of course Turner. Great landscapist though he was, he had little sense of space, of its recession and planes, of the orchestrated movement of the visible towards a virtual infinite. So it was that in 1824, in a letter to his friend Archdeacon Fisher, he could write, after a visit to Devil's Dyke, Brighton: 'It is the business of a painter not to contend with nature and put this scene (a valley filled with imagery fifty miles long) on a canvas of a few inches, but to make something out of nothing, in attempting which he must almost of necessity become poetical.'

It is all very well for an artist to adapt himself to his own limitations: the difficult thing is to make others adapt themselves to them and recognize what is novel in his work. Constable was merely an unskilled novice in the eyes of J.T. Smith, who persuaded him to return to the mill where, from 1797 to 1799, he worked in his father's counting house. But he persisted and early in 1800 he was back in London, studying in the Royal Academy schools. He was nearly twenty-four.

Some years before, about 1795, thanks to his mother (who was more inclined to indulge his taste for art than Golding Constable was), he met Sir George Beaumont, a mediocre landscapist, a pretentious and on occasion dictatorial patron but an enlightened collector, who when travelling often carried with him his principal treasures – a Claude landscape, *Hagar and the Angels* (now in the National Gallery), and thirty watercolours by Girtin. 'Their influence on him', wrote his friend Leslie in his indispensable *Life of Constable*, 'may be traced more or less through the whole course of his practice.' Yet his affinities with Girtin are not obvious. In London, the first painter he mentions in his letters is Ruisdael, and one notes that they both share a passion for atmosphere. Constable was also one of those who were much influenced by Rubens's *Château de Steen*, which belonged to Sir George Beaumont and was then being restored by Benjamin West. The influence of this picture was considerable in the history of English landscape painting. To acquire technical skill, he copied Ruisdael, Claude and Wilson. He knew, however, that the great and decisive question was: how to find oneself through others. Hence his well-known letter of 29 May 1802 to John Dunthorne: 'For the last two years I have been running after pictures, and seeking the truth at second hand. I have not endeavoured to represent nature with the same elevation of mind with which I set out, but have rather tried to make my performances look like the work of other men.'

In that summer of 1802 he accordingly returned to East Bergholt in search of a 'pure and unaffected manner... There is room enough for a natural painture. The great vice of the present day is bravura, an attempt to do something beyond the truth. Fashion always had, and will have, its day; but truth in all things only will last.'

And truth is solitary. So in 1804 he was at home rather than in London, painting cheap portraits for a living and expecting no benefit from them for his art. For the human figure was of no interest to him, which explains why he never mastered figure drawing, though he could handle it very well when the people represented were dear ones, bound to him by ties of affection. Witness the portrait of *Mrs Constable with Two of her Children* (Colonel J.H. Constable Collection). In the rendering of forms, particularly heads and faces, by a concentrated intensity of light alone, it is probably the most modern portrait painted in England before the twentieth century.

Family and friends may have had the feeling that he was stagnating. For this reason perhaps, a maternal uncle paid the expenses of a two months' tour of the Lake District in the autumn of 1806. There he made many sketches on paper which, says Leslie, 'abound in grand and solemn effects of light, shade, and colour, but from these studies he never painted any considerable picture... I have heard him say the solitude of mountains oppressed his spirits. His nature was peculiarly social and could not feel satisfied with scenery, however grand in itself, that did not abound in human associations. He required villages, churches, farmhouses, and cottages.'

But was his nature 'peculiarly social'? One wonders. Gainsborough's was, of course, even though he was a man of moods. But Constable? I see him rather as belonging to the same family as Rousseau, at ease among a small group of friends interceding between him and the world. Actually, the meadows and waters of Suffolk were his irreplaceable home, the only possible substitute being afforded through the warmth of a close friendship – as, for example, thanks to Archdeacon Fisher, Salisbury and its surroundings. Brighton he execrated, even while painting it. He was a man of sterling character, but not without his failings. His conviction that most painters are falsifiers, violating the morality of painting and blemishing its purity, only added to the bitter sense of frustration that he felt. His first reaction to any novelty was one of mistrust and rancour. How he went on in 1824 when the French made overtures to him (one of them was called Arrowsmith, but he was a Parisian). His character that year was not seen in the best light, in spite of his triumph at the Salon. It was then that he wrote: 'The world is rid of Lord Byron, but the deadly slime of his touch still remains.' As for David, his pictures are 'loathsome' and he 'seems to have formed his mind from three sources, the scaffold, the hospital, and a brothel.' Timidity and frustration rankled within him; he was a prey to morbid anxieties, to the point of physical and mental depression. In 1811 he fell in love with a local girl, Maria Bicknell, whose rich old grandfather Dr Rhudde strenuously objected to a match with an artist who had no visible prospects. He finally married her in 1816. That was also the year of his father's death; he seems thereafter to have been a man of somewhat firmer will.

From 1802, a practised eye might have detected the delicate texture of a new light in this or that canvas, but it is only about 1808, with the *View at Epsom*, that one begins to be aware of a significant creative advance. In 1809 with *Malvern Hall* he reveals himself. He ventured to seek his motif away from home, in Warwickshire, and he found it. Only in its very simple general design does this picture recall another landscape of the English school: Wilson's *Croome Court*. The latter is dazzling at first sight, with its great expanse of sky and its classical triangulation between the foreground oak in the sunset glow, the two trees in the middle distance and those at the back which support the pink mansion. The latter – Italy in England – is linked with the foreground figures by the contrivance of its expansive reflection in the water. Malvern Hall is also centrally sited, in a subdued pink instead of a luminous pink, between heavier clumps of trees. There are reflections in the water which have none of the iridescent sparkle of Wilson's. In front of the Hall, between a neutral, empty foreground and a light, simple background, extends a long band of the purest green – the first instance in Constable, and one of the most emphatic, of the presence of that green by which he set so much store. A simple, beautiful picture, entirely in a minor key. He painted only one *Malvern Hall*. As early as 1802 he painted his first *Dedham Vale* (Victoria and Albert Museum). The last dates from 1828. Dedham church, in both the first and last versions, stands nearly at the intersection of two diagonals drawn from the four

John Constable (1776-1837)

Barges on the Stour with Dedham Church, c. 1811 (?). Oil on canvas. (10¼ × 12¼″).

Victoria and Albert Museum, London.

corners of the picture. A morbid nostalgia for steeple and vale seems to pervade them both. The version of about 1810 shows him exerting himself to arrive at a broader, less stifling sense of space. The first successful version is the *Dedham Vale* of 1811 (Proby Collection), a completely different composition, with the church relegated to an inconspicuous position on the left, between the edge of the picture and the tree marking the foreground. The rest, stretching to the horizon, represents the most far-flung panorama ever painted by Constable.

About 1811, at the end of this unusually long formative period, he started producing those oil sketches for which he is today so much admired. He knew more or less what was expected of his exhibited pictures. But in them one may wonder whether he really satisfied himself, really rendered the truth as he saw it. Here one comes up against the basic dilemma of every artist in search of a public. Constable, all at once, seems to have set off on his own, and the *Lock and Cottages on the Stour*[20] is far indeed from the diluted, fluid, rather slack painting of the previous canvases. In his comments on this sketch,[21] Jonathan Mayne speaks of its almost expressionistic violence. In other words, it is not so much an attempt to 'render' a landscape as an impassioned outburst of self-expression prompted by contact with that landscape. The paper was primed with a chocolate brown which Constable did not quite cover and which shows through most effectively under the touches applied as if by an Oriental artist to convey the form of a tree or cloud, if one may speak of form here; for it would be more appropriate to speak of the movement or gesture of tree and cloud.

To the same period, around 1811, may be dated the *Barges on the Stour with Dedham Church* (Victoria and Albert Museum), an extraordinary symphony of greens. It is as if he were turning to conscious revolt the mild advice of J. T. Smith concerning the range of greens – greens veering to yellow on this side of the water, pure but muffled greens beyond, vertical blue strokes representing trees on the horizon, on a line with the usual church tower, square with raised corners (it figures in a hundred pictures by Constable), and greenish edging of the yellow cloud in the stormy sky. This quasi-monochrome, in which one admires the calligraphic firmness of the brush drawing, was executed in the same mood of vehement self-expression, though with a more sensitive appreciation of visual appearances, extending even to such details as the blades of grass in the foreground.

To the sketch of *Barges on the Stour*, one may add, in order to show the variety of his moods, that of *Willy Lott's House*, datable to around 1814. Curiously interesting in itself, it is even more so as it corresponds almost line for line, though in a counter-style, to the left side of *The Hay Wain*. Even the little dog in the sketch, who trots along with a superb stroke of black for a shadow, seems to be the same; seven years later in the finished painting he had only moved forward a few feet. But the sketch simply conjures up certain optical realities in the light which, reflected from the almost pure white of the sky where it blends with mauve clouds, impinges strongly on the edge and foot of a tall tree, on the shrubbery against the house and, even more, on the wall of the house wherever the shrubbery lets it through and there its impact is marked by a dazzling, almost overpowering white. In the equally luminous water, the reflected trees take on a faintly Cubist simplicity, which contributes to the authentic modernity of this superb sketch for a picture which, for all its charm, is much more staid.

At least from the time of these sketches, a dichotomy becomes apparent in Constable's work. These early sketches seem to answer to some ungovernable urge carrying the artist out of himself towards a higher level of art than had been imagined by the humble, complex-ridden Constable who in 1812 sought out Benjamin West, president of the Royal Academy. West had always given him good advice, reminding him as early as 1802 that 'light and shadow never stand still'[22] – a precept that obviously was not lost on Constable. Now, when he inquired of his illustrious elder 'whether he considered that [present] mode of study as proper for laying the foundation of real excellence,' West replied: 'Sir, I consider that you have attained it.'

It was now, about 1812, that Constable began to enjoy the decisive friendship of his life, with the young Rev John Fisher (who was sixteen years younger than the artist), then chaplain to his uncle, the Bishop of Salisbury. Constable sent him a small landscape, which gave rise to a discussion among Fisher's friends. 'What it wants', said one of them, 'is that what is *depth* near [at hand] should not be *gloom* at a distance.' And Fisher added: 'It is most pleasing when you are directed to look at it; but you must be *taken* to it. It does not

John Constable (1776-1837)
Weymouth Bay (unfinished), 1816. Oil on canvas. (21 × 29½″). National Gallery, London.

solicit attention; and this I think true of all your pictures, and the real cause of your want of popularity. I have heard it remarked of Rubens, that one of his pictures *illuminates* a room. It gives a cheerfulness to everything about it. It pleases before you examine it, or even know the subject.' Constable never of course attained to the musicality of Rubens, whose landscapes, as exemplified by the great *Rainbow Landscape* in the Wallace Collection, represent a height of achievement all too often unrecognized. But one may acknowledge in the English painter a deeper flow of passion.

A stay-at-home, with a constitutional tendency to that depression and frustration which marked his slow and uneasy career, Constable had some difficulty in renewing his powers, in opening himself to the new visual experience which he needed, preferring instinctively to keep to variations on familiar motifs. Pretexts had to be found to lure him away from them. Thus, after his marriage, his honeymoon took him to the Dorset coast, to Osmington and Weymouth. Rather gingerly he tried his hand at some new motifs, the most notable result being the three versions of *Weymouth Bay*. The staidest, the least touched by that sombre vehemence to which he periodically gave way, is the one in the National Gallery. Between his sky, beach and headland, Constable does not seem here to have found that basis of underlying unity which his long meditation on familiar landscapes had elsewhere made him hit on instinctively, so that the tonality swings this way and that, in an incessant exchange and interpenetration between all that is subjected to the same light. He has merely sanded his sea and his clouds. The result is lacking in poetry. In the Louvre variant he has shifted the dramatic centre of interest to the overcast sky and more strongly bound together the sky, the dark, livid water reflecting it, and the headland beyond, now skilfully diminished and thrust into the distance. The sea thus gains in prominence, and the picture is more stable and forceful. The format has changed (from $21 \times 29\frac{1}{2}''$ to $34\frac{1}{2} \times 44''$). The picture being distinctly higher, the sky has gained in breadth and interest.

The third variant (Victoria and Albert Museum) is again one of those miraculous small-size studies ($8 \times 9\frac{3}{4}''$) which seem to have been painted out of spontaneous delight with the scene before his eyes. The sky, quite as high as in the Louvre version, is more violent in tone and stormier, with the light bursting through a few pale breaks in the clouds. The cape has regained its importance in the tonal composition, its farthest point and the sea in the offing being so darkly overshadowed by the lowering sky as to be barely distinguishable from each other. The inland heights of the cape are lit up in livid green by a burst of sunlight through the clouds. The stretch of beach alternates in impassioned chiaroscuro between a pinkish and purplish brown, lapsing into indistinct shapes at either end. Such were Constable's changing moods. Clearly the small format, which he refrained from working up into a larger picture, did not correspond to a mood which he considered fit to bring before the public.

From his marriage dates a belated, uneasy but vigorous maturity, on the whole a cheerful one, with a shift to a lighter tonality. But the change was not always for the better. It seemed that Hobbema was far behind him, as he was even far behind Crome. But now, in the best-known painting of 1817, *Flatford Mill* (National Gallery), here, it seems to me, is Hobbema looming up again in this carefully contrived landscape and this commonplace lighting on decorous trees, sunny meadows and sound tile-roofs. This, one suspects, is just the kind of picture that offered Ruskin an example for his scornful contrast of

John Constable (1776-1837)

Seascape Study with Rain Clouds, c. 1827. Oil on paper mounted on canvas. (8¾ × 12¼″).

Royal Academy of Arts, London.

Constable with Turner. The issue has to be faced again, moreover, in a picture like *A Scene on the River Stour (The White Horse)* of 1819. It was his first 'big' landscape, the first of his 'six-foot canvases'. Exhibited that year at the Royal Academy, it earned him his election as an associate member of the Academy, a first, modest step on the way to recognition and honours. It is an appealing picture, with the charming motif that gives it its name – a horse on a barge pushed with long poles by two men seen in back view, as superbly posed as straining gondoliers. The blue water, a trifle sentimental, reflects the blue sky. Delicate trees, in a delicate play of light, are combined with a picturesque touch that balances the sentimental – the ragged, thatched roof of a broken-down shed. A contemporary critic compared it unfavourably with Turner, as failing to penetrate to the soul of nature or to raise the spectator's thoughts, but rendering only the appearance and complexion of things.

So already in 1819 had a pre-Ruskinian critic voiced his dissatisfaction with this unfortunate vein of diligent realism which is no more than a secondary feature of Constable's art, which should be ignored.

Circumstances offered him the change and renewal which he needed. A model father and husband, he lived only for his wife and children but all was not well at home. Maria was ill (she was to die of consumption in her early forties), and in search of better air he moved with his family to Hampstead, then relatively open country. Hampstead Heath provided him with an unfailing source of themes. The Victoria and Albert Museum has a particularly fine collection of the pictures made there, because they were studies painted for his own satisfaction and remained for the most part in the family collection which was bequeathed to the Nation by his daughter Isabel in 1888. Being unconnected with the places of his childhood, the significance of Hampstead for Constable was essentially pictorial. To express it, he drew on what he had learned elsewhere, particularly in the rendering of fleeting light effects, with flashes of sunlight and stormy glimmerings, conveyed as the case might be by small touches of bright pigment or abrupt, sweeping strokes. There is a suggestion of Rubens and Ruisdael in the *View at Hampstead*, in the windmill, the rainbow, the overall iridescence of the landscape. *Hampstead Heath* (Victoria and Albert Museum) is a fine intimation of stormy weather, with a dark ravine cutting across the foreground, which is brightened by the rump of a white horse. Further back, a gleaming pond where a black horse is drinking, and a gleaming slope. Still further back, rows of trees and verdure overshadowed by a large cloud. Then there is *Branch Hill Pond* (Tate Gallery), atmospheric, powerful, dramatic: mauve cumulus clouds on the left, balanced by a brown knoll on the right, in front of which, in a hollow, a cart and horses have halted. The landscape descends towards a bright pond, lying beyond the dark foreground. Working there between 1820 and 1825, he brought out the dramatic aspect of these hills and re-emphasized it in the *View on Hampstead Heath* (Tate Gallery): here is the same movement, with the hollow of the pond set between the foreground sloping down from the right and the rising ground in the middle distance on the left; the light-reflecting pond forms part of a curious rhythmic movement of light slanting down from the clouds. Now perhaps he may be said to match a Cozens or a Girtin in the poetic rendering of space, as it stretches indefinitely into the distance. The *View of Hampstead Heath* (Victoria and Albert Museum) is so vehement and aggressive in its dark assault against the light that it conveys a profound sense of desolation and hostility, in spite of the vegetation crowning the top of what is after all only a hill. It is as if his spirits were oppressed as much here as in the mountains of Cumberland and Westmorland. On the back he simply noted: '2 November 1821, Hampstead Heath, windy afternoon.'

Clouds and wind – he had always remained miller enough to be constantly observant of them, almost obsessively so. Since 1937 attention has been called to a book by one Luke Howard, *The Climate of London* (1820), containing a study of cloud formations, with which Constable seems to have been familiar, as he was, too, with Thomas Forster's *Researches about Atmospheric Phaenomena* (he mentions it in a letter to his brother George of 12 December 1836). Oddly enough, Howard's book also came to the knowledge of Goethe, who in 1820 published an article on 'cloud forms according to Howard,' with a poem to his memory and several on the various shapes taken by clouds. In Howard's study Goethe found confirmation of his view that all natural forms are symbols of eternity and bound together in certain strict relations. If attention has been drawn to the possible influence of Forster and Howard, it is because, after 1820, Constable seemed to move into another sphere, venturing into a new series of studies of an altogether different kind. Some may be described as rough sketches, hastily and urgently recording a unique moment of discovery, of self-expression, of revelatory contact. His cloud studies are at once similar, in their urgency of expression, and different, in the concern for objective precision which is essential to their value. This can be seen in the *Study of Sky and Trees* (1821, Royal Academy) and in the even more impassioned study of the same year, with the same title, in the Victoria and Albert Museum. Houses dimly seen through dark trees sustain a mauve-grey phantasmagoria in an expanse of blue. Essentially and fundamentally, that phantasmagoria corresponds to an exact state of the sky. But the technique with which it is rendered verges on Expressionism.

Constable was a keen observer of what he called 'the natural history, if the expression may be used, of the skies,' and on the back of his many cloud studies he carefully noted the date, time of day and other memoranda. On one is written: '1 August 1822, 11 o'clock a m, very hot with large climbing clouds under the sun, wind westerly.' On another: '5 September 1822, looking S E noon, wind very brisk and effect bright and fresh. Clouds, moving very fast, with occasional very bright openings to the blue.'

John Constable (1776-1837)

Study of Cirrus Clouds, 1821-22. Oil on paper. (4½ × 7″). Victoria and Albert Museum, London.

The culminating point, literally and figuratively, is the amazing little *Study of Cirrus Clouds* (1821-22, Victoria and Albert Museum). Here Constable seems to have been borne aloft in ecstatic levitation. No other painter has practised so curiously unreal a realism, none has so wonderfully rendered the weightlessness of these wisps of cloud scudding across the sky. Such a picture gives a very different idea of Constable from the rather sentimental and edifying image of him which he himself did so much to convey. Such work as this is what he called his 'skying' (letter to Fisher of 23 October 1821). In the same letter he writes that the 'landscape painter who does not make his skies a very material part of his compositions neglects to avail himself of one of his greatest aids... The sky is the source of light in nature, and governs everything... The difficulty of skies in painting is very great, both as to composition and execution; because, with all their brilliancy, they ought not to come forward, or, indeed, be hardly thought of...'

His stay at Hampstead seems to have brought a real renewal and purification of his sense of light, as he observed it from hour to hour on his sketching walks. Another little (10 × 12″) picture of genius is the *Study of Trees at Evening* (1823, Victoria and Albert Museum). This shows a golden sunset flooding out behind the houses, glowing on certain

John Constable (1776-1837)

Brighton Beach with Colliers, 1824. Oil on canvas. (5¾ × 9¾″).

Victoria and Albert Museum, London.

trees, setting off the dull green of others which stand in shadow, and filtering through the leafage in shimmering points of light.

His next phase is marked by a more complete discovery of the sea and coast than had been possible during his short stay at Osmington in 1816. By 1824 Maria's health was failing. Hampstead no longer sufficed. The sea air was needed and so he installed his wife at Brighton. Though he disliked Brighton, he nevertheless painted it very well. He was too fastidious not to be disgusted at the vulgarity of seaside life. It is true, too, that he did not care for the charming Regency architecture of the place: but then Constable was no architect. What he could accept wholeheartedly was the breakers and sky, together with the sandy beaches and the picturesque fishing boats, though he found them less so than the Hastings boats. But his fastidiousness made him wary of marine subjects, which he considered 'hackneyed' and 'easier than landscape'.

Fortunately he resigned himself to tackling them and made a virtue of necessity. Fortunately, because some of these studies are delightful examples of pure painting. Perhaps the most striking of them all (though again of absurdly small dimensions, just under 6 × 10'') is *Brighton Beach with Colliers* (1824, Victoria and Albert Museum). Today, almost as a matter of course, Boudin comes to mind, because anything impressionistic pre-dating the seascapes of the Impressionists themselves is associated with his name. But the powdery lightness of this painting and the subtle interchange of pinks and blues between sky and sea, the mauve pinks of the sky passing into the pinkish tan of the beach, bring to mind other names as well, right up to Monet. It is curious to find such lavish impasto in so small a picture. Whatever his feelings about Brighton, one senses his sheer delight in the paints as one follows from ship to ship the re-echoing touches of pure black and pure white. This picture overshadows everything else that Constable painted on the Sussex coast, with the notable exception of another small oil sketch (just under 8 × 12''): the *Coast Scene at Brighton* (Victoria and Albert Museum). It shows, almost disconcertingly, all that Constable let slip from his grasp because he did not sufficiently believe in it. In the exact centre of the picture is a white sun, casting over the surrounding sky an uneven glow of warm yellow and orange to the left and round about, and streaky pink to the right; above the grey cloud where these tones mingle, extends a more or less pinkish mauve. This whole sky is built up over the pure outline of a stretch of land running out beyond the bay. This evening landscape is so far simplified as to do away with the town altogether. There only remain a few bright, indistinct figures oddly silhouetted against the delicate bands of colour that form the whole landscape. *Hove Beach* (Victoria and Albert Museum) is an accurate rendering of the sea light filtering through clouds over grey-blue breakers flecked with white.

While it has become almost a cliché to equate such pre-Impressionism with Boudin, it is only fair, nevertheless, to point out the unmistakable analogies that exist, despite an interval of thirty-five to forty years. They may be most tellingly suggested by a quotation from Baudelaire's review of the 1859 Salon, referring to Boudin: 'On the margin of each of these studies, so rapidly and so faithfully sketched from the waves and the clouds (which are of all things the most inconstant and difficult to grasp, both in form and in colour), he has inscribed the date, the time and the wind: thus for example, *8th October, midday, North-West wind*... In the end, all these clouds, with their fantastic and luminous forms; these ferments of gloom; these immensities of green and pink, suspended and added one upon another... in short, all these depths and all these splendours rose to my brain like a heady drink...'[23]

The pictorial saga of Constable's native Suffolk was continued, however, as he had vowed it would be. After *Stratford Mill* of 1820, the third of his 'six-foot canvases' or large exhibition pictures was the famous *Hay Wain* of 1821 (National Gallery). While not the best (far from it, indeed), it is certainly the best known of his works.

There is hardly any need to describe the very characteristic, very traditional setting of this picture, a much more subtle work than may be supposed by those who are only familiar with it from calendars and postcards. On the whole, a good black-and-white photograph best conveys the tonal values and the forcible distribution of the lighting, the impact of the chiaroscuro. All this may be fatally blurred by a poor reproduction in colour, and a picture in which the artist put so much faith, passion and patience becomes no more than an agreeable piece of popular imagery.

It is very much more than that, but it is also a work in which the artist did his utmost to win over a stubbornly unresponsive public. He deliberately checked his instinctive boldness, his quest for a revelation, a deeper insight into actual reality. Here he set out to re-experience the sensations of his childhood. Mention has already been made of the admirable sketch of *Willy Lott's House*. It stood on the Stour, near Flatford Mill. Its owner, Willy Lott, was said to have spent hardly four whole days away from it in a life of eighty years. He himself thus seems like a figure of childhood legend, with something of that reassuring permanence which provides a foil to the fugitive effects of time and light. The intensity of that first small sketch is sustained in the full-size sketch of *The Hay Wain*, actually a little over six feet in width, in the Victoria and Albert Museum. It glows with a mossy effect on the leafage, with a snowy effect on the shrubbery beside Willy's house. Everything is reduced to luminous correspondences. The water reflecting the light from the broad sky sends it back from the boy on a horse, who articulates the foreground, to the hay wain crossing the ford. Shimmering and gleaming in the foreground from object to object, the light then flows softly and lazily over the water and along the meadow. There is scarcely a shadow in all this brightness. The question of picturesque objects no longer arises; a roof and leafage merge by subtle contagion into the same vigorous impasto. This unity of expression stems from a close-knit texture of vivid, broken touches often firmed up with the palette knife. Here already, overlaying some broad high-lights, is the first light fall of what came to be known as 'Constable's snow', originally a term of ridicule. These white flecks, which he carried even into the zones of shadow, vouch for the omnipresence of light. His 'snow' appears again and again, from Brighton to Salisbury, almost like a signature.

The exhibition version of *The Hay Wain* kept to the same composition, except that Constable eliminated the boy and his horse. If objects were not to be absorbed in a glow of light, his picture space had to be carefully constructed; however shallow, it had to give free passage to the eye and mark the correspondence of one plane to another between the serene expanse of the water and that of the meadow. The wain itself remains unchanged and suffices to turn a landscape into a scene, enlivened with a few touches of bright colour on the carter and his horses.

With *The Hay Wain*, Constable's career assumed an international dimension. Seeing it at the Royal Academy exhibition of 1821, the French author Charles Nodier wrote an

John Constable (1776-1837)

Study for the Hay Wain, c. 1821. Oil on canvas. (54×74″). Victoria and Albert Museum, London.

enthusiastic appreciation of it. This brought the Parisian art dealers to his door, and it was none too soon, for the painting of such large pictures was time-consuming and expensive. Neglected at home, he began to enjoy some recognition across the Channel and in 1824 he was invited to take part in the Salon in Paris. There he exhibited *The Hay Wain, A View on the Stour* and a small *Yarmouth Jetty*. They were much admired by, among others, Géricault and Delacroix, who is said to have repainted the background of his *Massacre of Chios* after seeing them. Constable was still on his guard, but after all his three pictures were sold in Paris for £250 and others were ordered from him. He could not but be flattered by the appreciation in France of his freely handled paintings. 'They... acknowledge the richness of texture, and attention to the surface of things. They are struck with their vivacity and freshness, things unknown to their own pictures.' French criticism, though not always favourable, was nevertheless more imaginative than in England. Some critics likened his canvases to 'the full harmonious warblings of the Aeolian lyre' or 'high flowery

John Constable (1776-1837)

The Leaping Horse, 1825. Oil on canvas. (56 × 73¾″). Royal Academy of Arts, London.

conversations affecting a careless ease'. To which Constable replied: 'Is not some of this blame the highest praise? What is poetry? What is Coleridge's *Ancient Mariner* (the very best modern poem) but something like this?'

It is a pleasure to find Constable, who was all too prone to lean towards the rather narrow, evangelical intimism of Cowper, thus associating himself spontaneously with a great Romantic poet, the one who perhaps had ventured farthest into the world of dreams. So Constable himself acknowledged the attraction of that world.

He was at the height of his powers in 1825, and *The Leaping Horse* (Royal Academy of Arts) is perhaps the picture in which he reveals himself most completely. The history of *The Hay Wain*, both sketch and exhibition picture, is meagre in comparison with that of *The Leaping Horse*. A remarkable study by Lord Clark, published in the *Sunday Times* of 12 October 1958, admirably clarifies the matter, even though some problems concerning the origin of the picture call for further consideration. What seems certain is that Constable started out from a drawing now in the British Museum which shows exactly the same spot, with a clump of trees on the left, then the barge, the bank of the canal and the lock, with the willow beside it. And the horse is there as well, but not leaping. But since the drawing is a sketch of an actual scene, it seems probable that Constable intended from the start to show the horse leaping, for the locks along the towpath were surmounted by barriers, erected to keep the cattle from straying, and the barge horses were trained to jump over them. But a curious fact is that there is a version of the picture (Willoughby Collection), not mentioned by Lord Clark, showing two horses instead of one, and they are standing perfectly motionless, with the hauler beside them. Here, having no rider to animate the horizon line, Constable shifted the tower of Dedham church well into the picture, from its position on the far right in the final painting. The heaviness of the effect makes his purpose obscure here and focuses attention on the admirable study in the Victoria and Albert Museum and the fine exhibition picture shown at the Royal Academy (where it still is).

Lord Clark's essential conjecture – and it is only a conjecture, in view of Constable's meagre artistic culture outside the history of landscape – is that the painter's imagination was kindled by the position of the horse on the wooden platform over the lock, and that he saw that platform as the plinth supporting a sculpture, an equestrian group. Such, indeed, is the surprising impression conveyed by the picture.

There was not much difference in general design between the study and the painting. When the latter came back from the exhibition, he made a significant change. The willow originally stood on the right, leaning *towards* the fine equestrian group and seeming to counter its movement. So now he decided to transplant it. A little clumsily, he proceeded to set it up to the left of the lock, behind the horse. The gain in dynamism is undeniable. An external dynamism so to speak, for as usual Constable had put into his first version an irreplaceable passion and drive. It is a matter of texture, of the spirited handling of the palette knife and the shimmer of his 'snow' over everything represented. In 1825 Constable was at the peak not only of his vigour but also of his courage and determination. Thus it is that the handling and texture of the paints in the Royal Academy picture seem to me singularly fine, if more delicate than in the study; instead of the broader movements of the palette knife, there is a contained, incessant, overall trembling of the brush (though it is clear, too, that the knife has also been brought to bear), which sets up fine ripples of colour, particularly in the rendering of the water; and which, in the end, results in a textural consistency so delicately granular that one is tempted to speak of form-consuming pointillism.

The *Cornfield* of 1826 has a number of great ancestors, from Ruisdael on. Objects are rendered with realistic precision, and by catching the light serve to keep it up throughout to a full pitch of brightness. By calling the picture *Drinking Boy*, Constable draws attention to the picturesque motif of the boy in a red jacket.

From 1811, Constable was a frequent visitor to Salisbury, first as the guest of Dr Fisher, the Bishop, then, even more often, of his nephew the Rev John Fisher, up to the latter's death in 1832. After the countryside of his native Suffolk, Salisbury Cathedral with its great spire is one of his favourite themes. To enter truly into its surrounding landscape, any piece of architecture must be accurately absorbed into the atmosphere, to the point where it is barely allowed to subsist. The sketch in the Victoria and Albert Museum, known simply as *Salisbury Cathedral*, is in this respect a masterpiece. The spire rises up like a pointed flower, of the same nature as the trees that surround it.

Some of these impressions are rather overgrown with vegetation; others are memorable, in particular the sketch usually dated 1827 of *Salisbury Cathedral and Archdeacon Fisher's House from the River* (National Gallery). Following his usual sketch technique, he prepared the canvas with a brown priming coat, which he covered over, more or less, with broad, strongly massed strokes of the brush, especially noticeable in the great tree which all but conceals Fisher's house – apparently so small in the perspective he has chosen – and which in itself spans nearly half the width of the picture. The cathedral spire joins with other trees, in particular the tall poplar beside it, to form a sort of pyramid; but again the perspective is such that the poplar seems to dwarf the spire just behind it. The foreground consists entirely of the dark reach of the river – which *would* be dark, rather, were it not enlivened by the white, crescent-shaped boat and its enlarged reflection in the water.

This is one of those pictures to which Constable gave no further thought, once they were finished. It was quite otherwise with the large painting of 1831, *Salisbury Cathedral from the Meadows*. It remained unsold and he worked on it again in 1833; references to it abound in his correspondence, often concerning the print made from it by David Lucas. The great rainbow arching over the cathedral is a rather polyvalent symbol for Constable. It has of course a religious import; it also expresses his sense of indebtedness to certain masters, of belonging to a select fraternity, and his desire to invoke them in certain works. One thinks of Rubens, who stands in the first rank of rainbow painters. Here the cathedral is given due prominence, with nothing to attenuate the mighty upsurge of the spire, nor to mask the noble design of its triple pediment, lit up like a promise of grace in the glare of a stormy sky. Between the rainbow and the tall, inclined tree-trunk, which also receives its share of light, the cathedral is caught and held in a sacred orb. And the extraordinary wealth of motifs, though knit together in a tonal unity so strong that nothing slips from its grasp, suggests that this is something in the nature of an artistic testament. The cart, which is almost as prominent as the cathedral, is drawn by three horses, the first being a reincarnation of *The White Horse*, and looking at them is the dog from *The Hay Wain*; splashing their way through the marsh waters, cart and horses move towards the willow which, in the original version, almost checked *The Leaping Horse*. And the slimy posts sticking up out of

John Constable (1776-1837)

Salisbury Cathedral and Archdeacon Fisher's House, from the River (sketch), 1827. Oil on canvas (20¾ × 30¼").

National Gallery, London.

John Constable (1776-1837)

Hadleigh Castle (sketch), 1829. Oil on canvas. (48½ × 65¾″).

Tate Gallery, London.

the water in the foreground are doubtless those, so full of memories, which Constable, when he saw them on a walk, wished he had in his studio.

Such a picture reveals not only the artist's deeper vision, but also his discerning powers of self-criticism. On 15 February 1836 he wrote to his engraver Lucas: 'The *Salisbury* is much admired in its present state, but still it is too heavy, especially when seen between the *Lock* and the *Drinking Boy*.[24] Yet we must not break it up, and we must bear in recollection that the sentiment of the picture is that of solemnity, not gaiety, nothing garish, but the contrary; yet it must be bright, clear, alive, fresh, and all the front seen.'

His marriage in 1816 had made Constable a happy man. But as the years passed the state of his wife's health was a cause of growing concern. She died on 23 November 1828 and from then until his own death nine years later he remained in mourning. His painting grew appreciably darker. In 1829, at the age of fifty-three, he was made a full member of the Royal Academy. The President, Sir Thomas Lawrence, told him bluntly that he was lucky to be elected at all, seeing that there were 'historical painters of great merit on the list of candidates'.

The picture of 1829 was *Hadleigh Castle* (Tate Gallery), a peak of tragic expression, worlds away from the reassuring *Cornfield* of 1826. It represents a wild spot in Essex, at the mouth of the Thames, the morning after a stormy night. The picture as it exists today is a spare and rugged study for a canvas which seems to have been lost. Here almost all that is not livid is dark, on the perilous borderline between the visible and the opaque. The memory of some great upheaval seems to brood over this melancholy scene, so compellingly, however, that the imagination accepts and shares its gloom. From the crag bathed by indistinct waters rise the two shattered towers of the ruined castle. A shepherd can be discerned with a dog; there may be some animals somewhere, but one can only be sure of the white sea birds wheeling round the crag, while above and beyond the towers some rooks stand out against the clouds. The brightest part of the picture is the livid horizon line.

'Can it be wondered at, then, that I paint continual storms?' His melancholy was thus tinged with bitterness. As an Academician, he was no better understood than he had ever been by the men who were now his colleagues. As a member of the hanging committee, he no longer had to submit his pictures for acceptance at the annual exhibition. But when his *Watermeadows near Salisbury* accidentally found itself among the paintings of outsiders and the jury cried out against it, he took it under his arm and walked out. When in 1833 he exhibited his *Englefield House*, the President objected that it was 'only a picture of a house and ought to have been put in the Architectural Room.' Constable replied that it was 'a picture of a summer morning, *including* a house.'

The first mention of the 'opening of Waterloo Bridge' as a picture subject occurs in his correspondence in 1819. In December 1823 he refers to it as being prepared for exhibition in the following year. Subsequently he speaks of a smaller and a larger version, but seems to have had great difficulty in working out the subject to his satisfaction. He appears to have lacked a power of objective construction when away from familiar places and themes. On 27 September 1831 he wrote to Lucas about engraving it for a book of mezzotints after his pictures: 'The ships are too commonplace and vulgar, and will never unite with the general character of the book.' The judgments of Leslie, Constable's biographer, are both incoherent and revealing.

In the *Waterloo Bridge* he had indulged in the vagaries of the palette knife (which he used with great dexterity) to an excess. The subject challenged a comparison with Canaletti (*sic*)... and the comparison was made to Constable's great disadvantage; even his friend, Mr Stothard, shook his head and said, 'Very unfinished Sir,' and the picture was generally pronounced a failure. It was a glorious failure, however... and I will venture to say that the noonday splendour of its colour would make almost any work of Canaletti, if placed beside it, look like moonlight.

At a later page, summing up the history of the picture, Leslie writes: 'The expanse of sky and water tempted him to go on with it, while the absence of all rural associations made it distasteful to him; and when at last it came forth, though possessing very high qualities – composition, breadth, and brightness of colour – it wanted one which generally constituted the greatest charm of his pictures – *sentiment* – and it was condemned by the public; though perhaps less for a deficiency which its subject occasioned, than for its want of finish.'

Constable suffered painfully from rheumatism in the last feverish months preceding the exhibition of 1832. When the pictures were hung, his *Waterloo* was beside a grey seascape by Turner. As Constable, at the last moment, was touching up the bunting with vermilion and lake, Turner stood watching him; then, taking up his palette, he added a round spot of minium, a little bigger than a shilling, to his grey sea, and Constable's vermilion and lake at once seemed dim beside it (Turner later made his red spot into a buoy).

Naturally Turner was right in asserting the supremacy of values against colour, and the flaring, flickering colours to which Constable resigned himself partly conceal his misgivings. Nevertheless, and this applies to the version in the Glenconner Collection even more than to that in the Victoria and Albert Museum, the vibrant touches of colour result in a glorious expansion of light. 'What would he have felt,' writes Leslie, 'could he foresee that, in little more than a year after his death, its silvery brightness was doomed to be clouded by a coat of blacking, laid on by the hand of a picture dealer... by way of giving tone to the picture.'

Such in brief was the career of John Constable up to 1832, and there were some admirable works still to come in the last five years of his life. His art assimilated aesthetics to moral excellence, to a narrow notion of what truth means to an artist. No art at its best was more subjective than that of Constable; no art was intended to be more objective, to the point of mediocrity if need be. If recognition came slowly, it was due as much to his own uncertainties, hesitations and contradictions as to the inevitable incomprehension of the public. As early as 1802, when he was twenty-six, he had written: 'There is room enough for a natural painture.' By that, he meant, on the one hand, a more sincere and authentic painting, closer to the nature of the artist himself; on the other, a painting uninhibited by the old conventions and school recipes by which landscape art was then hedged in, the insistence on browns and patina, the taboo regarding a foreground in a cold colour, etc. 'Where do you put your brown tree?' he was asked by Sir George Beaumont. He took as his guide not the knowledge or memory of other pictures, but the sight of nature as he saw it with his own eyes. Constable's art was based on his rejection of a hackneyed, crippling culture. But did that make it any more 'faithful to nature'? His own passion carried him away from the docile rendering of visual appearances at which he aimed in his exhibition pictures. So nature for him was rather an essence than an existence, and the visible things he painted were a means of reaching the invisible things he felt rather than tamely record-ing what he saw. Even in his most personal sketches and studies, can Constable really be said to have painted in a green key? Browns, more or less livid yellows, mauves, violets, blues and vehement grey-greens with certain favourite accords of mauve and pale green appear to be much more characteristic of his palette than any forthright green. Of course nature offered him her colours; he seized on them avidly and, like Gainsborough, collected in the course of his walks 'flowers, feathers of birds, and pieces of bark with lichens and mosses adhering to them, which he . . . brought home for the sake of their beautiful tints.' On a visit to a friend, he 'brought from Fittleworth Common at least a dozen different specimens of sand and earth, of colours from pale to deep yellow, and of light reddish hues to tints almost crimson.' This, it may be said, justifies him; well might he love these in-tensely real things, because they are part of nature and nature is divine. Constable needed to be thus reassured. An existential world would have alarmed and baffled him. He needed to feel that he was at one with the world in the shelter of the divine mantle. His Wordsworth-ian religion of nature went deep: 'The landscape painter must walk in the fields with an humble mind. No arrogant man was ever permitted to see nature in all her beauty.'

Not surprisingly, he was taken at his word, and in the often disconcerting dichotomy to which I have referred, the whole personal interaction of impression and expression has often been ignored in favour of a naturalism which, in its purest form, is quite unusual in him. Constable is no Sandby, and yet it is of him that Fuseli said: 'I like the landscapes of Constable; he is always picturesque, of a fine colour, and the lights always in the right places; but he makes me call for my great coat and umbrella.' And his brother Abram Con-stable said to Leslie: 'When I look at a mill painted by John, I see that it will go round.'

'Nothing can exceed the beauty of the country', wrote Constable from Suffolk. 'It makes pictures appear sad trumpery.' So they may appear; but then why write, 'Art pleases by reminding, not by deceiving'? There was of course something of rapture in his appreciation of nature; it is said that he sat so still while painting in the open air that he once discovered a field mouse in his coat pocket. As he put it himself: 'The trees and the clouds seem to ask me to try and do something like them.' But rapturous appreciation does not necessarily bring insight with it, and the artist, as he said, must learn to see nature as the scholar learns to read Egyptian hieroglyphs. He attached little importance to the subject, to incident or anecdote: 'I have to combat . . . the plausible argument that subject makes the picture.' Nature is a mystery and the artist its interpreter. In nothing was he more modern than in denying the individuality of an object in painting: 'I never saw an ugly thing in my life, for let the form of an object be what it may, light, shade and perspec-tive will always make it beautiful.'

He was the least consciously egoist of painters. He tried with genuine candour to record the rapture he felt, and it sometimes seemed to him that he had succeeded: 'My *Lock* is liked at the Academy . . . and its light cannot be put out, because it is the light of nature.'[25] And again: 'My *Lock* is now on my easel; it is silvery, windy, and delicious; all health, and the absence of everything stagnant.'

He saw his predecessors and their art like his own; political prejudice alone prompted him to speak ungenerously of the French revolutionary David; instinctively, he was warm-hearted, enthusiastic and admirably fair-minded. In his third lecture at the Royal Institution, he praised 'the Rainbow of Rubens': 'I mean, indeed, more than the rainbow itself, I mean dewy light and freshness, the departing shower, with the exhilaration of the returning sun, effects which Rubens, more than any other painter, has perfected on canvas.' A picture by Ruisdael 'haunts my mind... the whole so true, clear, and fresh, and as brisk as champagne; a shower has not long passed.' He admires 'a truly sublime Cuyp; still and tranquil, the town of Dort is seen with its tower and windmills under the insidious gleam of a faint watery sun.' Two French masters were among his gods. One was Claude, whose 'characteristic excellence' was 'brightness, independent of colour, for what colour is there here? (holding up a glass of water).' The other was Watteau, whose *Bal champêtre* (Dulwich) 'seems as if painted in honey; so mellow, so tender, so soft, and so delicious... this inscrutable and exquisite thing would vulgarize even Rubens and Paul Veronese.' Among English artists he especially admired Wilson ('a large, solemn, bright, warm, fresh landscape by Wilson, which still swims in my brain like a delicious dream') and Gainsborough (on looking at his landscapes 'we find tears in our eyes, and know not what brings them'). He paid tribute to Rembrandt's *Mill*, 'a picture wholly made by chiaroscuro' – that chiaroscuro which he had resolved would be the essence of his own pictures.[26]

Constable or Turner? With that question I began this survey. It may fittingly be closed with two comments of the former on the latter:

'Turner has some golden visions, glorious and beautiful; they are only visions, but still they are art, and one could live and die with such pictures'; and 'Turner has outdone himself, he seems to paint with tinted steam, so evanescent and so airy.'

They are only visions: that is the gist of the matter.[27]

7

From Pre-Romanticism to Ultra-Romanticism. Hellenism and the Sublime.
The Temptations of Visionary Art and the Supernatural:
Loutherbourg, Ward, Martin, Danby, Etty, Fuseli.

AROUND 1760 the mood changed and some curious dichotomies appear; the cult of Greek art, for example, veered in two directions, contributing both to Neo-classicism and to Romanticism. John Flaxman (1755-1826) was the typical neo-classical artist, imitating the design of Greek or, as it was then called, Etruscan vase painting. His sculpture is of no concern here. As a draughtsman, however, he is of some account, chiefly because he influenced Blake. Flaxman's style of outline drawing was formed during his years in Italy (1787-94), in imitation of the antique. His Dante illustrations are an important source, firstly because Blake found them consonant with his theory of the unbroken line, expressing essential truth in contradistinction to the chaotic illusion of appearances; secondly because his line is dynamic, representing a play of energies and forces; thirdly because it is rhythmical, marked by correspondences, repetitions, concords. The pre-Romanticism also present in Flaxman is typified by his *Chatterton Receiving the Bowl of Poison from Despair*. The first thing one notes is that this Chatterton is a self-portrait – a rather grim touch of narcissism. The second is that he is wearing a kind of classical tunic, which would have pleased Reynolds. The third is that Chatterton's suicide, archetypically romantic, is interpreted here in a setting of undisguised mythology; a supernatural breath holds up a sinister black drapery over the two figures, the grimacing spirit offering the bowl and Chatterton receiving it. A forbidding or supernatural drapery is a stock feature of the pre-Romantic style, which will be found again in Etty.

Philippe Jacques de Loutherbourg (1740-1812) was an Alsatian artist who emigrated to England. Born in Strasbourg, he was precocious and showed great facility. From 1760, he exhibited landscapes, seascapes, battle pieces and rustic scenes at the Paris Salon; Diderot praised their dexterity and deplored the crudeness of the colouring. In 1767 he was elected a member of the French Academy of Fine Arts, and in 1771 he moved to London, bringing with him a letter of introduction to Garrick, whose stage and scenery designer he soon became, remaining with the Drury Lane Theatre until 1785. There is certainly something of the stage set in his landscapes, the parts being arranged in a stereotyped manner. After his arrival in England, he embodied some of the observed realities of English life in his work, as for example his *Midsummer Afternoon with a Methodist Preacher*. But as time passed he lost interest in reality. Ellis K. Waterhouse observes severely: 'He could paint anything he liked out of his head, but was too lazy to refer back to nature.'[28] It may not have been a case of sheer laziness; he is one of those painters who is put out by nature, and his art is variously compounded of skilful imitations of his predecessors, self-assertion and a falling in with the new moods of the day. The *Lake Scene in Cumberland: Evening* (1792, Tate Gallery) shows what he was capable of. The subtle gravity of the lighting, the mild tonality conveying the hush of evening, and the restraint of his Romantic treatment of water and rock are worthy of a great landscapist.

The term pre-Romantic may aptly be applied to him. Natural forces overshadowing man are evoked and exalted. His mountain scenery, therefore, is essentially made up of torrents and waterfalls. The *Falls of the Rhine at Schaffhausen* (1775, Victoria and Albert Museum), with their rushing waters seemingly intent on sweeping away the boulders that stand in their path, was a stock theme both in painting and literature. A related theme is that of the *Avalanche* (Tate Gallery). Here indeed is a natural force that nothing can withstand: it is the spectacular image of a cosmic catastrophe. Loutherbourg is at his best in this intermediate zone. In an era which saw artists busily illustrating Macklin's Bible and contributing to Boydell's Shakespeare Gallery, he tackled the great biblical themes and produced a *Deluge*. The result was, however, anything but cosmic; it merely shows three

Philippe Jacques de Loutherbourg (1740-1812)

Lake Scene in Cumberland: Evening, 1792. Oil on canvas. (16¾ × 23¾"). Tate Gallery, London.

people, a man, woman and child, being caught in a terrible storm which has darkened the sky. Loutherbourg, nonetheless, certainly contributed to bring the cosmic side of the Bible into fashion and to make it a characteristic feature of English Romanticism. He was one of the first to make the white horse of the Apocalypse (Revelation, VI) the subject of a painting. His grandiloquence prepared the way for that of Martin and Danby. He was, moreover, a talented illustrator who knew how to combine the topical and the sublime. In the *Battle of Camperdown* (1799) and the *Battle of the Nile* (1800) he renewed the Dutch tradition of painting sea-fights. The smoke billows impressively among the great sails, and it is all very vigorous and dramatic.

Loutherbourg's career is not a simple one, but its various aspects are significantly connected with each other. In keeping with the mood of the times both in France and in England on the eve of the French Revolution he became interested in the occult. He was a friend of Cagliostro (as also, oddly enough, of Gainsborough) and about 1789 he took up faith healing. The results were disappointing and, as magicians are apt to do, he resigned himself to being an illusionist. For many years, especially after 1790, he devoted himself to devising, exploiting and improving the Eidophusikon, a spectacle of panoramic scenery and shifting light, which gave the illusion of movement in dramatic displays of battles and shipwrecks. The most exciting moment was the firing of a distress signal, and there were even sound effects. One of his stock scenes was 'The Cataract of Niagara'. In *Coalbrookdale* the bursts of fire and smoke from behind houses shrouded in semi-darkness produce a chiaroscuro worthy of his Eidophusikon. The way for this work had already been shown by Wright of Derby's industrial night-pieces. The dim pinkish glow of *Arkwright's Cotton Mill* had blended into the moonlight; *Coalbrookdale* sets the night ablaze, like a premonition of Martin's apocalypses. A superb team in the foreground completes the arc of the circle supporting the scene with all its contrasts.

It is significant of the mood of the period when one finds an honest genre painter of middling abilities like Julius Caesar Ibbetson (1759-1817) turning, in 1798, from his usual themes of daily life to paint his *Phaeton in the Storm* (Leeds), a scene as vehement as any of Loutherbourg's. Was there ever a wilder, more cataclysmic Wales than this? The wretched carriage, apparently on the point of collapsing, is dwarfed by spectral and forbidding pillars of rock; the cliff-edge road seems to be heading for the abyss and the angrily surging waters below; the black, livid sky is rent with lightning, and thunder rumbles among the eerie chiaroscuro of the mountains. Even if such a vision is an accident in Ibbetson's career, that accident is nonetheless significant. But then there is *Conway Castle by Moonlight* (Wallace Collection), a characteristic night-piece, and *The Mermaids' Haunt* (Victoria and Albert Museum): they, too, suggest the imaginative variety of the period, with an undercurrent of pagan sensuality that was soon to disappear.

James Ward (1769-1855) is an impressive if finally unsuccessful artist who must be approached with caution. An important feature of his strong sincere personality was his sense of the supernatural, which led him to believe in the spirit world and made him an admirer of Blake. If he painted horses, it was not in the spirit of an enthusiastic anatomist, like Stubbs, or that of a genre painter, like his brother-in-law George Morland, but rather in the spirit of a mythologist. The horse seems like an apparition: such are *Monitor* (Royal Collection) and *Marengo*, Napoleon's horse (Guest Collection). The most fantastic of these

Philippe Jacques de Loutherbourg (1740-1812)

Coalbrookdale by Night, 1801. Oil on canvas. (26¾ × 42″). Science Museum, London.

pictures is the *Fall of Phaethon* (1808, Leicester-Warren Collection): Phaethon, with his chariot and horses, whirls giddily through the abyss of space in a vast sheet of flames. Never was a difficult subject approached more boldly. Blake is not far off.

But there is nothing here of what might be described as Ward's personal mythology. This is to be found in a 'landscape' like *Gordale Scar, Yorkshire* (1811-15, Tate Gallery). Its very size (nearly 11 × 14′) is significant and corresponds to the painter's candid ambition and rugged energy, for it was the reply to Sir George Beaumont's assertion that Gordale Scar was unpaintable. The whole lower part of the picture is full of animals – the deer filing in from the gorge; the cattle opposite, massed together in the sole focus of light; two stags fighting in front of the herd of deer; with, on the right, a stately white bull.

The bull, for Ward, is a mythical animal and reappears in picture after picture; not a motif but a leitmotiv. It stands in the familiar surroundings of *Regent's Park* (Tate Gallery), under a yellow sky dominated by a dark cloud. In the *Lake and Tower in Tabley Park*, the white bull stands near the tower, near the dark water, under thick clouds. Finally, and above all, there is the *Bulls Fighting, with St Donat's Castle* (1804, Victoria and Albert

Museum), a picture roughly of the same size as Rubens's *Château de Steen*, which Ward saw in Benjamin West's studio in 1803 and set out to emulate. The castle is there, it has changed its name and moved from left to right, but has the same role; and Ward was fascinated not only by the immense sweep of horizontal space (replacing the upward sweep of *Gordale Scar*) but also by Rubens's virtuosity in arranging his various incidents and knitting them together in a strong spatial unity. But Ward's picture is dominated by his favourite motif, by the fierce clash of two wild-eyed bulls. It was not admitted to the Royal Academy exhibition of 1804; one wonders if there was not here an early outbreak of Victo-

James Ward (1769-1855)

Gordale Scar, Yorkshire, 1811-15. Oil on canvas. (131 × 166"). Tate Gallery, London.

rian decorum which was offended by its force and violence. A gnarled, uprooted, fantastic tree-trunk marks the scene of the fight; sharing the focus of light with the white bull, it constitutes an almost supernatural presence in the picture – indeed, a kind of Laocoön. This is a finer painting than *Gordale Scar*. In the *Deer Stealer* (Tate Gallery) there is the same weird vegetation, the same snaky stems of trees.

Apart from Rembrandt and Soutine, how many men have been as successful as Ward in tackling a theme like the *Quarter of Beef* (Tate Gallery)? Before so impressive a work, one wonders if Ward is not a painter in need of rehabilitation.

Just such a rehabilitation has recently occurred in the case of John Martin (1789-1854). In 1935 the three huge pictures of his *Last Judgment* were sold for seven pounds; today he is enthusiastically compared to Delacroix. This suggests that fluctuations in artistic taste are influenced less by the considered judgment of experts than by broad movements of the collective imagination. Born in Northumberland and trained in Newcastle, he came to London in 1806, working initially as a painter on china and glass; his inventive mind was also occupied with hydraulic schemes for improving the water supply and sewage system of London. In 1811, however, he began exhibiting at the Royal Academy and there, in 1816, showed his *Joshua Commanding the Sun to Stand Still*. He painted a series of biblical scenes ranging from Genesis to Revelation, grandiose phantasmagorias showing unusual visionary power, with their Roman cohorts and fantastic architecture. In 1821 appeared his *Belshazzar's Feast*. It created a sensation, both at home and abroad, and for the next thirty years Martin was one of the most famous of English artists, a familiar name all over Europe. In the form of prints his *Deluge* and *Destruction of Sodom* hung on the walls of every home. Exhibited at the Louvre in 1834, the *Deluge* was awarded a gold medal. In his essay on the 'Productions of Modern Art', Charles Lamb wrote of Martin: 'His towered structures are of the highest order of the material sublime... they satisfy our most stretched and craving conceptions of the glories of the ancient world.' In 1863 Thoré-Bürger could still write: 'Of all English painters, he was perhaps the most famous on the Continent.'

It is obvious that he was not an isolated phenomenon. The way had been prepared for him by the night and fire effects of the Eidophusikon and paintings by Loutherbourg; by Blake; and by Turner's landscapes and the early history paintings by which he made his name, including two *Plagues of Egypt*. But for Martin the appeal of the irrational, the grandiose, the far-flung and fantastic was irresistible. Fire, in all its cosmic splendour, was not only *his* element; it seemed to run in the family, for in 1829 his brother Jonathan set fire to York Minster. In the end, John Martin gave up painting to devote himself to his vast schemes for the improvement of London, publishing pamphlets and plans dealing with the metropolitan water supply, sewage, docks and railways.

Martin's 'architectural' powers have been overrated. He likes to pile up titanic mountains to dizzy heights, but so does Gustave Doré; and indeed (though it may be said that anyhow Martin came first) I am reminded of Doré when I see *The Bard* (1817, Newcastle), on the very edge of a beetling crag, hurling defiance at the army of prancing knights far

John Martin (1789-1854)

Sadak in Search of the Waters of Oblivion, 1812. Oil on canvas. (30 × 25″). Southampton Art Gallery.

below on the other side of the stream, at the foot of a slope covered with a strange mossy overgrowth of trees and surmounted by the castle of childhood dreams. Unlike literature, painting is too explicit an art to admit of this kind of thing. Martin in fact learned to be less explicit, to conjure up the architectures of a dream-world in a more elementary, more schematic chiaroscuro. One of his fascinations lies in the simple relation between fabulous structures extending *ad infinitum* and the teeming humanity connected with them. His *Fall of Nineveh*, if the picture still existed and not just the print, would doubtless be an excellent example.

The small night-piece of 1843 entitled *Solitude* (Mrs Charlotte Frank Collection) would probably be dismissed by the true devotees of Martin. Yet there is perhaps a more acceptable super-reality in its eerie moonlight, the precision of the lighting and the situation by dark waters of the couple which it illuminates, than in certain phantasmagorias. Among the earliest of his fire pictures ('my first work', he terms it) is *Sadak in Search of the Waters of Oblivion* (1812, Southampton Art Gallery). It shows how effectively, as early as 1812, this amazing contriver of the impossible could devise his infernal vistas, his incandescent lakes, glowing crags and forbidding heights towards which Sadak vainly scrambles, clinging to a ledge overhanging the chasm. Again and again Martin returns to his favourite structure, the beetling crag, and the sensation that goes with it, giddiness. Together they spell out man's inexorable fate: the descent into darkness.

The Great Day of His Wrath (c. 1853, Tate Gallery) is simpler and therefore perhaps more satisfying. The world bursts asunder and goes up in flames, and beneath the fiery sky yawns the pit of darkness into which the last of living beings tumble headlong.

In conclusion, two comments on Martin, the first by Théophile Gautier: 'Surely no one can deny the genius, the inventiveness, the sublimity of his conceptions. He has all the makings of a poet. He lacks but one small and simple thing, which is to painting what style is to literature: execution and craftsmanship.'

The other is by Lord Clark: 'In Martin the colour scheme and the handling are often somewhat insensitive, but there is such a sweep and power to his imagination that one easily understands why his work delighted his contemporaries, much as a spectacular film might have done.'[29]

Francis Danby (1793-1861) was born in the south of Ireland, near Wexford, and studied art at the Royal Dublin Society's schools. After working for some years in Bristol, he came to London in 1824. He was elected an associate member of the Royal Academy in 1825 (defeating Constable by one vote). Because of a now obscure marriage scandal, he left England in 1829. For some years he lived on the Lake of Geneva, returning to London in 1840. From 1847 until his death, he lived at Exmouth, painting and building boats. In his art and his life, Danby was a responsive, imaginative and decidedly romantic personality. One of his first pictures to attract attention was *The Upas Tree* (1819). This poisonous tree, whose shadow was fatal, was a theme also taken up by Byron. *Disappointed Love*, exhibited at the Royal Academy in 1821, stands on the borderline between sentimentalism heightened by emotive symbols and Romanticism marked by a generalization of the theme. The pretty figure of the forlorn girl in white is set off by the deep shadows behind and around her. This kind of sentimental appeal was to become all too common in nineteenth-century English art, especially among the Pre-Raphaelites.

John Martin (1789-1854)

The Great Day of His Wrath, c. 1853. Oil on canvas. (77⅜ × 119⅜″).

Tate Gallery, London.

There is, however, another side to Danby who, like John Martin (but not in imitation of him), also treated the apocalyptic themes that were then so popular, for example, the *Opening of the Sixth Seal* (1828, Dublin). The following year he painted another *Subject Inspired by the Apocalypse:* 'And I saw another mighty angel come down from heaven, clothed with a cloud: and a rainbow was upon his head, and his face was as it were the sun, and his feet as pillars of fire' (Revelation X, 1).

There is no lack in these pages of 'romantic' landscapes from artists as varied as Loutherbourg, Martin and the watercolourists, and even Gainsborough and Stubbs. Rugged crags silhouetted against the sky are a stock feature of them. It is usually obvious, except with a Towne or a Cozens, that the artist had never actually *seen* such things and does not expect anyone to believe that he had. But Danby, like Towne and Cozens, was a traveller, and while as an artist he 'generalizes' in order to disengage the essential character of a landscape from its insignificant accidents, he nevertheless bases it firmly on an actual place and scene. On that basis his imagination sets to work. Such is the case with his *Liensfjord*

Lake in Norway (Victoria and Albert Museum). Danby had visited Norway in 1825, and with its sinister, vaguely menacing waves and lurid lighting, this desolate spot seems to suggest the imminence of some supernatural apparition.

William Etty (1787-1849) is one of those painters whose stature is difficult to appreciate, because few English artists, beneath the surface of an apparently successful career, have been more fundamentally at variance with their time and country; so it is that his very real gifts were to some extent misapplied and wasted. He was born in York, where his father was a baker and confectioner. He was small and ugly and he resolved never to marry: 'In which resolution I pray to God to help me that I may devote myself more purely to my Art, my Country, and my God.' But in fact he had been an unsuccessful suitor in his youth; later he repeatedly fell in love with his models and offered them marriage. He seems to have lived in a state of mental confusion, of shifting and undefined aims; perhaps because those by which he really set store would have isolated him too completely. The best, the only enduring part of his work centres on a single theme: the female nude. For this devout and conscientious artist, woman was 'God's most glorious work'.

Many of his contemporaries, however, felt uncomfortable at what they considered an obsession with nudity. Of his *Toilet of Venus* exhibited at the Royal Academy in 1835, one critic wrote: 'A brothel on fire, which had driven all the Paphian nymphs from their beds into the courtyard would be a modest exhibition compared to him, for they would at least exhibit *en chemise*. Several ladies we know were deterred from going into the corner of the room to see Leslie's, Webster's and other pictures of merit there, to avoid the offence and disgrace Mr Etty has conferred on that quarter.' In a letter to Archdeacon Fisher (11 June 1828) Constable refers caustically to his *World Before the Flood*: 'Etty has a revel rout of Satyrs and lady bums as usual, very clear and sweetly scented with otter [*sic*] of roses – bought by an old Marquis (Ld Stafford) – coveted by the King (from description), but too late.' Another critic likened his goddesses to chambermaids.

Poor Etty. And yet the best of his individual nudes – the *Nude* of 1825 and the *Bather*, both in the Tate – are glowing and vital works. They prove that he was one of the finest colourists of his time. He knew what he was doing. 'Paint', he said, 'with one colour at a time, in flesh, or at most with two – 'twill give cleanness and clearness of tint. And let each layer of colour be seen through. Or, in other words, manage it so, by scumbling, that the tints underneath appear. It will give depth, and a fleshiness of effect, impossible to get by solid colour.' However, like almost all his contemporaries, he used bitumen, so that many of his pictures have darkened. Behind him of course stand the Old Masters, Rubens, Titian, Veronese, whom he tirelessly copied to train his hand; and by that means he acquired an admirable technique. Yet there is something amiss. Take the *Nude with Skull and Crucifix* (Victoria and Albert Museum). Here is something more than a naked woman, but has the imagination been brought to bear on it? Whether the model was a chambermaid or not, she remains simply a model and does not care a pin for the skull and crucifix. Not far away, in the same museum, is *The Deluge*. But why *The Deluge*? It is a pretty girl, seen from above, who has been sunbathing, on a towel apparently. Inevitably one is reminded of the academic 'masterpieces' of late nineteenth-century art in France, of Bouguereau. Ingres or Bouguereau? That is the question.

Francis Danby (1793-1861)

Liensfjord Lake in Norway, exhibited R.A. 1841. Oil on canvas. (32½ × 46″). Victoria and Albert Museum, London.

It is not a matter of sensuality; the nude has been sensual as long as art has been representational. It is a matter of painting. Etty's practice is indeed as he describes it; but the key word in the passage quoted above is 'flesh'. His one concern, anyhow in his painting of nudes, is the rendering of flesh; he gives no thought to relating that flesh to its surroundings. He does not see the body he paints as part of a whole, he fails to place it in a composition. The *Nude* in the Tate Gallery, leaning against a column, with a red drapery stretched behind her, stands there like a full-length Van Dyck portrait. The modelling is flawlessly smooth; the trace of the brush cannot be detected. 'Titian', it has often been said. It would be quite enough to say 'Guido Reni'.

So certain problems are raised by what one might call the spontaneous painting of Etty. But it must be added that he also set up as a 'history painter'. The history of England, first of all, with *Youth on the Prow and Pleasure at the Helm*, a quotation from Gray relating to the shipwreck of King Henry's son. Etty was fond of drownings and shipwrecks;

they were good dramatic subjects. Like Turner, he painted a *Hero and Leander* (1829). The diagonal layout of the two bodies, the dead Leander and the dishevelled Hero expiring upon him, gives the picture a compact expressive power. *The Storm* (1830, Manchester Art Galleries) seems to hold the same fate in store for this couple, except that the quotation from Psalm 22 ('They cried unto Thee, and were delivered; they trusted in Thee, and were not confounded'), printed in the catalogue when the picture was originally exhibited at the Royal Academy, at least promises spiritual succour to these two pious souls. Here one is struck by the extent to which the drapery, particularly the one blowing out behind the figures, evokes the Venetian school, as does the rather garish intensity of the combination of green and red.

While the realism of most of his nudes is apt to be disconcerting, *The Storm* has more of allegory than realism. The boat and the oar are copied from the antique, and the danger to this couple does not come from the water. But the compelling power and sure touch of this picture, the way Etty has built up and suggestively enriched this fateful storm, show the mark of a true painter. Nor were his talents limited to the nude and history painting. Judging by his self-portrait, he had the makings of a great portraitist.

Johann Heinrich Füssli, who came to be known in England as John Henry Fuseli (1741-1825), is the least English of English painters. For of all the foreign artists who migrated to England none had a stronger personality and offered stouter resistance to assimilation. On the other hand, he would not have become an English painter if he had not had such deep affinities with the country of which he became the most eccentric adoptive son.

He was born in Zurich in 1741, of a cultivated German-Swiss family. His father, Johann Caspar Füssli, was a painter, collector and author of some note. He grew up in the midst of those conflicting intellectual tendencies and tensions which then characterized the German-speaking countries. Destined by his father for the Church, he received a good classical education and studied theology, of the liberal, Zwinglian variety. But at the same time he came under the influence of Johann Jakob Bodmer, a friend of his father and one of the prophets, in Switzerland at least, of *Sturm und Drang*, with its new emphasis on individualism and self-expression. Bodmer called for the free exercise of the imagination, unhindered by the restrictions imposed upon it by French classicism; he transmitted to the world of German culture the vivifying and liberating influence of English thought and literature. Rousseau counts for something, but Bodmer, the editor of the *Nibelungenlied*, the translator of Milton, Shakespeare and Dante, all of whom were to provide Fuseli with themes, brought the vital stimulus to bear on his youthful imagination. Another mentor was the Zurich scholar Johann Jakob Breitinger, who opened his eyes to the more perilous temptations of the occult and supernatural.

Or perhaps Fuseli discovered them for himself. Already, from the age of ten to sixteen, he was poring over his father's collections, not only copying but making childish yet often inventive drawings of his own; and already it is a world of brutalities, dreams and nightmares, of battles, murders and similar phantasms. One notes that even then he was firmly installed in a world of fantasy, turning his back on observed realities and feeding his mind on the art and even more on the literature of the past. His imagination was fired by the heroic, obsessed by the titanic (at eleven he drew a *Fall of the Titans*), the monumental, the dynamic pressed to an extreme pitch of violence. The grotesque, too, was a prominent feature of this vision, and the erotic was soon to become another. Through Bodmer, he also became a close friend of Lavater and later translated into English his *Essays on Physiognomy*.

Ordained as a Zwinglian minister, Fuseli preached but one sermon (1761). Soon afterwards, acting with the characteristic ardour of his *Sturm und Drang* temperament, he joined Lavater in exposing a corrupt magistrate, whose family, however, were still powerful

William Etty (1787-1849)

The Storm, exhibited R.A. 1830. Oil on canvas. (35 ½ × 41 ½″). City of Manchester Art Galleries.

enough to take vengeance on them, and they were forced to leave Zurich (1763). Fuseli went to Berlin. Paradoxically (and his life was full of paradoxes), this proved to be the first step towards his Anglicization. In Berlin, for an Anglo-German society, he made some drawings after *Macbeth* and *King Lear* (including 'Lear and Cordelia' of course). The British Ambassador in Berlin, Sir Andrew Mitchell, encouraged him to visit England, and by the beginning of 1764 he was in London. In 1766 he accompanied a young man of quality to France and met Jean-Jacques Rousseau in Paris. Already he was an English writer and in 1767 wrote his *Remarks on the Writings and Conduct of Jean-Jacques Rousseau*. Back in London, he met Reynolds in 1768: this proved decisive and he became a painter – an English painter.

So in 1770 he left England for Rome, where he frequented a circle of artists that included Romney, Northcote, Alexander Runciman, John Brown (whose art, in its rather perverse appeal, owes something to Fuseli), Jacques-Louis David, and several sculptors, including the Dane, Nicolai Abildgaard (Fuseli shows a strong sense of sculptural values). It may have been then, in Rome, that another Anglicized Swiss, P. H. Mallet, with his *Northern Antiquities* (1770), acquainted him with the heroic legendry of the Edda and the Sagas. Did he ever really learn Icelandic as he is alleged to have done? Certainly there is no need to assume that he did.

Not surprisingly, the great revelation that Italy brought him was that of Michelangelo, the very embodiment of heroic and titanic action at its most intense. Artists of lesser genius, like Giulio Romano at Mantua, offered him the same vision on coarser but more accessible terms. Herder met him in Rome and hailed him as 'a miraculous painter of character'. By 'character' he presumably meant expression, carried to the point of expressionism. Anyhow, in 1775, Zimmermann wrote to Herder that out of millions only a few knew how to speak the language of *Sturm und Drang*: 'Füssli, yourself, Lavater and Goethe'. To acquire the Michelangelesque sense of muscles and sinews playing under the skin, he dissected corpses. It is characteristic of his work that, under their clinging garments, the musculature of his figures shows through conspicuously. Such is notably the case in his drawings and sketches, like *Hamlet with the Skull of Yorick* (Auckland, New Zealand). Hamlet is a sculpturesque figure with enormous thighs and overwrought forms. The gravedigger, apart from an inexplicable sleeve, is a nude study of back and buttocks. In a picture of 1806-07, *A Mother and her Family in the Country*, purporting to illustrate Cowper's *Retirement*, but with vehement gesturing wholly out of keeping with the poet's placid humours, the little boy is more naked than clad.

It has been suggested that the female busts in the Capitoline Museum in Rome, with their outlandish coiffures, may have influenced his obsession with fanciful and elaborate hair-styles. They may account for it in part. The fact remains that, at that time, he had only to open his eyes in the street to be struck by the absurd fashions that reigned in women's hair-styles. But personally it is my conviction that with Fuseli everything came from within. Hair and hats held an obvious fascination for him, with unmistakably erotic overtones. *Mrs Fuseli out for a Walk* still has a certain traditional stylishness, but the *Courtesans* (1807, Belfast) are outlandish and unreal inventions. Something there may be of Carpaccio and the Italian Renaissance generally, and doubtless other antecedents could be found among the German or German-Swiss mannerists of the sixteenth century. Outside painting, it is probably only in Africa that such elaborately contrived hair structures could be found, mingled and interwoven moreover with other, unidentifiable materials. Looking at these compact, symmetrical coiffures, with their horns, their inflexible parallel bands, their flawless nodules, carapaces and varnished corselets, all perfectly dehumanized,[30] one casts about for a significant analogy. And one finds it. These women are delightful insects. He is known to have been fascinated from boyhood by the world of insects, to him a symbolic emanation of nature's moods, messengers from another realm bringing a mysterious animation into the silence of nature. He himself bred moths, especially hawk-moths. In this pre-Romantic period, when occultism and magic mingled with the early workings of the scientific spirit, he was among those who shared in the impassioned confusion between the two which subsisted in men's minds. The works of that bizarre poet Erasmus Darwin, *The Temple of Nature* and *The Botanic Garden*, provided him with matter for illustrations.

In 1778 he had left Italy. Stopping in Zurich, he fell madly in love with a young woman named Martha Hess, whose fine, if rather severe and haughty features figure in many paintings and drawings. But her father refused to have him as a son-in-law and he left his native city for good. By 1779 he was back in London, and from this time on his serious work as an artist may be said to begin. It soon commanded attention. While his meeting with Reynolds years before had sealed his resolve to become a painter, the opposition of Reynolds failed to prevent his election to the Royal Academy in 1790. He was appointed professor of painting to the Academy (1799), and then keeper (1804). In 1788 he married one of his models, while at the same time having an affair with the feminist writer Mary Wollstonecraft (whose daughter was to become Mary Shelley).

'Hang Nature, she puts me out,' said Fuseli. By Nature he seems to have meant the natural, for life offers more than enough to choose from. One thinks of Baudelaire, who ignored or overlooked Fuseli but would, one fancies, have had every reason to be delighted with his perverseness and his modernity, fantastically distorted perhaps but unmistakably proclaimed by these female figures. One is not surprised to learn that the artist took a keen interest in women's fashions. True, they are more often courtesans than ladies, but he may have found the former more amusing to look at. There is more interest shown in Fuseli in Switzerland than in England and one has to go to Zurich to see his best pictures and study his art. Certain English critics regard his perverseness as an inverted puritanism, his vision as the denunciation of a flawed and tainted world. The Swiss critic and collector Paul Ganz shares this moralizing view and has developed it even further: 'His cynically mocking sketches of the life and doings of London's demi-monde and his obscene erotic drawings... reveal contempt for the physical side of love. In this contempt he does not content himself with depicting the fashionable follies of the age, the fantastic coiffures, half rococo and half classical, and shameless dresses, but he seeks to depict the moral inferiority and depravity of woman.' This misguided interpretation of Fuseli puts him down as a homosexual because of 'his admiration for the male superman'.

Fuseli's admiration for the human body on the heroic scale is of course obvious; and Michelangelo was probably a homosexual, and Winckelmann certainly was. And if the taste for the heroic was in the air at the time, there were just not enough super-women available to satisfy it. But Fuseli found at least one whose humiliation of the male is complete: Brunhilda, from her bed, gloating over the sight of the wretched Gunther tied up and hanging from his hook (1807). His *Lady Macbeth* (1784, Louvre), a shade too eager perhaps, in a movement that owes more to Fuseli's dynamic temperament than to her own situation, but superb, sculptural, intense, can scarcely be called a figure of degradation. On the other hand, no one denies that Fuseli all too often (but not here) mistook the theatrical for the dramatic, as in *Macbeth* (1812, Tate Gallery) approaching with the daggers; here it looks as if his friend Lavater had given him rather too sketchy an outline of the 'physiognomy' of horror.

'Nature puts me out.' Blake was to say much the same thing, only using other words. Both in fact lived in the world of the intellect. Working from narrow foundations, which consisted chiefly of the Bible, Blake himself invented the themes of his imaginative world. Fuseli had read widely and made the most of it in his art; but though his reading may supply the starting point, he never illustrates anything but his own vision. He ranged over antiquity from Homer to Ovid, and it is with him that the old legends of the North appear for the first time in painting, as in *Thor Fighting the Dragon of Midgard in Hymir's Ship* (1790): like all the Romantics Fuseli felt that mythology needed refurbishing. Unlike Blake, he found little that appealed to him in the Bible, but English poetry gave him all he wanted, from Spenser to the merest ballad of Sir Walter Scott (*The Fire King*, Victoria and Albert Museum). Nothing in all Shakespeare seems to touch so personal a note in Fuseli as *A Midsummer Night's Dream*. Producers today are aware of the erotic undertones of the play. Fuseli's Titania is the first of Shakespeare's women to be shown in her sensual nudity, caressing Bottom with his ass's head. But this is nothing. The fairies around Titania have always seemed to belong to an innocent childish mythology. Fuseli's fairies are amazing little monsters anticipating the strange figures imagined by Dadd, which are illustrated at the end of this book. Bosch and Bruegel invented only what seemed best calculated to intimidate St Anthony. It is the spectator who is ill at ease when confronted by this horribly miniaturized world, where several scales come into play simultaneously and various permutations take effect on these gnomes, giving one with a baby's body the head of a grey beard, another the features of a grinning child, dovetailing and mixing them together in repulsive caresses. Such are the three *Titanias*, the one in London (Tate Gallery) which is the most perverse and most teemingly peopled, the one in Winterthur, and the one in Zurich which is the most concentrated, most pictorial and least horribly suggestive.

The most unexpected conjunction of all is that of Fuseli and Cowper. Fuseli, the arch-Romantic, even declared that Cowper, the intimist, the pious poet of ladies and their tea tables, was the best poet of the age. How did he happen to illustrate a scene from Cowper like *The Dressing Room*? The poem is full of sanctified airs. Fuseli shows two tirewomen fitting a gown on the beautiful heroine, contriving of course to bare her breasts. Ruthven Todd has this to say: 'His tall fantastic women clad in parodies of the long clinging dresses of the period are as Haydon suggests procuresses and whores, haggling and tempting, rather than figures from Cowper's poems.' This is, in effect, a repeat of Ganz's criticism. But then, more interestingly (and more divergently), Todd adds that 'all their everyday and trivial

Henry Fuseli (1741-1825)

Titania, Bottom and the Fairies, 1793-94. Oil on canvas. (66½ × 53⅛'').

Kunsthaus, Zurich.

actions have become charged with the significance of magical rites – even the placing of a cup upon a table seems to have some terrible hidden significance.'[31]

Indeed, with Fuseli, all nature is hemmed in by the supernatural; to it clings an evil spell. *The Changeling* shows, with a full display of horror, a fiendish presence in the cradle where the child should be. On his return to England Fuseli had begun turning out his *Nightmares*, erotic visions of incubi and succubi, whose victims are always beautiful young women convulsed with fear, much like the tormented heroines of gothic novels. For it is the gothic spirit that prevails here. The *Nightmare* (1781) in the Detroit Institute of Arts is superior to the one of the same year in Frankfurt; it holds together in its fine, more sculptural composition the body of the victim and the horse, which is no longer a horse but a nameless apparition.

The fiends in Fuseli's œuvre are continually there, lurking or flitting about. For example, he depicts a woman, who is said to be Mrs Fuseli (and whose pudendum is indicated under the clinging dress), standing beside a chimneypiece; to right and left kneel two little fairies, denizens of another world, one in front, the other in back view, with malevolent features, figures of fashion and figures of evil. Behind Fuseli plainly looms the Mannerism of the sixteenth century, and Antal[32] has pointed to the influence of Bandinelli, Rosso, Parmigianino and Primaticcio in particular. He observes that there was already something of Parmigianinesque mannerism in Reynolds. I would add that in Fuseli, perhaps by way of Reynolds, there would seem to be a reminiscence of various equivocations of Correggio, especially in the dusky, languishing gaze of the eyes, which in Fuseli becomes more suggestive than ever. And Antal might have mentioned the Germanic source: Bartholomeus Spranger, Niklaus Manuel Deutsch, Hans Baldung Grien.

Fuseli cannot be called an eclectic; he is too singular for that. But his is a composite art, drawn from many sources. In Berlin, when he first came under the spell of Hogarth, he enriched the German language with a new verb: *verhogarthisieren*. He was a restless seeker after novelty. Antal writes: 'He sought to create vehement expressive attitudes and striking compositional patterns resembling streaks of lightning.' Antal also notes the 'emphatic but usually general expression [of] faces at once agitated and mask-like.'

In other words, he did not work from nature; he was not interested in external realities but only in the realities of his private world. And surely it is obvious that the private world of this Mannerist enamoured of the heroic is more complex than has been supposed. He is, moreover, a marvellous calligrapher, with something of Gillray's expressionism (though he stops short of caricature). The way in which *Mrs Fuseli Out for a Walk* holds her glove and the linear patterning of the glove are a revelation. In his 'subjects', the lines of force, not the outlines, are drawn taut and if necessary cut across the figure in order to suggest the momentum and direction of the movement. At the same time, the autonomy of his calligraphy is such that the lines tend to reduce this movement to an arabesque, thus giving rise to a secondary tension between the reduction of movement to line and the extreme thrust of the line towards a passionate vehemence, a Dionysiac or martial dynamism which in turn is subordinated to an overall rhythm. Violence, after all, is more telling if set to rhythm like a dance.

Yes, but can Fuseli be called a great painter? It is hard to say. He does not seem to have been spontaneously, or normally, interested in colour. The whole point of a picture like the *Nude Woman Listening to a Girl Playing upon the Spinet* (1799-1800, Öffentliche Kunstsammlung, Basle) was to display his virtuoso powers; at the same time, there is an appealing impudence in the way he takes over the theme and layout of Titian's *Venus and the Organ Player* (Prado, Madrid) and turns it into another picture. Everything about it is so typical of Fuseli, from the tilted figure of the slender musician, with her brown bodice and her insect-like coiffure, to the flow of her gown sweeping down to the feet of the voluptuous nude; and yet the whole pattern is Titian's, including the principle of active rhythm found in the placing of the hands on the keyboard, both of them thrown out to the left.

'Genius may adopt but never steals.' This aphorism of Fuseli's should be remembered before too much is made of his quip, 'Blake is damned good to steal from.' If more attention had been paid to dates, it would have been seen that in most cases Blake naïvely

Henry Fuseli (1741-1825)

The Nightmare, 1781. Oil on canvas. (40 × 50″). The Detroit Institute of Arts, Gift of Mr and Mrs Bert L. Smokler and Mr and Mrs Lawrence A. Fleischman.

borrowed both his motifs and his rhythmic principles from Fuseli. The spellbound faces in the grip of overwrought emotion, the hallucinated eyes starting out of the head – all this appears in Fuseli before it does in Blake; see his *Lady Constance* (1783), her head between her two symmetrical arms, and the *Job* of 1786. It would be unfair and doubtless untrue to suggest that either of them borrowed his fine Satan from the other, but one cannot help noting the kinship between Blake's picture *Satan Calling up his Legions* (1808) and *Fuseli's Satan and Death Separated by Sin* (1799). Fuseli's wonderful *Silence* (c. 1800, Private Collection), a crouching woman shown full face, symmetrically, her head bent low, her arms crossed between her legs, is evidently the source of the very striking attitude of Blake's Eve

Henry Fuseli (1741-1825)
Nude Woman Listening to a Girl Playing upon the Spinet, 1799-1800. Oil on canvas. (28¼ × 36¼").
Öffentliche Kunstsammlung, Basle.

in *The Body of Abel Found by Adam and Eve* (*c.* 1826). To Fuseli's *Three Witches* from *Macbeth* (1783), with their three caps and their three parallel, outstretched hands, may be traced the reiterated rhythm and cruel, inflexible parallelism that is found in Blake's admirable *Stoning of Achan* (*c.* 1800-1805).

The globular, staring eyes and brutish, over-sized figures that occur so often in Fuseli, for example in his *Fire King* (Victoria and Albert Museum), are equally characteristic of Blake's evil figures (*Good and Evil Angels Struggling for a Child*, 1795). Possibly Fuseli owes them to Blake, but he made them very much his own.

When the *Sturm und Drang* had passed, Goethe came to frown on Fuseli as the embodiment of all that art should not be – exhibitionism of feelings and passion, and demonism unleashed. But he went on buying Fuseli's drawings whenever he could find them.

WILLIAM BLAKE (1757-1827) is that rare thing, rare anyhow since the Renaissance: a man of dual genius. (Something of that remarkable duality will be found again in the case of Rossetti, who in fact was prone to regard himself as a reincarnation of Blake.) It is difficult to separate Blake's painting from his poetry and to decide how the initial image shaped itself in his imagination. I should say, however, that this visionary was first of all a visual artist, and as such he will be dealt with here, with no more than allusions to the poet.

He was the son of a London hosier who, like many humble folk at that time, had remained a devout Christian in an age of cut-and-dried rationalism. The Blakes were Nonconformists, which meant that their Christianity opened on a much richer, more intense spiritual world than that of the established Church. So it did not seem outrageous when, at the age of four, William saw angels walking among the haymakers, and at seven a tree whose boughs were spangled with angels' wings. As he was a sensitive, highly strung child, his parents made no attempt to send him to school. Noticing his gift for drawing, they bought him prints to copy and at fourteen he was apprenticed to the engraver James Basire, with whom he remained for seven years. He was not a boy of easy temper, and to avoid conflicts with other apprentices Basire sent him off by himself to make drawings of the tombs in Westminster Abbey. Gothic art as he studied it there made a lasting impression on him, both aesthetically and spiritually. At twenty-one he attended the Royal Academy schools for a time, where he seems to have met with little encouragement from Reynolds (whom, as man and artist, Blake could never abide). He took to doing engravings for the booksellers and watercolours for himself, and published his first volume of poetry, *Poetical Sketches*, in 1783. In 1782 he had married Catherine Boucher, the daughter of a market gardener at Battersea, who signed the marriage register with a cross. She proved an admirable wife and an affectionate and understanding helpmate who preserved Blake from loneliness and maintained his mental equilibrium.

In 1780 he had engraved *Glad Day*, which he was to interpret again in the form of a colour print in 1794, but already the fine figure of the early engraving, emitting rays of light, is the first sign of the mystical world of Blake. A classical, Apollonian representation, it also has another antecedent; with its outstretched arms it is the Cosmic man transmitted from Vitruvius to Athanasius Kircher; it is the initial form of Albion, the Eternal Man of Blake.

He became friendly with the painter Thomas Stothard, who introduced him to Flaxman; he soon met Fuseli, too, a man he respected and always remained particularly fond of. Fuseli, with his interest in the occult, and Flaxman, as a Swedenborgian, may well have stimulated his visionary interpretation of reality. Some account must also be taken of the traumatic events of these early years, which must have impressed themselves on so sensitive a nature: the Gordon Riots in 1780 and the burning of Newgate Prison, bringing him the revelation of violence; then, in 1787, the death of his younger brother Robert, whose spirit he saw ascending and clapping its hands for joy, and who in 1788 appeared to Blake in a dream revealing to him a new method of relief engraving. This system, which meant engraving with varnish on a copper etching-plate, enabled him to reproduce not just a drawing but a whole page, with both its written text and surrounding design. Fuseli acquainted him with Lavater's aphorisms, which are one of the sources of his Romanticism, opposing an active Evil to a passive Good. Thence sprang his notion of energy. In 1789 he published the incomparably fresh and idyllic poems which he called *Songs of Innocence*, extolling the ineffable delights of childhood and its state of union and harmony. Using his own method of relief engraving, he published them himself, hand-written and illustrated with his own ethereal, Flaxmanesque designs.

This was the first of his illuminated books. It was followed by others similarly produced, all issued in very small editions: the *Songs of Experience* (1793), the *Marriage of Heaven and Hell*, etc. Once the page with its text and design had been engraved and printed, Blake coloured it by hand; so that each copy of the edition is a unique work of art.

Blake undoubtedly sympathized with the French Revolution, and is said to have gone about the streets of London in a red cap. If he did, he failed to attract much attention, for in 1795 he was offered the post of drawing master to the Royal family. Needless to say, he declined the offer. This is the period when, as an artist, he was most appreciated and received a commission to illustrate Young's *Night Thoughts*. The failure of this great project, involving immense exertions on his part (he produced over five hundred watercolours for it), marks a turning point. In spite of various schemes to set him up, which only resulted in fresh conflicts and even a trial on trumped-up charges of sedition, following a quarrel with an unscrupulous dragoon, Blake lapsed into a period of solitary aloofness which lasted more than twenty years; this left its mark on him very strongly and sharpened the idiosyncrasies of his personal vision.

In 1793 he moved from Poland Street across the Thames to Lambeth. There he crossed a threshold beyond which ordinary, everyday things changed their aspect and Lambeth became in his eyes a place of mystical sojourn, from which emanated vast, cataclysmal cosmogonies which he presented as projections of the spirit: they are great, cruel epics illustrating the strife which the individual discovers within himself, his conflicts, passions, shortcomings and separateness. Already in his father's home he had learned something of Swedenborg and Jakob Boehme; of the latter, Coleridge was to say that in an arid age his influence had maintained the moral and imaginative integrity of more than one man.

Boehme has represented Creation as actually a Fall – the fall of being into the world of existence, of unity into multiplicity, of the individual into the incomplete half of the sexual couple. At the same time Boehme regarded the world of appearances as a complex of signs and symbols – *signatura rerum*, the visible, legible 'signature' of reality. Blake in turn came to look upon the tangible world in this way. He blamed Swedenborg for having conversed only with angels and men, never with devils. *The Marriage of Heaven and Hell*, after the *Songs of Experience*, is a voyage into the world of unfolding energies, and presupposes the Fall. In the world of being, desire is an abomination and sexuality can only be conceived of as a disaster. In the world of existence, desire is good, freedom to satisfy it must be absolute and abomination attaches to the Law, the Decalogue imposed by the sinister Nobodaddy, who is the chastising God of the Old Testament. It is law that makes brothel and whore, rebellion and crime. In Blake are to be found all the basic tenets of modern anarchism, combined with a vision that harks back to Milton and the fundamental belief that 'the body' is a manifestation of spiritual energy.

Man's estate is the Experience resulting from his lapse into existence. The initial crime is that of Elohim who, under his great metallic wings, like those of an Assyrian god, created Adam in his own image and at once trammelled him in the serpent coils of time and matter.

The illuminated books were only a part of his production as a pictorial artist. At the same time he produced his pictures, done in various forms of tempera which he was fond of likening to fresco.

In 1805 a publisher named Cromek commissioned him to illustrate Blair's poem *The Grave*, but his designs were considered too austere and the engraving work was given to another man, Schiavonetti, who made them less extreme. Calling on Blake and finding him at work on a picture of Chaucer's Canterbury Pilgrims, Cromek went off and craftily suggested the same theme to the painter-illustrator Stothard, who innocently accepted, painted the picture and exhibited it before Blake had finished his. Stothard had been a friend of Blake's. After this incident he became an enemy in Blake's eyes, and to make matters worse Flaxman took Stothard's side. So it was that Blake, in a final effort to break out of his solitude and win recognition, decided in 1809 to hold a public exhibition of sixteen works, including the *Canterbury Pilgrims, Satan Calling up his Legions* and *The Body of Abel Found by Adam and Eve*. He wrote for it a Descriptive Catalogue which amounts to a manifesto. 'Chaucer's characters', he wrote, 'live age after age. Every age is a Canterbury Pilgrimage; we all pass on, each sustaining one or other of these characters; nor can a child be born, who is not one of these characters of Chaucer.'

The exhibition was a complete failure. A 'liberal' journalist, Leigh Hunt, the future friend of Shelley, described the author of 'these wretched works', as 'an unfortunate lunatic whose personal inoffensiveness secures him from confinement.' The catalogue, Hunt went on to say, is 'a farrago of nonsense, unintelligibility and egregious vanity, the wild effusions of a distempered brain.'

Southey, in 1811, refers to Blake as 'evidently insane... possessed.' In 1824, seeing his poem *The Chimney Sweeper*, Charles Lamb supposed him dead. But in fact the all but forgotten poet and painter, so poor that in 1821, at the age of sixty-four, he had to sell a portfolio of prints that he had been collecting since his boyhood, had been given a new lease of life in 1818. A young painter, John Linnell, was introduced to him and became an

William Blake (1757-1827)

Elohim Creating Adam, 1795. Colour print finished in pen and watercolour. (17 × 21 ⅛″). Tate Gallery, London.

admiring disciple. He was soon to bring with him a whole set of young men, all of them artists. In the glow of their admiration, Blake became expansive, whereas before he had been aloof. His style of engraving grew more mellow and he tried his hand at the simpler, more expressive medium of wood engraving. The resulting illustrations (1821) of Thornton's version of Virgil's first eclogue are schematized landscapes in a quaint, pastoral vein, mostly night-pieces with the soft play of moonlight. They provided inspiration for the young

William Blake (1757-1827)

The Ghost of a Flea, c. 1819-20. Tempera on panel heightened with gold. (8½ × 6⅜″). Tate Gallery, London. ▷

artists, gaily styled 'The Ancients', whom from 1824 Linnell grouped around the master. Linnell also introduced into their circle an older man, John Varley, astrologer, watercolourist and drawing master, who stimulated Blake to draw his visionary heads or spiritual portraits of the illustrious dead. Varley encouraged him to cultivate his gift of inspired vision, and since human beings like other creatures were to his mind but transient incarnations of eternal characters, Blake proceeded to paint in tempera the *Ghost of a Flea* (c. 1819-20, Tate Gallery), attesting that he had seen it – a massive, obtuse creature, with brutish brow, burning eyes and darting, pointed tongue, holding in its claw-like hand a bowl of blood. The colour scheme of sparkling green and brownish gold was described by Allan Cunningham as 'curiously splendid'.

In 1823, for Thomas Butts, the only patron who had given him any material and moral support during the years of solitude, he designed twenty-two illustrations for the *Book of Job*. On the basis of these watercolours, he made at Linnell's suggestion a series of engravings. In 1824 the same idea was taken up and applied to the *Divine Comedy*. At sixty-nine Blake began studying Italian and produced a series of a hundred watercolours. Towards the end, as his final illness gained on him, he worked in bed. One day he stopped, looked up at Kate and said: 'Kate, you have been a good wife, I will draw your portrait.' This was probably the first time that he looked with his earthly eyes at what he set out to draw or paint. A few days later, in August 1827, three months before his seventieth birthday, he died serenely and joyously, after singing Hallelujahs to the glory of his Maker, with an energy that made his voice resound throughout the room. He was laid to rest in an unmarked grave in Bunhill Fields burying ground, Finsbury.

'A man without a mask', was how the youngest of the Ancients, Samuel Palmer, described him. 'A saint among the infidels, a heretic with the orthodox,' said Linnell, adding, however, some reservations which made him out as a man of dangerous tendencies, a threat to Christian morality.

Blake was a candid believer in his visions; his poems, he said, were dictated to him. 'Mad or Not Mad?' is the title of a chapter in Gilchrist's Life. Some thought him to be possessed, even his friend and executor Frederick Tatham, evidently, since he took it upon himself to burn some of Blake's manuscripts on the ground of religious scruples. The portrait of him by Thomas Phillips (1807, National Portrait Gallery) is interesting, with the large, bright, globular eyes and the snub nose that led Blake to write: 'I always thought that Jesus Christ was a snubby or I should not have worshipped him if I had thought he had been one of those long spindle nosed rascals.' This odd remark speaks for an attitude which underlies the self-proclaimed egocentrism that informs the whole of his pictorial and poetical mythology.

In 1854 Emerson declared that it was the age of Swedenborg – spirit makes the world and nature is its symbol. One cannot attempt or presume to appreciate Blake's art until one has first penetrated into Blake's world. It is a world where death does not exist, since everything is equated with spirit. But with Blake, again, one cannot really undertake to distinguish the literal from the figurative, as when he declared: 'Milton loved me in childhood and showed me his face... Shakespeare in riper years gave me his hand; Paracelsus and Behmen [sic] appeared to me.' His position may perhaps be summed up as follows. For Blake there is no culture as normally understood, but a communication of spirits on an equal footing. There is no nature either. The 'vegetable world' is but a shadow and reflection, and Wordsworth, who so extolled nature, was in his eyes a pagan philosopher: this is a long way from the peaceful, dreamy contemplation of the watercolourists, his peers. Blake, though an older man than most of them, was much more advanced and absolute in his Romanticism, his firm rejection of external appearances: 'Natural objects always did and now do weaken, deaden and obliterate imagination in me.' In the Descriptive Catalogue of 1809 he wrote: 'He who does not imagine in stronger and better lineaments, and in stronger and better light than his perishing and mortal eye can see, does not imagine at all... All the copies or pretended copiers of nature, from Rembrandt to Reynolds, prove that nature becomes to its victim nothing but blots and blurs.'

How then did he see his art? 'The painter of this work asserts that all his imaginations appear to him infinitely more perfect and more minutely organized than any thing seen by his mortal eye.' Here is the heart of the matter. Art is discovered to have an underlying affinity with reality itself. He believed in line and proclaimed his belief: 'The more distinct, sharp and wiry the bounding line, the more perfect the work of art.' Its tension unfailingly maintained conveys the pulse of life. It is the form thus defined, form and shaping force, that distinguishes eternal substances and the artist renews the act of creation by rediscovering original form. Of course there is no general line of beauty, no master key attesting to an aesthetic order: 'The harmony and proportion of a horse are not the same with those of a bull. Every thing has its own harmony and proportion.'

Blake spoke out vigorously against every form of art that depended on the visible world and the sensations or impressions conveyed by it. The invention of oil painting coincided with the cult of the visible. He denounced the Venetian and Flemish masters as 'demons' because of their 'infernal machine called chiaroscuro' and their 'broken lines, broken masses and broken colours'. A Monist like Milton, Blake re-echoes the words of the angel Raphael explaining to Adam that spirits (and our vision of them) 'are not a cloudy vapour, or a nothing; they are organized and minutely articulated beyond all that the mortal and perishing nature can produce.' So that the artist's delineation can attain to the spiritual only by the closest attention to minute particulars. Blake moved towards a mystical expressionism of outline which took the body as its means: 'That called body is a portion of Soul discerned by the five Senses.'

But it is not with the five senses that Blake creates, it is not with the eyes of the body or single vision that he paints:

> Now I a fourfold vision see,
> And a fourfold vision is given to me;
> 'Tis fourfold in my supreme delight,
> And threefold in soft Beulah's night,
> And twofold always. May God us keep
> From single vision and Newton's sleep.

The world of Swedenborg and Blake is a world of analogies where the transfer from one register to another is immediate. The eye sees an insect; the imagination sees a fairy:

> With my inward eye 'tis an old man grey;
> With my outward, a thistle across my way.

'Man's perceptions are not bounded by organs of perception; he perceives more than sense (tho' ever so acute) can discover.' Thus twofold vision means

> To see a world in a grain of sand
> And a heaven in a wild flower,
> Hold infinity in the palm of your hand
> And Eternity in an hour.

'Single vision and Newton's sleep': with Newton the sense of Eternity was lost and he represents for Blake a mediocre, material philosophy of the five senses. Blake depicts him drawing with the compass, repeating the gesture of the *Ancient of Days*, in the admirable frontispiece to *Europe* (1794), as he leans out of a sun or a fiery nebula and with his out-stretched arm opens his compass wide in the darkness. *Newton* (1795) is shown seated, apparently underwater (and water is the element of matter and death) on an iridescent rock whose grainy texture is well rendered by Blake's distemper, and on which one divines the shapes of sea urchins, sea anemones or perhaps cuttlefish. Crouching nude over a scroll, he draws geometric forms with a pair of compasses. He is a slave to geometry and reason; he embodies single vision. The intent gesture of the hands and the intent gaze of the eye fixed on its task are compellingly expressive. The body has that overwrought musculature which Blake may owe to Fuseli and which carries a hint of violence and menace.

Blake based himself essentially on his view of the great biblical vision and his opposition to the morality derived from the Bible. But around him, impinging on him, were the developments of pre-Romanticism and Romanticism, and the occultist deviations from the great system of Platonism and Neoplatonism. The Monist dynamism which on a large scale of being raises or degrades stems from the *Phaedo*, as transmitted by Milton. The frightening *Nebuchadnezzar* (1795, Tate Gallery), with his animal claws and bare sinews, his beard trailing on the ground, the horror of his condition written on his face, obviously represents the degradation of man, in bestial enslavement to matter. The *Ghost of a Flea* adds to it a further touch of cruelty.

But the biblical system predominates and the bearded God is his predominant obsession. In *Elohim Creating Adam* (1795, Tate Gallery), the latter is not yet in God's image; but in *God Judging Adam* (1795), seated in his fiery chariot, Adam is wholly in his image, even to the flowing beard. The most terrible of Elohim's apparitions is in the *House of Death* (1795), a hovering head with large sightless eyes and vast beard, the outstretched arms holding out a long streamer (on which perhaps the Law is inscribed) ending in arrows pointing towards the prostrate (and of course sinewy) bodies of the dying. One of the dying, as if dazed, lifts himself up on his elbows, with his head thrown back, and gazes at the God of Death, while an executioner standing on the right, with a knife in his hand, seems to await his turn. Such is the Jehovah-Urizen of Blake. Although Blake emphasizes the play of dialectics throughout the conflict ('without contraries no progression'), it cannot be said that the figure of Satan ever becomes positive. *Satan Calling up his Legions* (1808) is a fine sculpturesque figure, but the face and gaze are those of a destroyer, even though the attitude is not unrelated to that of *Glad Day* (1794). The composition is very fine but still traditional. That of *Satan Smiting Job with Sore Boils* (c. 1826-27, Tate Gallery) is even finer, and superb in its mystical unity. The thighs of the fiend seem to be coated with scales and his bronzed colour is not that of flesh. Standing on the prostrate body of Job, he powerfully occupies the whole centre of the composition, his arms held out at full length (one of them pouring down the boils) under reddish bat's wings set off by a corresponding cloud pattern in darker tones, whose scalloped edges recede and overlay each other, forming the blackish red and white and blue aureole of an enormous setting sun, all these colours and motifs being characteristic of Blake's visions. Blake could say of Milton that he was 'of the Devil's party without knowing it.' One cannot say the same of Blake, because for him both the Devil and the God of the old religions were together the symmetrical instruments of man's oppression.

William Blake (1757-1827)

Satan Smiting Job with Sore Boils, c. 1826-27. Tempera on mahogany. (12⅞ × 17″).

Tate Gallery, London.

William Blake (1757-1827)

Hecate, c. 1795. Colour print heightened with watercolour. (17 ¼ × 22 ⅞″). Tate Gallery, London.

Milton was a prime source of inspiration for Blake the artist, but while Milton fell in line with the thought and imagery of the Bible, Shakespeare stood apart, grand and independent. He inspired two of the large colour prints, finished in pen and watercolour, of 1795, both of them illustrating passages in *Macbeth*. One is *Pity*, a hauntingly strange and beautiful allegory, which refers to the lines:

> And pity, like a naked new-born babe,
> Striding the blast, or heaven's cherubin, horsed
> Upon the sightless couriers of the air,
> Shall blow the horrid deed in every eye,
> That tears shall drown the wind.

One of the two soaring figures leans down to take up the 'new-born babe', while a woman, apparently dead, lies at full length on the ground. The other is the famous *Hecate* or *Triple Hecate* (one version in London, another in Edinburgh). Presumably it refers to the scene in Act III where Hecate and her three witches concoct their evil spells. Two fair-haired figures, their faces hidden from view, kneel behind the dark-haired Hecate, one on either side, without impairing the sculptural beauty of her form. Hecate is covered in part by a night-blue robe under which her legs are crossed, only the powerful feet being visible. Over her hovers a Fuseli-like creature with a fiendish face and bat's wings. At her right are her three beasts: an enormous red-eyed toad, an owl and a beige-coloured donkey who grazes quietly as if unconcerned with the scene but who shows plainly that, like the others, he is not a creature of the real world.

The influence of Flaxman was not salutary; it accounts for a certain affectedness in Blake's early designs. Subsequently he arrived at a style which may be described as sculptural, and which springs from manifold but converging sources: Fuseli, Michelangelo, Gothic and the Italian Renaissance engravers Bonasone and Marcantonio. An overwrought intensity of features, gesture and attitude marks its starting point; an often threefold repetition of the same gesture and attitude is characteristic of it (*The Stoning of Achan*). The dynamism of Blake's figures seems to proceed on the one hand from the example of Michelangelo and the soaring, straining, plunging figures of the Sistine Chapel; on the other, from a psychological peculiarity of his own, for the visionary, even in the intervals between his hallucinations, was not a man like other men. In the case of Blake, imagination supplied the driving power. In the illustrations to his *Book of Urizen*, one is struck by the fact that the figure in plate 14 and the one in plate 27 show the same momentum (so strong that in the latter it makes the robe stream out by the force of its own motion), with this difference, that in plate 14 the figure is head down, its arms braced against a rock in an athletic balancing act, with the hair in this momentary pause still streaming out behind the head, just as the robe streams out in plate 27. This airborne movement, once he had arrived at it, remained so strongly impressed on Blake's imagination that he reverted to it in his illustration of *The Simoniac Pope* (1824-27, Tate Gallery) in Dante's *Inferno*. One has only to turn the plate upside down for the falling figure to assume an upward momentum.

Blake's esoteric symbolism gives a meaning to every detail of position, gesture, colour and the compositional relationships. The whirlwind does not bear the same meaning if it goes from left to right, or from right to left like the whirling figures of the lustful in Dante's *Inferno*. Blake's symbolism is too complicated a subject to be dealt with in this book, and in fact there is no need to go into it, for Blake's art can be appreciated for its own sake, without reference to the complex symbolism underlying it, or to the antecedents behind it. After all, it was thought for a century that *God Judging Adam* represented Elijah in the fiery chariot. And in the case of the *Good and Evil Angels Struggling for a Child*, one can overlook the fact – unless one notes the chained foot – that the evil angel was meant for Orc and the good for Los, whose jealousy enchained him and made him a figure of revolt.

In the printing process which he used for his illuminated books one may distinguish two main techniques employed by the artist: one consisted of a printed design or a kind of monotype, which he then finished off in watercolour; the other consisted of various combinations of watercolour and tempera. Proceeding from the light and delicate effects of

William Blake (1757-1827)

The Simoniac Pope, 1824-27. Watercolour. (20¾ × 14½"). Tate Gallery, London.

William Blake (1757-1827)
Beatrice Addressing Dante from the Car, 1824-27. Watercolour. (14⅝ × 20¾″). Tate Gallery, London.

watercolour on the one hand, and the reworked designs of his illuminations on the other, Blake in 1794 began a new production of separate illustrations, detaching them from the text with regret, 'for they, when printed perfect, accompany poetical personifications and acts, without which poems they never could have been executed.'[33] The design was painted on millboard or similar material, in very thick colours mixed with a strong glue medium; it was then printed off on paper, under low pressure, in two or three copies. The rich grainy texture as, for example, in his *Newton* was the direct outcome of this process. Blake then worked over this rich mottled surface while still wet, on each print, to make it more expressive; finally, he finished the prints with pen and watercolour. *The House of Death, God Judging Adam, Pity, Hecate, Newton* and *Nebuchadnezzar*, all dated 1795, speak for the happy results that Blake achieved in this medium. The results were not so good in his tempera paintings, which he liked to call frescoes; here the colours have often altered and darkened, especially when applied to copper.

Needless to say, one will look in vain in Blake for local colours. But his emotive and symbolic colouring is, as Rossetti was the first to note, indispensable to an appreciation of his art. Swedenborg may have supplied the starting point, with the red of love, the blue of wisdom and the yellow-white of the celestial world. But it has always seemed to me that with Blake it is rather the relationships of colours than individual colours, rather their accords and dissonances, that are significant and memorable. In the last works there is a wonderful lightening of the surface texture, as for example in the diaphanous and radiant watercolours illustrating Dante, such as *Beatrice Addressing Dante from the Car* (1824-27, Tate Gallery).

Blake was an inspired visionary, and for that very reason cruelly vulnerable, liable to an aching sense of emptiness and spiritual death when inspiration failed, but also responsive to the exultation of recovering it again. His letter to William Hayley of 23 October 1804 strikingly suggests these states of mind: 'Suddenly, on the day after visiting the Truchsessian Gallery of pictures, I was again enlightened with the light I enjoyed in my youth, and which has for exactly twenty years been closed from me as by a door and by window

John Linnell (1792-1882)
Kensington Gravel Pits, 1811-12. Oil on canvas. (28 × 42″). Tate Gallery, London.

shutters... Dear Sir, excuse my enthusiasm or rather madness, for I am really drunk with intellectual vision whenever I take a pencil or graver into my hand, even as I used to be in my youth...'

The Blake of those inspired moments gave rise to the image of the painter-prophet which in 1818 attracted disciples to him. The first was John Linnell (1792-1882), and it is all to his credit, for neither the source nor the nature of his attachment to Blake is quite clear. Linnell was not a man of warm or generous sympathies. But, though narrow-minded and (as the sequel proved) harsh, he believed in Blake and helped him. Around 1815 he painted some vigorous portraits and some landscapes like the *Canal at Newbury* (Fitzwilliam Museum, Cambridge) which, though focused on externals, at least shares with Blake a sharpness of design like that of Dürer or the Flemish masters. Although after Blake's death his career became distinctly worldly, Linnell continued to show a sensitive response to nature, as one may note in a rather Palmerian landscape like the *Harvest Moon* (1855, Victoria and Albert Museum), with its procession of harvesters and the cornfield with its curving edge seen in eerie light. *Before the Storm* (Tate Gallery), with its great recession of sheep, driven as it were by the rising wind that sweeps over the plants, may be compared with the landscapes of the Pre-Raphaelites, like Holman Hunt.

Linnell was fond of minute, expressive detail in the manner of Dürer, and this is part of his influence on Palmer.

Samuel Palmer (1805-81) was a painter largely forgotten, until a great revival of interest began with the exhibition of his work at the Victoria and Albert Museum in 1926. Since then, he has become as interesting a painter for England as Odilon Redon for France.

He was the son of an unworldly Baptist who, from love of books, became a bookseller, cared tenderly for his frail, asthmatic, hypersensitive child and (as his son recounts) shed 'delicious tears' at the sound of organ music. His maternal grandfather was also a Baptist but, unlike his father, a tyrant in religious matters; in opposition to this, Samuel later turned to the ritualism of the High Church. He was one of those men who are destined to be surrounded by women; in his childhood he was much influenced by his mother and his nurse, Mary Ward. Of the latter, he wrote: 'When less than four years old, as I was standing with her, watching the shadows on the wall from the branches of an elm behind which the moon had risen, she transferred and fixed the fleeting image in my memory by repeating the couplet:

> Vain man, the vision of a moment made,
> Dream of a dream and shadow of a shade.[34]

I never forgot those shadows, and am often trying to paint them.' And with them, all the mysterious interplay of shadow with light, forever promising and withholding a revelation.

From childhood he drew and painted and felt 'a passionate love – the expression is not too strong – for the traditions and monuments of the Church; its cloistered abbeys, cathedrals, and minsters, which I was always imagining and trying to draw.' Thirty years before the Pre-Raphaelites, he copied the Campo Santo frescoes in Pisa (after engravings). When he was thirteen his mother died, a shock that left its mark upon him. At fourteen, in 1819, he exhibited for the first time and by then fancied himself a free-thinker. These early shocks and crises prepared the way for the later fits of anguish and remorse.

There followed a phase of what he felt to be aimless and fruitless effort; the more he learned of painting, the less capable he felt of being a painter. Then, 'it pleased God to send Mr Linnell as a good angel from heaven to pluck me from the pit of modern art.' That was in 1822. Linnell showed him engravings after Dürer and Lucas van Leyden; also prints by Bonasone, some of them illustrating the emblems of Bocchius (1555) and containing elements that were to reappear in Palmer's work – dark, rolling clouds, a sheep-shearing (symbol XXXII), a shepherd under a tree with a dog in the foreground and sheep outlined against each other. He was struck by a marble in the British Museum of *Endymion Asleep*, and it inspired the *Sleeping Shepherd* of Shoreham. The conclusion of these early studies and discoveries was that, for him, allegorical Christian landscape came to represent the highest form of art.

In October 1824 Linnell took him to Blake's house, known to the young men as 'The House of the Interpreter' (from the *Pilgrim's Progress*). For Palmer this was an unforgettable event. In 1822 Blake had made his exquisite wood engravings for Thornton's *Pastorals of Virgil*, with their thin crescent moons, elongated figures and solitary silhouettes with a shepherd's crook. There are many elements in them that the feminine genius of Palmer took over, above all the idea of a double vision of the pastoral – symbolic and mystical as much as real. Blake brought him, in the blank and despondent intervals of inspiration, the mystical sustenance he needed. But such were Palmer's alternations of mood that three of the Blake paintings he owned were found at the end of his life 'stored away in the basement with a lot of rubbish.'

More would be known of Palmer's states of mind, were it not that his son, after writing his father's life, burned practically all Palmer's papers and sketchbooks, embarrassed no doubt by these frank records of his inner life. Describing the 1824 sketchbook, his son noted that 'there are thirty-three moons in this one volume, and vast flaming suns; but never a cast shadow from beginning to end.' Palmer was obsessed by the play of light in open fields and effects of reflected light, from a cornfield, for example, on the surrounding trees. This is the complete opposite of Constable and his moving lights. Here is the restful glow of light, the sudden transparency of objects in twilight, a *quality* of lighting. He alternated feverishly between art and nature in quest of small revelations. 'Look for Van Leydenish qualities in real landscape, and look hard, long and continually.' He also looked in books, and in his copy of Milton all the references to the moon have been noted. The reading of Bocchius and John Flavel encouraged him to see the 'World below' as a reflection of the 'World above.' But Satan kept intervening and cutting off the sources of light: 'I cannot execute at all . . . I feel ten minutes a day the most ardent love for art, and spend the rest of my time in stupid apathy, negligence, ignorance, and restless despondency; without any of those delicious visions which are the only joys of my life.'

To counter-balance those slack periods he cultivated the doctrine of excess, a Blakean doctrine deriving from Milton and the angel's words to Adam:

> . . . thy desire, which tends to know
> The works of God, thereby to glorify
> The great Work-master, leads to no excess
> That reaches blame, but rather merits praise
> The more it seems excess.

In 1826, thanks to a legacy from the tyrannical grandfather who had now died, Palmer bought a house at Shoreham, in Kent, a mystical Barbizon, which, surprisingly enough, remains today very much as it was then. From 1826 to 1832 it was the Valley of Vision, a place of metamorphoses whose swelling hills and dipping hollows between sun and moon, between shadow and light, hold out undefined promises and call up undefined memories. Six years and one place gave rise to these illuminations, but it may be that to some extent the time and place simply answered to Palmer's mood and were not entirely responsible for it. For in 1825 he had painted the exquisite little *Rest on the Flight into Egypt* (Ashmolean Museum, Oxford) and it is already a vision. The tonal harmony between the muted red of the Virgin's dress and the trees and crops is so mellow that the picture, already with its pattern of slopes and shadowy hollows, entrances the eye. Palmer may be said to stand on an equal footing with the Siennese, without imitating them in the least. From 1826, after a series of fine sepias, he worked steadily in a mixed technique, usually oil and tempera rather than watercolours, producing a rich, grainy texture that is one of his great charms.

One of the finest of the Shoreham pictures, all of them small-sized, is the *Valley Thick with Corn*. In the foreground, amongst the heavy ears, is a kind of womb-like cavern with a reclining figure. The background here, as so often, rises sharply, with an enormous moon hanging over it. The *Valley with a Bright Cloud* bathes in a visionary light. His notebooks record his efforts to finish *Naomi Before Bethlehem*, and show the extent to which he lived in a Swedenborgian world of analogies and transmutations: 'Now I go out to draw some hops that their fruitful sentiment may be infused into my figures.' Of this composition, of which all trace has been lost, his son showed little appreciation or, one suspects, understanding: according to him, 'The wildest conceptions of Blake and Fuseli combined with the most extravagant symbolism of early art could not be more wild and extravagant than this.' The death of Blake in 1827 was the death of a father figure. Though Palmer had revered him, it came as a release, enabling him to open his eyes to nature, to look at his valley, to enjoy the caressing play of sunlight and moonlight on its rounded hills and to express what he saw with a new exhilaration. 'Universal nature', he wrote to Linnell in 1828 from Shoreham, 'wears a lovely gentleness of mild attraction; but the leafy lightness, the thousand repetitions of little forms, which are part of its own genuine perfection... seem hard to be reconciled with the unwinning severity, the awfulness, the ponderous globosity of art.'

As before he had struggled obscurely against the inward vision of Blake, so now he stood out against Linnell's attachment to externals: 'Tho' I am making studies for Mr Linnell, I will, God help me, never be a naturalist by profession.'

The *Cornfield by Moonlight with the Evening Star* (watercolour and pen, *c.* 1830, Collection Lord Clark) is again a Blakean vision, owing much to the wood engravings for Thornton's Virgil. Palmer admired those engravings. 'They are visions', he wrote, 'of little dells, and nooks, and corners of Paradise... I thought of their light and shade, and looking upon them I found no word to describe it... There is in all such a mystic and dreamy glimmer as penetrates and kindles the inmost soul.' Following the very Blakean shepherd with his great staff, as he strides with his dog towards the centre of the picture, the eye sweeps over the long streak of lunar gold that glistens on the standing sheaves. A peculiar glitter on the left marks another patch of moonlight which, passing over the leaf-fringed hill, shimmers again on the right-hand slope. The red of sheaves and hills sets off the greenish grey of the

Samuel Palmer (1805-81)

A Hilly Scene with Church and Moon, 1826-28. Watercolour, pen and tempera, varnished, on panel. (8⅛ × 5⅜″).

Tate Gallery, London.

sky; and the great crescent of the moon which creates this whole picture, far from seeming arbitrary or improbable, takes on the heightened reality of a dream.

Two pictures of this period (1826-28), both in the Tate Gallery, are closely related not only in design but in spirit and vision: *A Hilly Scene with Church and Moon* and *Coming from Evening Church*.

The first (tempera, watercolour and pen) is built up within a gothic arch of trees, their branches meeting in a point at the top, just above an enormous crescent moon. One appears to be an oak, the other a horse-chestnut in flower, a tree that Palmer loved and drew again and again. Through this arch appears a great round hill on which an attentive eye can discern tiny 'primitive' motifs, including a sheepfold. The moon whitens the peaks beyond, which, apart from the northern motif of a windmill, seem to hark back to Giotto. The squat church in the middle distance, with its conical tower, rises over the corn which, by an effect of perspective, is as high as the church walls. The corn on the right has a hieratic stiffness, while on the left the heavy ears bend over slightly. Turning to the second picture (tempera and oil, a combination characteristic of Palmer which Blake would have abhorred), one finds a more velvety, less spare but also less luminous effect than in the first. The enormous full moon slumbers in a neutral sky. Under the same arch (but not the same trees), it glows dimly on the steep hills behind the church, this time with a sharply pointed spire, from which comes the procession of the faithful (ears of corn transmuted into men and women) marked by a pious mannerism: the tall foreground figures, the woman in muted red, the man in faded yellow (a contemporary equivalent of Joseph and Mary with the Child), dwarf the figures behind. The moon obsessed him all his life and in 1860, long after he had done his best painting, he could still note: 'Thoughts on rising moon, with raving-mad splendour of orange twilight glow on landscape. I saw that at Shoreham.'

From a thin crescent he moved on to a full moon, less surprising in its effects. After 1830 there seems to be a new gravity and receptivity to the world which rules out certain excesses, a new mood of rapt meditation. The picture still mistakenly known as *The Harvest Moon* (c. 1833, Tate Gallery) should probably be called *The Gleaners*. It conveys the mellowness of the twilight hour to exquisite effect. The cornfield, still in the light, falls off towards a clump of trees on a lower level, where the shadows are gathering. A laden wagon and team of oxen link the two levels. Over the foreground sheaves, as well as over the gleaners, wagon and oxen, the fading light still glows. In the *Yellow Twilight*, on the other hand (or *Orange Twilight*, as his son misleadingly called it), the scale of colours is much more emphatic. Palmer sought out different light effects, nowhere catching them with more subtle intensity than in *The White Cloud*, which exists in two forms, a brush drawing in indian ink, sepia and body colour of 1831-32 and a picture of 1833-34. The theme of clouds is referred to in a letter to Linnell: 'Those glorious round clouds which you paint, I do think inimitably, are alone an example how the elements of nature may be transmuted into the pure gold of art.' The picture, which keeps closely to the study but falls short of its magic, brings to mind Bruegel's *Harvesters*, with the figures walking amidst the corn. The composition, with the ground falling away from right to left, recalls Palmer's *The Harvest Moon*; the jutting gable of a house on the right has become the slanting edge of a rick on the left. But beyond a light screen of vegetation, lighter still in the picture, the vast luminous cloud, which in the study is a powerful source of light, dominates the whole composition.

The Magic Apple Tree (watercolour and pen) has the rapturous intensity of a Van Gogh. Again set within arching tree-trunks and branches, it is built up, more so than any other picture by Palmer, in separate, forceful touches of colour knitted together in a singular unity of texture. Can one speak of planes? This, rather, is the idiom of naïve art, with big woolly sheep resting in the foreground beside the exquisite, fair-haired shepherd boy in white and blue. The spire of *Coming from Evening Church* rises behind, but there is an involuntary symbolism in the fact that it is submerged by the red-gold profusion of apples, re-echoed in the tints of gold rippling over the landscape to the horizon. It is a hallucinated vision of nature with unmistakable sexual undertones.

Palmer was a sensitive observer of the variations of light and texture, in, for example, an apple tree in sunlight: 'General effect in bright sun, the whole tree, apples and leaves, very golden; in the same tree will be some boughs of darker apples dim in relief but exquisite in finish; boughs next in size to smallest twigs are I think of a crusty texture and a pale dead gold.'

Two points are constantly observed and analysed in his notes and letters: light and texture. He made an unremitting scrutiny of the diaphanous effects of twilight in both morning and evening: 'All was low in tone as preparing to receive the still and solemn night, yet the tower on which the last light glimmered, seemed luminous in itself and rather sending out light from itself than reflecting it.' Again in his notes for 1824 (when he was only nineteen), he wrote of 'summer evenings when venerable buildings seem no longer to be brute matter but with a subdued solemn light which seems their own and not reflected, send out a lustre into the heart of him who looks – a mystical and spiritual more than a material light.'

One could hardly be further from the modern movement than Palmer when he pays tribute to Bonasone, and to a lesser degree Claude and Alexander Cozens, for having taught him, not to emphasize the value of shadow, but to see 'shadow in its poetic sleep.'[35] And one could hardly be more in advance of one's time than Palmer in his sensitive feeling for textures. For I should say that the beauty of *The Magic Apple Tree* is above all a matter of texture, as is also true of the *Pastoral with Horse-Chestnut* (1831-32, Ashmolean Museum, Oxford), which in fact is like a variant of it with the same shepherd lad and sheep, the heavy blossoms replacing the apples. This had already been true of *In a Shoreham Garden* (1829, Victoria and Albert Museum), where the flowering tree projects its enormous pink buds right into the sky, amidst a richly varied pattern of vegetable textures, both grainy and prickly; the figure of a woman in the green recess at the back is an ambiguous apparition. There would seem to be plenty of matter for psychoanalytical study in Palmer's work, particularly his obsession with lush and richly grained textures. Palmer's own references are suggestive enough: 'Why,' he asks, 'does the parsley, with her frizzled locks, shag the border; or why the celery, with her whitening arms, perforate the mould?' Moss and lichens fascinated him. *A Barn with a Mossy Roof* is like a manifestation of his mystical, Dubuffet-like obsession with all that is clotted, curdled, gritty, spawning, pimply, ocellated, with nature 'sprinkled and showered with a thousand pretty eyes, and buds, and spires, and blossoms gemmed with dew, and clad in living green.'

In 1832 Palmer left Shoreham after six years in the heart of its pastoral simplicity, but from 1832 to 1834 he returned often to renew his inspiration there. In 1837 his old nurse

Samuel Palmer (1805-81)
Cornfield by Moonlight with the Evening Star, c. 1830. Watercolour, gouache and pen. (7¾ × 11¾″).
Collection Lord Clark.

and second mother, Mary Ward, died, and that was doubtless the end of his vision of childhood. The following year he married Linnell's daughter. Gradually he came to paint like Linnell, only not so well, and the last long years of his life (he did not die until 1881) are on the whole a melancholy story of stagnation and failure.

'My father', wrote his son A. H. Palmer, 'valued the Calverts more highly than he did his Blakes.' Born in Devonshire and brought up in Cornwall, Edward Calvert (1799-1883) spent five or six years in the navy before devoting himself to art from 1820 on. His woodcuts and etchings have always been appreciated for their vitality and sense of rhythm. His fresh and appealing watercolours vouch for both culture and sensibility. As a hellenist, a pagan, a pantheist, he pursued an arcadian vision, alternating with a mood of Christian pastoralism deriving from Blake. His watercolour *A Primitive City* (British Museum) is dated 1822. Though the enormous moon, the shepherd and the sheep mark him as a follower of Blake, the picture is dominated by the delicately mannerist and sensual figure of a woman, all but naked in her flimsy drapery.

After his oil painting *The Nymphs* (1825) he veered away from paganism and engraved his *Christian Ploughing the Last Furrow of Life* (1827), inspired by the *Pilgrim's Progress*. By 1828 his pagan ideals had regained the upper hand, as evidenced by his *Bacchante* and *Cyder Feast*, both woodcuts. 'I have a fondness for the earth,' he wrote, 'and rather a Phrygian mood of regarding it.' But the best of his work had been done by about 1831-32 and thereafter he lapsed into a vapid idealism.

George Richmond (1809-96) was for a time very close to Blake, whom he met when he was sixteen; at seventeen he painted his tempera picture of the *Creation of Light*. But he was something of an eclectic, and it has been said of him that he took his sheep from Blake and his corn and trees from Palmer. His *Christ and the Woman of Samaria* (Tate Gallery) may be cited to confirm it, but in spite of all the debts to others it is a graceful, well-designed and well-executed picture. Christ and the beautiful woman exchange a subtle glance in which there flickers a discreet sensuality. Between them, from the well to the horizon, rises a delicately modulated spatial perspective. A work of secular inspiration, like the early Blake-like *Eve of Separation*, shows that Richmond had taste and talent enough to weave around the couple a spell of tender melancholy.

8

J.M.W. Turner. The Phases of his Art.
Turner and Claude. Turner and Holland. Turner and Italy.
Gulfs of Shadow and Gulfs of Light. The Sea and Monsters.
The World Seen and Construed as Cosmos.

JOSEPH MALLORD WILLIAM TURNER (1775-1851) was born in London, in Maiden Lane, Covent Garden. He was the son of a barber and wigmaker, and as he was very much attached to his father – it has been said that he was never the same man after his father's death – he came to take a kind of challenging pride in this humble extraction. He began drawing early and the barber proudly hung the boy's drawings in his shop, on one occasion announcing to a customer, 'My son is going to be a painter.' Between them there grew up a profound understanding. A time came when Turner had to choose between his father and society, and he chose his father. He was less attached to his mother, a woman of ungovernable temper; she became insane and had to be confined in 1800. Of education in the formal sense he received little. At the age of nine, following an illness, he was sent to Brentford for the country air, living there with his uncle, a butcher, and attending the local school; at the age of thirteen he attended another school for a short time at Margate. But Turner was self-taught and self-made, and he possessed his full share of the naïve enthusiasms and eccentricities which such men often have. The favourite poet of this great Romantic was the first of the pre-Romantics, James Thomson, who in a style still conventional and hackneyed as compared with that of Turner's contemporaries, Wordsworth and Coleridge, extolled the beauties of nature in *The Seasons* – a nature divine and considerate even in its wilder moods. The greatest of Romantic painters, for all the meagreness of his literary baggage, was himself led to write a long moralizing poem, *The Fallacies of Hope*; he liked to add poetic quotations to the titles of his pictures, and quotations from his own poem are hardly less frequent than those from Thomson.

An an artist, his school was London, its suburbs and the sea off Margate. Ruskin's *Modern Painters* is an elaborate defence of Turner and the fifth volume contains an admirable passage on the resonances of London to be found in the work of a painter who, projected by his genius into the supranational world of European art, remained to the end a child of the London streets and a true Cockney. He spent the most impressionable years of his boyhood in the neighbourhood of Covent Garden market, and Ruskin made the most of this fact: 'His foregrounds had always a succulent cluster or two of greengrocery at the corners. Enchanted oranges gleam in Covent Gardens of the Hesperides; and great ships go to pieces in order to scatter chests of them on the waves.[36] That mist of early sunbeams in the London dawn crosses, many and many a time, the clearness of Italian air; and by Thames' shore, with its stranded barges and glidings of red sail, dearer to us than Lucerne lake or Venetian lagoon, – by Thames' shore we will die.'

Like a true child of the streets, he was precocious. A view of Margate Church dates from his ninth year. At thirteen he executed two watercolours with considerable skill. At the same age he was receiving lessons from Thomas Malton, a perspective draughtsman. Shortly afterwards he was sent to Paul Sandby's drawing school in St Martin's Lane, worked for a short time under Sir Joshua Reynolds and briefly studied architecture. But from 1789 to 1793 he was a student at the Royal Academy Schools. Two of his drawings were exhibited at the Academy in 1791, and that same year he set off on his first sketching tour.

The primary gift which he possessed and fully exercised even in this early period was a visual memory of astounding power. Seeing a print in a shop window, he could return to his room and reproduce it down to the last detail and tone. The most fleeting impressions of light playing on things remained fixed in his mind. So retentive a memory – and one recalls the importance Hogarth attached to this faculty – enabled Turner to devise and *create* mentally. (One suspects that Constable's was not a visual but rather a tactile memory.)

In 1793 Dr Thomas Monro saw one of his drawings and invited him to come and work in his house in Adelphi Terrace. 'Dr Monro's house is like an Academy in an evening', wrote Farington (30 December 1794). 'He has young men employed in tracing outlines made by his friends.' The essential part of the doctor's collection consisted of watercolours by John Robert Cozens. It was certainly here that he first heard of Alexander Cozens' *New Method*; it is known that he owned some of Cozens' blot drawings. At Dr Monro's house he met Girtin, the valued friend of his youth; having but a few years to live and working as if he knew it, Girtin forged a style of his own more quickly and brilliantly than Turner did, moving towards an ever greater warmth and richness of tone, while Turner was already cultivating his peculiar taste and genius for violent and dramatic contrasts.

Turner was very soon to realize that, for the sake of his own prestige, it was in his interest to mask landscape as history painting. But he was content in these early days merely to emphasize the dramatic aspect of landscape. Probably certain night scenes by Wright of Derby, such as the *Lighthouse on the Coast of Tuscany*, gave him help in composing his first seascapes. *Fishermen at Sea* (1796, Tate Gallery) is thought to be his first oil painting. In a sky black with clouds, the moon glows dimly, a semicircle of light, shining more intensely on the surface of the sea; to this semicircle corresponds a diamond-shaped patch of water dramatically swept up by a squall, it would seem, but a limited if not an artificial squall, and there in the same glow of moonlight floats a boat. This work by the twenty-one-year-old painter is more remarkable for forcefulness than for subtlety. But in 1797 the river scene entitled *Moonlight: a Study at Millbank* (Tate Gallery) seems already to outdo Crome in the broad conception of sky and water spread out beneath and around a full moon viewed straight on. Detail is reduced to a minimum, two boats on the right and a dark reach of shore on the left. This is a work of serene and appealing poetry; would there were more like it!

The early Turner shows the influence of Richard Wilson, but it does not seem to me that that influence was ever very pervasive. Looking at what may be justly considered Turner's first major work, *Buttermere Lake* (1798, Tate Gallery), one is reminded rather of J. R. Cozens; quite apart from the contrast between the darkening lake-waters and the opaque or faintly luminous forms of the mountains beneath a lowering sky, one recognizes what was, with Turner, already an obsession – to strike out light from darkness and blazon it forth. 'A shower', continues the picture title. Everything is wet and dimmed. Yet, from the heavens, light surges forth anew in an iridescence culminating in a rainbow. But it is a rainbow which Turner, unlike Constable, refrains from making polychrome; a green translucence is its most expressive feature. It arches down lighting up the lake shore in two long, thin, golden bands; then, all in green streakings, it runs over the water around a small boat. One is amazed at the technical mastery evident in every part of this fine picture.

To this same year or early in 1799 dates an initial drawing of *Norham Castle*, which he regarded as marking the real beginning of his career. And in fact this subject seemed to haunt him to the very end; he came in time to strip it down to the bare essentials, leaving but an aerial, transparent form. In 1799, when he was still only twenty-four but had already been exhibiting there for seven years, he was elected an Associate of the Royal Academy, his undeniable abilities carrying all before them. But his ambitions did not stop there; he dreamed of great painting and thus of a mutation of his art, for he now had a revelation: the sight of two famous paintings by Claude Lorrain, the *Sacrifice to Apollo* and the *Landing of Aeneas*. Brought to London in the spring of 1799, they were purchased by William Beckford. Farington records Turner's opinion of the *Sacrifice to Apollo*, that 'it seemed beyond the power of imitation'. Jack Lindsay[37] has stressed, perhaps overstressed, the importance of the figure of Aeneas for Turner, a son passionately devoted to his father and also to his mission. However this may be, the changing of his art, into landscape and history painting combined, after the manner of Claude, began with *Aeneas and the Sibyl* (*c.* 1798). Now, and for the next few years, he drew his subject-matter from both Graeco-Roman mythology and the Bible. Thus, in 1800, he painted *The Fifth Plague of Egypt*, in which a swirling cloud-form makes its first appearance. It is by no means easy in this case to discover the decisive influence; but there would seem to be a reminiscence of Wilson's *Niobe* (more probably the destroyed rather than the extant version) in both the imploring figure and the prostrate figures, and even in the great swirling cloud which looks like a skilful and more meaningful reinterpretation of the curiously gigantic tree which fills so much of the sky in Wilson's picture. Now, moreover, Turner had been able to see the best of the Dutch masters, adding to what he learned from Claude and preparing a new synthesis of the thing seen and the thing imagined; Jan van Goyen's *Storm*, for example, seems to me closer to Turner than anything by Richard Wilson. And from this time on, the influence of Rembrandt was undoubtedly at work on Turner, stimulating him in his dream of striking out light from darkness.

At the end of 1800 father and son were finally relieved of Mrs Turner's stormy presence; she was interned at Bedlam and died there in 1804. At the Academy exhibition of 1801 Turner showed an oil painting, *Dutch Boats in a Gale*. Fuseli admired it, describing it as 'quite Rembrandtish', while the president, Benjamin West, went even further: 'It is what Rembrandt thought of but could not do.' Constable, still marking time at the threshold of his career, thought highly of it too, but candidly observed that he knew the picture by Willem van de Velde on which it was modelled. After this chorus of praise, Turner's election to the Academy followed as a matter of course. Already a passion for the sea was growing on him. In 1802 he painted *Fishermen upon a Lee Shore, in Squally Weather*. The sea is rough, and in rendering the surging power of the waves the painter was led towards a looser treatment of form and volume. Before becoming a dedicated watercolourist, he handled oils with vehemence, skilfully combining the opposite effects to be obtained from impasto and the bare grain of the canvas. In this year begins his characteristic alternation between mythological subjects and his fascinated concern with the sea. The mythological picture of 1802 is *The Tenth Plague of Egypt*, and in aiming at a severity which did not come to him naturally, and a structural soundness which in fact was alien to his genius, he was trying to follow the example of Poussin. The principle of the composition is architectural in the firm positioning of the planes, especially the background planes, and in the presence of fabulous buildings ranged in tiers on the right – which, however, in their effect, point forward to John Martin rather than back to Poussin.

On 15 July 1802, during the brief interval of the peace of Amiens, Turner sailed for Calais. As chance would have it, the weather was rough and off Calais the packet had to wait outside the harbour for high tide before it could cross the bar and land at the pier. Turner, with a few others, instead of waiting, went ashore in a small boat which, however, was nearly swamped in the heavy seas; he seized every opportunity for an emotional experience connected with the sea. From Calais he crossed France and headed for the Alps, in his eyes a further source of drama and emotional experience which he could turn to account in his art. On the way home he stopped in Paris and spent some days in the Louvre, studying, analysing and copying Ruisdael, Rembrandt, Titian and above all Poussin. In the sketchbook in which he copied them, he added written comments, often critical, on the pictures that attracted his attention. Ruisdael's *Burst of Sunlight* he seemed to take as a cautionary example: 'The sky rather heavy... usurps too much of the picture and the light. Objects near to the light poor and ill-judged. Foreground dark, violently so near the bright light that gives a crudeness inconsistent with the purity of the distance.'

He examined Poussin with an equally critical eye, disapproving of the contrasts in *Orpheus and Eurydice*, to his mind overdone and destructive. But in front of the *Gathering of Manna* he discovered 'the grandest system of light and shade in the collection'. He was fascinated by the colour scheme, by its power to define lines and forms, establish proportions and illuminate the subject; Poussin's power of suggestion held him spellbound. But this did not prevent him from writing a lengthy criticism of *The Deluge* (i.e. *Winter*). Nor was he satisfied with Rubens' *Landscape with a Rainbow*; he found it 'defective as to light and the profusion of nature', and the lines of the landscape he described as 'confused and ill-judged'. 'Rubens', he said, 'throws his colours about like bunches of flowers.'

These notes, recording his first impressions of the Old Masters in the Louvre, were jottings set down on the spur of the moment; they were never meant for publication. But one cannot read them without feeling how unusually lucid, acute and, in a word, *intellectual* was Turner's view of painting. It is safe to say that the same critical vigilance presided over the organization of his own works.

He returned to London late in 1802, and in the following year exhibited the first of his canvases to gain fame: *Calais Pier, with French Poissards Preparing for Sea*. Turner was too familiar with Dutch seascape painting not to borrow some characteristic effects from it before fully developing his own powerful style. The point here was to convey an immediate sense of man's confrontation with the elements, and with danger, as suggested by a dramat-

234

ic variation from the norm. Thus a mast, normally upright, is given a dizzying tilt to one side. And all the rest follows. The sky is fraught with threatening contrasts between the dark, lowering clouds and the sunlit gap in the midst of them, through which a burst of light comes down over the sea; at the same time there is an upward movement in the Romantic vein from sea to sky which already heralds future trains of movement centred on the human element. In the case of a painter with so powerful a vision as Turner, one may assume that he began very early to project on to the canvas, differently disposed each time, the elements of a picture already composed in his own mind. In the present instance, one is surprised not only by the upswept sea but by the obscure animation, hardly quite realistic, of the figures on the pier. In spirited contrast with it, these figures are trying to hold their own against the elements. When the picture was exhibited at the Academy, Sir George Beaumont, the then arbiter of taste, was outraged. The younger men admired it, with one significant exception: Constable, the advocate of 'natural painting', who shook his head at its forced values and disregard of nature. Turner saw clearly enough what would be in store for him at each display of his boldness. He had a mind of his own, and if his presence in the Academy's collective exhibitions was to raise a storm of criticism, then he would exhibit privately. Where his art was concerned he was bold enough to scorn half-measures and he knew how to get his own way, by cunning if necessary. Laurence Binyon has likened him in this respect to Shakespeare playing cynically on the understanding, ranging over several levels, which he had arrived at with a heterogeneous public. The two cases may not be strictly comparable. For Turner, like Constable though more deliberately and extensively, chose to keep his best painting to himself and to live by selling the ordinary run of his production; hence the huge accumulation of unsold works which he left at his death, and which is in fact the central core of his œuvre. It must be added that in order to make himself respected, even while administering a shock, Turner had a weapon at his disposal which Constable never would or could learn to use: the sublime, as prophetically formulated by Burke in England and Diderot in France, and vainly prefigured in 'history painting' from 1760 on. The elemental was extolled by a respectable amateur aesthetician, the Reverend William Gilpin, in his *Observations Relative Chiefly to Picturesque Beauty*. According to him, 'To see a conflagration in perfection we must see the *elements engaged*. Nothing is eminently grand but the exertion of an element.' Turner, in contradistinction to a man like Fuseli, had the insight to realize that a painter's true task lay not in illustrating Shakespeare or Milton but in giving visual shape to the great elemental dramas played out in water and more particularly in fire. Mythology and the Bible were not to be disdained, but whatever the themes they supplied, whether the plagues of Egypt or a pagan legend, they always set the painter the same problem: to find the right fragment of nature in upheaval which should express the theme suitably, and which that theme in turn should emphasize by giving it a name and function.

In 1805 the subject implicit in *Calais Pier* was treated explicitly in *The Shipwreck*, and in its power and suggestiveness, the organic unity of its construction and the dramatic effectiveness of the lighting, this picture stands out as Turner's first great seascape. Here the entire sky is dark, though not uniformly, for through the gloom one can make out the shapes of clouds; and the background to right and left is shot with livid gleams. Nearly all the light is focused on a diamond-shaped patch of raging sea curiously reminiscent of the heaving patch of sea in his first oil painting, *Fishermen at Sea* (1796, Tate Gallery); it is as if Turner, sparing of his imagination, had deliberately reverted to this expressive form, from the realization that he had failed to make the most of it the first time. To the right of the lozenge a boat comes to the rescue, its mast and sail more extravagantly tilted than in *Calais Pier*; it is trying to take in tow a longboat full of frail-looking figures; this Turner took more or less literally from Rowlandson (*Distress*, 1799). This longboat marks the lower left corner of the picture, while another boat draws the eye, in a line symmetrical with the sail on the right, upward into the dimmer area where the ship is foundering. This quadrilateral, outside which the sea again becomes uniformly inky, performs its dramatic function so perfectly that one could hardly ask for more in the way of realism. The substance and fury of these foaming waves, their sinister transparency as they tower over the troughs, their fiendish perversity in hindering the heroic efforts of the rescuers, all this shows a painter sure of his power. The curious thing is that he had perhaps never given so much expressive, not to say expressionistic force to so many figures, to so many bodies either tensed in strenuous effort or sinking in passive exhaustion; never had he drawn them with such precision, such vivid colours, such unusual lighting.

In 1808, to close this cycle of stormy seascapes until he took it up again with renewed vigour in 1830, Turner exhibited *Spithead: Boat's Crew Recovering an Anchor* (also known as *Spithead: Two Captured Danish Ships Entering Portsmouth Harbour*). This canvas reverts to the picturesque and dramatic aspects of *Calais Pier*; the water is again heaving with those great waves, here rather over-dramatized. But the stately sails towering undaunted over the untamable sea long continued to haunt him.

Paintings like the *Fall of the Rhine at Schaffhausen* (1806) and the *Cottage Destroyed by an Avalanche* (1810) show Turner vying with Loutherbourg. It is more interesting to find him stubbornly emulating Claude as in a sequence of history pictures: *Aeneas and the Sibyl*, the *Destruction of Sodom, Narcissus and Echo, Jason in Quest of the Golden Fleece*, and the *Goddess of Discord Choosing the Apple of Contention in the Garden of the Hesperides* (1806). This same year, as if feeling assured that the mantle of Claude now fell to him, he began his *Liber Studiorum* in imitation of Claude's *Liber Veritatis*; it was intended to comprise a hundred engravings of his pictures, but never went beyond seventy etchings and mezzotints, many of them done by Turner himself.

Though he had never had the benefit of a formal education, and though his work met with opposition, Turner was elected professor of perspective at the Royal Academy in 1807, and the painter John Landseer declared that he had never had a better teacher. In 1812, in order to have more room for his private exhibitions, he took a large house in Queen Anne Street West; he also had a small country house at Twickenham, near the Thames, and though he was not much of an open-air painter, this was a convenient place to work out of doors, directly from the motif, whenever he felt inclined.

He also turned now from ancient myth to contemporary history. There was of course nothing new in this; West, after all, had painted his *Death of General Wolfe* as long ago as 1770. It was in February 1808 that Turner exhibited his *Battle of Trafalgar as Seen from the Mizen Starboard Shrouds of the Victory*. West in his great picture had kept to the convention of placing the protagonist in the foreground and fixing attention on him by a suitable heroic attitude. But Turner would have none of this, and with him there is a conspicuous

J.M.W. Turner (1775-1851)

Snowstorm: Hannibal and his Army Crossing the Alps, 1810-12. Oil on canvas. (57×93″). Tate Gallery, London.

absence of heroics. From the unusual angle of vision which he had chosen, the eye looks down on a mass of figures grouped in the middle distance round the dying Nelson, but without grandiloquence or any over-emphasis of detail, all forms being simplified for the sake of an overall organic and tonal unity. Around this focus of dramatic interest extends a grand view of the great naval engagement, with glimpses of the Spanish and French ships and a crowd of sailors and marines before the mainmast of the *Victory*. The multiplicity and variety of the scene is kept under perfect control.

The painter John Landseer fully appreciated the novelty of this style which subordinated the vainglory of the subject to the peculiar veracity of painting. Landseer wrote of Turner, in connection with this picture, that 'the brightness of his lights is less effected by the contrast of darkness than that of any other painter whatever, and even in his darkest and broadest depths of shade, there is... a sufficiency of natural clearness.' And he added: 'In the pictures of the present season, he has been peculiarly successful in seeming to mingle light itself with his colours.'[38]

A certain number of mythological and historical paintings, together with a personal vein of dramatic realism connected with the sea – was this all for a painter who was already over thirty? By no means, for by this time he had also done some excellent oil sketches painted with a full brush, of the same order as those of Constable, representing peaceful river landscapes. *Walton Bridge* (*c.* 1807, Tate Gallery) is in much the same vein as *Malvern Hall*, but lighter and more luminous in tone. In it Turner succeeded in obtaining colour modulations that are at once accurate and lyrical, the river varying with exquisite nicety from blue to pink. Did he, at this time, feel the need to make himself more receptive to reality or indeed to public taste? Was he simply attempting to become more saleable, or was he intent on pursuing certain tonal experiments based on closer observation of reality in order to bring his imagination under stricter control and arrive at a more authentic expression of his sensibility? Before, he had been something of a Shelleyan painter; now, passing back beyond Wordsworth, he moved towards a milder, more reassuring, more Thomsonian view of nature and man's place in nature, of the simple, unaffected joys of human life.

As regards the style of his painting, it moved closer now to the Dutch school, as in *Sun Rising Through Vapour: Fishermen Cleaning and Selling Fish* (1807, National Gallery). *Caversham Bridge* (*c.* 1807, Tate Gallery) is a delightfully pale and suggestively vague sketch. With its light tonality, reminiscent of watercolour, it seems to indicate one particular direction in which these experiments were carried. Turner was one of those who, in these early years of the century, had taken over from watercolour the practice of using a white priming coat, at least for the parts occupied by sky and water. Sir George Beaumont, the arch-academic, severely disapproved of these 'white painters'. The Pre-Raphaelites in their ignorance thought they had invented this practice. Characteristic of Turner's new orientation are *The Blacksmith's Forge* (1807) and *The Cobbler's Shop* (1808). The culminating work of this phase was *Frosty Morning* (1813, Tate Gallery). It is frankly anecdotal in the manner of the fancy pictures which Turner extolled in the lectures given in his capacity as professor of perspective. It was exhibited in 1813 with a quotation from Thomson: 'The rigid hoar-frost melts before his beam.'

The *Frosty Morning* is a scene on a country road, with the figures of men, women, horses, dogs and a child with a hare draped round her neck (she may have been Turner's daughter), all playing their due part in this superbly painted picture. 'A masterpiece of careful construction and atmosphere, with an effect of casual directness,' wrote Lindsay,[39] with more admiration than I myself can feel; for I must confess that this scene, however well painted, fails to touch me. Writing in 1939, in a book on Turner as conservative as it is useful, A. J. Finberg described the *Frosty Morning* as the last work in which the artist's inspiration rings completely true and in which form and content are indissolubly one. I should say rather that it is a work in which the significant does not prevail over the signified; in which, in a word, Turner is careful to offend no one.

But already, by about 1812, there were signs that this curious interlude was coming to an end. Now again he portrays the inhuman sea in *Devonshire: Fishing in Rough Weather*, originating in the sketchbooks in which he jotted down his first impressions of the elemental violence of wind and sea. Now, above all, came such a picture as *Snowstorm: Hannibal and his Army Crossing the Alps* (1810-12, Tate Gallery). This is the counterpart, in terms of mountain-scape, of the *Shipwreck* done several years before and of the cataclysmic seascapes yet to come. It is a great picture, but it is not beyond criticism and indeed it brings to mind the adage: 'Nothing is great but by deceiving.' To deceive in this case means making play inordinately with indistinct forms, with figures blurred beyond recognition: this is at the opposite pole from the *Shipwreck* and its precision. Yet Turner knew what he wanted and knew what he was doing, and one may doubt whether he stands as much in need of psychoanalysis as Lindsay thinks. But·it is clear that he subscribes to the idea of human guilt and sin entailing punishment; his attitude is the reverse of Blake's militant struggle against all the forces of darkness opposed to the liberation of man. I fear we must conclude that this arch-romantic is a marvellous obscurantist, and that the notion of punishment is central to his view of things. It has been pointed out that he was led, perhaps as a result of a visit to David's studio in Paris in 1802, to identify Napoleon with Hannibal; and that all his life he was obsessed with the history of Carthage, doomed to extinction from the beginning owing to a moral flaw – a flaw which of course he also read into the moral fibre of France. It must be admitted that this picture, painted some months before the retreat from Russia in 1812, is curiously prophetic, even though its actual theme is not a retreat but an invasion whose force was ultimately spent in the delights of Capua.

The vast, dimly lit cavern hollowed out above the human forms in his *Hannibal* is surrounded by a dynamic structure which issues from the right and passes without a break from the near-black of the rock to the near-black of the sky and juts downward sharply like a sinister beak, the sun looming eerily through the gloom like a malevolent eye. One is reminded of Turner's admiration for J. R. Cozens, whose only oil painting was a landscape representing *Hannibal on his March over the Alps, Showing to his Army the Fertile Plains of Italy*. This picture, wrote Leslie, was 'so fine that Turner spoke of it as a work from which he learned more than from anything he had then seen.' But he treated it in quite a different spirit, passing from the suggestion of hope which greets the eye at first to the promise of doom implicit in this swirling gloom. To his Hannibal painting he appended some lines from his *Fallacies of Hope* alluding to both the exactions and the sufferings of this army.

It was time for him to settle his account with Claude. In 1809, at the British Institution, he exhibited *Apullia in Search of Apullus*. (When the picture went to the National Gallery after his death, the keeper R. N. Wornum changed the title to 'Apuleia in Search of Apuleius'; but inscribed on the frame in Turner's hand is 'Apullia in Search of Apullus. V. Ovid.') The composition, set out breadthwise, is emphasized by a long bridge extending horizontally and separated from the foreground by tall trees; the tiered buildings on the right are characteristic of classical landscape; the figures, more prominent than those of Claude, owe something perhaps to Poussin.

Then came a *Dido and Aeneas* and in 1815, a decisive work, *Dido Building Carthage* (National Gallery). In painting the latter he had had Claude's *Embarkation of the Queen of Sheba* in mind, and in his will he stipulated that his picture should always hang beside it – one of his most vulgar gestures, according to one historian; but, as visitors to the National Gallery may see for themselves, his wish has been respected. The long gleam falling across the water and the grey stone glinting in the sun made quite a fine Claude. The latter's *Embarkation of St Ursula* of 1646 had a fine bright sky with small clouds which catch the light. Turner had only to produce a subtler lighting effect. He did so to his own satisfaction and no one will dispute this point with him. In 1817 came the *Decline of the Carthaginian Empire*, another pre-Martinesque work, but much more strict in design and execution. The sea, rendered in rippling wavelets, is an obvious reminiscence of Claude; the sky, with its hue of dull gold, is pure Turner. The monumental constructions on either side would suggest Claude, were it not that Turner has contrived to give all this an unmistakable aspect of pretentious and ungainly decadence. Where Martin comes to mind is in the new element on either side: the tremor of a mysteriously agitated crowd. Broken in spirit, the Carthaginians have just consented to surrender their weapons and their children to the Romans: their downfall is at hand.

He was obsessed throughout his life with Carthage and with Troy (and its aftermath in Aeneas), and it is strangely moving to find him in 1850, at the age of seventy-five, exhibiting a *Departure of the Trojan Fleet* in which, though others may speak of senility, I find an abiding, unquenchable vitality, bursting forth in a gorgeous display of iridescent waters and fabulous boats overlooked by lustrous architectures of pale gold.

In 1827, with the *Embarkation of St Ursula*, Turner reverted once more not only to a theme used by Claude but to its very composition; but, ruthlessly dissolving reality, he leaves behind only a gleaming wraith of it.

I cannot say whether the *Parting of Hero and Leander* (1828-37, Tate Gallery) should be included in this cycle. Was Turner, at this period, trying to do his own version of Martin? This landscape seems to be a prey to some all-embracing conflagration, presided over by an apocalyptic moon. This is doubtless Turner's most melodramatic and theatrical work.

With *Crossing the Brook* (1815, National Gallery) Turner may have wished to settle his account with Rubens. So, anyhow, one is tempted to infer, for despite its mastery one cannot clearly identify the intention behind it. Again he has painted a large landscape which is also a genre painting, with anecdotal interest. Who is fording the brook? A dog carrying a basket in his jaws, sent across by a girl on one side to her companion on the other. This of course is a mere pretext, for these three figures are absorbed in the landscape. It is a characteristically English one (an idealized view of the Tamar, looking towards Plymouth), sweeping and graceful. Three slender trees, which had been much used since Giorgione's time and which Turner was to restore again to Italy after 1819, dominate the waterscape in the foreground and remain beholden to Claude; the wooded middle distance carries the eye downstream through a gap to a faraway bridge and the ever fainter reaches of the landscape, with the sea dimly glistening beneath the sky. This subtle luminous picture, with its strong foreground light and its skilful gradations of tone ending in the pale greens and hazy blues on the horizon, looks like a synthesis of all the tonal experiments which had occupied Turner from 1807 to 1812. On the other hand, it may simply have been made, like others before it, with an eye to attracting a wider public as a very fine piece of painting, much as Constable was to do twelve years later with his *Cornfield*. It is, at all events, yet another work of which John Landseer might have said that the brightness of the lights is not obtained by the contrast of darkness. And one remembers the comments he made in the 1802 sketchbook on seeing Rubens's *Kermesse* in the Louvre: he marvelled at finding it quite devoid of shadows, in complete opposition to Rembrandt's manner.

It was however at this very time, when Turner was open as never before (and never again) to contact with visual reality, that Hazlitt chose to attack him in one of his 'Round Table' essays. Turner's pictures, he wrote, were 'too much abstractions of aerial perspective, and representations not properly of the objects of nature as of the medium through which they were seen... They are pictures of the elements of air, earth, and water... All is without form and void.' Hazlitt's hostility seems to have led him to foresee the direction Turner's art would take, for his charge of formlessness is more applicable to the later pictures. In another essay he went so far as to speak of daubs, and while allowing, with his usual insight, that Turner was 'the greatest landscape-painter of the age', he warned him that the public had seen 'the quackery of painting trees blue and yellow to produce the effect of green at a distance'.

In 1817 Turner made a tour of the Low Countries and the valley of the Rhine. In the following year he exhibited a *View of Dort*, very much in the Dutch style, as coppery toned as a Cuyp, and also a *Field of Waterloo* which is not so successful as his *Battle of Trafalgar*. In 1819 he exhibited the last work of this tour and it attracted attention: the *Entrance of the Meuse: Orange-Merchant on the Bar, Going to Pieces*. This painting came as a revelation to the young Samuel Palmer, who was then only fourteen years old. The year 1819 marks a turning point in Turner's career. Writing to Farington from Rome, Sir Thomas Lawrence expressed his conviction that Turner was the only painter who could do justice to the Italian landscape. Turner had in fact been intending to visit Italy for some years, and now at last, in August 1819, at the age of forty-four, he went. He travelled by way of Mont Cenis, Turin, Como and Venice and reached Rome apparently in early October; then, hearing that Vesuvius was erupting, he hurried to Naples to see it. In those few short weeks in Rome he did some 1500 pencil sketches. Italy was a revelation to him, a visual shock. For hitherto he had sought a quality of light, alternating between what might be described as militant light and victorious light. And now, all at once, he found himself bathing in that light of the South which he could render only by radically lightening his tones and altering his technique of oil painting in order to incorporate and maintain the white ground of watercolour painting. He thus came to employ a whole range of golden tones, of reddish browns, light, tender, fluid browns, forthright blues, and pale hues by which light consumed colour. It was by confronting Italy now and experiencing it to the full, in purely personal terms, that he freed himself at last from the classic Italy of Claude Lorrain and Richard Wilson. It would be a mistake to conclude, from the works that for years were to stem from this encounter, that one may so far simplify one's view of Turner as to see in him a gloomy, self-centred 'isolationist' alienated from a world he loathed. The main interest lies after all in his great achievement as a painter, and not in the doggerel which he liked to append to his pictures, however self-revealing it may be, and however useful in clarifying the story or anecdote behind them. For what the eye finds in these pictures, first and foremost, is sheer delight; and however pervasive the 'fallacies of hope' may be, the painter holds the key to the one reality which gives them their appeal – colour and light.

Among the next paintings are the *Arch of Titus and the Campo Vaccino*, done about 1820 and exhibited in 1823, and the *Bay of Baiae with Apollo and the Sibyl*. Sparing of his creative powers as he had always been and never ceased to be, Turner went on for ten years bringing out his landscapes and visions of Italy, and though in the meanwhile he had revisited the country, it seems to me that the lightness of key in *The Golden Bough*, first exhibited in 1834, belongs in fact to his first journey to Italy. Everything here smacks of Mannerism, particularly in the slenderness and elongation of the figures, including the priestess holding out the bough.[40] Tall slender pines produce at the same time what might be described as a parallel elongation of the landscape, whose natural beauties are set off by

J.M.W. Turner (1775-1851)
Ulysses Deriding Polyphemus, c. 1829. Oil on canvas. (52¼ × 80″).
National Gallery, London.

an improbable cluster of towering buildings behind the priestess. The lake in this picture is a white, staring eye, as in the sketch of *Lake Nemi* of about 1830; for Turner this eye seems to hold intimations of the infinite.

On the frame of the *Bay of Baiae* a wag wrote the words: *splendide mendax*! Splendidly false it may be in relation to a conscientious attempt to render a reality, external not just to the artist but to art itself. Such, more or less, was to be the case henceforth with all Turner's 'visions', to use Constable's term for them. But, for the matter of that, what Turner was trying to render was not an external reality but a poetic reality, described as follows by Ruskin: 'The Cumaean Sibyl, Deiphobe, being in her youth beloved by Apollo, and the god having promised to grant her whatever she would ask, she, taking up a handful of earth, asked that she might live for as many years as there were grains of dust in her hand. She obtained her petition, and Apollo would have given her also perpetual youth, in return for her love; but she denied him, and wasted into the long ages; known at last only by her voice.'

For Turner, henceforth, it was pictorial form and that alone that mattered. It evolved somewhat over the years, but whatever came his way in all that time was recast in accordance with a pictorial conception. So that Turner's Rhine and Turner's Italy are very much alike, as may be seen by comparing these Italian landscapes with the *Ehrenbreitstein* of 1834-35. The comments of the French critic Gustave Planche in the *Revue des Deux-Mondes* re-echo the verdict of *Splendide mendax*, but they also take due note of that lightness of key which Turner owed to Italy: 'I find it impossible to believe that any such landscape has ever existed anywhere but in fairyland... Is this mountain made of gold, mahogany, velvet or porcelain? The mind is wearied out in conjecture and hardly knows where to stop. The sky in which the horizon lines float is luminous and diaphanous. But neither Spain nor Italy nor the shores of the Bosphorus could have provided Turner with any model for the creation of this gorgeous atmosphere...'

In 1828 he made a second journey to Italy, and it was on his return, in 1829, that he exhibited *Ulysses Deriding Polyphemus* (1829, National Gallery), which may rightfully be

J.M.W. Turner (1775-1851)

Calais Sands, Low Water, Poissards Collecting Bait, c. 1830. Oil on canvas. (28½ × 42″).

Bury Art Gallery, Lancashire.

J.M.W. Turner (1775-1851)
Interior at Petworth (unfinished), c. 1837. Oil on canvas. (35¾ × 48″). Tate Gallery, London.

described as one of Turner's finest paintings and, more generally, as one of the finest 'history paintings' ever made, not only in England but in Europe as a whole. I have said that Turner used his powerful imagination sparingly, and here, it seems to me, is further proof of that. It is as if the painter had said to himself: 'I have found under these skies the light of my dreams, but I have forgotten what I was looking for around 1805; I have forgotten the grandeur to which I aspired after Claude.' For what in fact Turner has produced once again is a prodigious super-Claude; and of course Poussin had painted a *Polyphemus* of his own, departing somewhat from his usual manner, a rockbound Polyphemus[41] whose huge shadowy figure reappears here, hardly distinguishable from the rocks and almost towering over the ship. The light comes from the setting sun, going down in glory just above a strip of sea intensely blue beneath a foil of light clouds ranging in colour from pink to gold. With all the skill and resourcefulness on which he could now draw, Turner calculated the extent to which he could safely alter the traditional structures and proceeded to do so with unexpectedly happy results. Claude's sources of light are nearly always in the centre of the picture. Turner, for his part, shifts the sun as far to the right as possible, with a single galley, already sinking into the shadows, placed there to indicate the middle distance on this side. On the other side, powerfully occupying the left centre of the picture, is the ship of Ulysses, all in ruddy golds, from the sailors to the oars and flames, set off by the near-white of the sails. Swarming figures occupy the rigging nearly up to the mast-heads and ply the oars. Draped in red, Ulysses scoffs at Polyphemus and flings up his arms to emphasize his words. The sea is divided between the broad path of gold laid down by the

J.M.W. Turner (1775-1851)
Norham Castle, Sunrise, c. 1835-40. Oil on canvas. (35¾ × 48″). Tate Gallery, London.

setting sun, with the added gold reflections of the ship, and an expanse of dark blue flecked with foam. The horizon has been kept down as low as possible.

Turner's great imaginative paintings alternate with exquisite impressions of visual reality, worthy of a Cox or a Bonington of genius. A fine example of the latter is *Calais Sands, Low Water, Poissards Collecting Bait* (*c.* 1830, Bury Art Gallery, Lancashire) in which the hourglass of the setting sun glows on the wet sand and illumines the daily toil of the 'poissards': again a Dutch picture, but one that only Turner could have painted.

In 1830 his father died. The bond between them had been unusually close; they had always lived together and lived in harmony. It was recorded at the time that Turner felt as though he had lost an only child. The close and loyal relationship which he had maintained with his father all his life had naturally tended to cut him off from other people; but even if the complexes created by his mother's insanity (whose impact may easily be exaggerated) had never come into play, it is doubtful whether a man of Turner's stamp would ever have been integrated into the society of his time. Lindsay, dwelling on the oddness of his having remained a bachelor, emphasizes his strong sensuality, his erotic drawings of love-making couples, and his preoccupation with the female back; and Lindsay adds, 'He gets something of the sexual suggestiveness out of this viewpoint that Fuseli does.' Turner had for years had a mistress, Sarah Danby, widow of a musician and composer, and by her he had two daughters. Why did he never marry her? No doubt he remained a bachelor because of his father, with whom he shared his home, and perhaps another reason why he held aloof from women is, as Lindsay suggests, that, though he was sexually attracted to them, they inspired him with an unreasoning fear and mistrust due to the traumatic memory of his mother's madness.

However this may be, his father's death left him free to accept the friendship of Lord Egremont, the eccentric master of Petworth, and it was of some consequence in his career. He was allowed to come and go in the house as he wished; a studio was fitted up for him and he often went there to work. Legend credited Lord Egremont with forty-three children, all living at Petworth House with their respective mothers. One might almost suppose that in the fascinating *Interior at Petworth* (*c.* 1837, Tate Gallery), the mothers and their brood have been metamorphosed into these indistinct, puppy-like shapes scattered over the floor in the foreground. Everything in the picture has the vagueness as well as the intense suggestiveness of a dream, and the uncertain patch of white looming up in the arched doorway brings to mind the strangely white lustre of the Italian lakes. A warm harmony of yellows, dull reds, pinks and light greys conveys the shifting uncertainties of that dream. A whole series of tiny watercolour sketches (about $4\frac{1}{2} \times 6''$) in the British Museum preceded the Petworth pictures in the Tate Gallery, among which is the *Music Party, Petworth* (*c.* 1830), where the dissolution of forms is less extreme and some graceful female figures are sufficiently worked out in strokes of colour, with some accurate curves firming their undefined bodies and some telling detail (ruching around a neck), for them to convey a distinct impression. Turner used colour not to construct an external reality but to create the truth of each picture as an aesthetic experience. So the question he had to ask himself was: how much black does a dress require to balance the red of an arch?

Comparing, at the same date, the exteriors with the interiors at Petworth, one notes that the former retain their solidity longer, forms dissolving more quickly and completely

indoors. Gradually the exteriors lapse into the same state of luminous reverie. Few are more exquisitely lyrical than the *Bridge and Tower* landscape in the Tate (after 1830), an inimitable pattern of pinks and mauves, with the palest of yellow accents, shimmeringly undefinable, in the sky. One is not far from a late Monet. I have referred already to the evolving theme of *Norham Castle*, treated first in 1800 as a real enough ruin on a dark hill; rocks, cliffs, watercourses and boats are there clear and distinct. In the third interpretation (after 1835) it has become a blue phantom hovering between sky and water, between the sulphur-yellow glow of the sun and its reflection, encircling that of the castle. *The Thames Upstream from Waterloo Bridge* (1840) is of the same order of vision – a dream of water with a recollection of a bridge.

May one say that the first journey to Italy had resulted in the ascendancy of light over forms, the second in the destruction of forms by light? The question arises because some of the most glorious manifestations of his art are connected with Venice. And Venice, with its peculiar quality, the hazy mildness of its light, may account for that evolution. But on the

1828 journey he did not go to Venice, and after 1819 did not return there until 1835. Yet, even though the forms are still quite distinct, the *Salute and Dogana* (1834) belongs in its tonality to the later series. The Venetian evocations are an enchantment; they span the period 1835-42 but cannot be dated with any precision. Particularly fine is *A Venetian Scene: San Benedetto, Looking Towards Fusina* (Tate Gallery) in a dominant key of sulphur yellow; it is a dream through which glide the long-beaked gondolas with their wraith-like figures, while ideal buildings loom in the distance. Fine, too, is the *Bridge of Sighs: Boats Before the Riva* (c. 1842, Tate Gallery), an Oriental procession amidst creamy structures, with patches of lightest blue enclosed in the ring formed by the bridges and their reflections. Then there is *Boats on the Lagoon* (Victoria and Albert Museum): are these really the

J.M.W. Turner (1775-1851)

Snowstorm: Steamboat off a Harbour's Mouth, 1842. Oil on canvas. (36 × 48″). Tate Gallery, London.

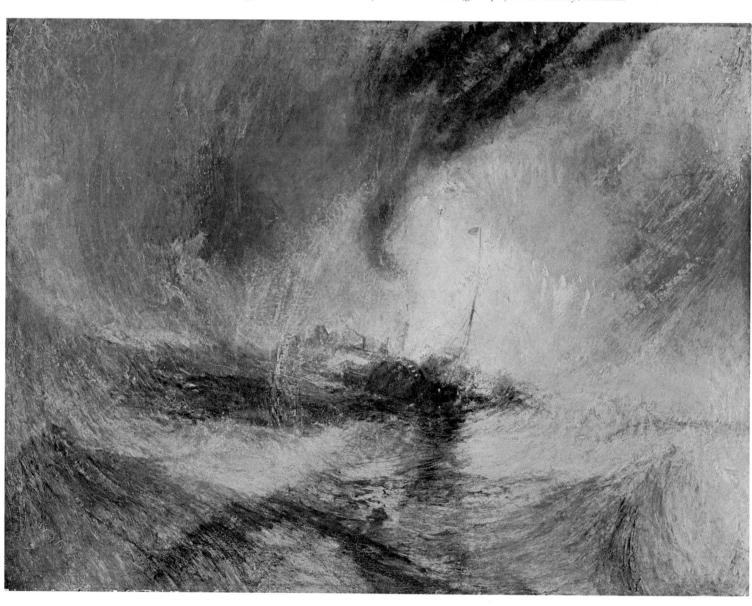

boats mentioned in the title, or is it the moving water around them? And this golden-hued Orient glowing like that of Delacroix, can one not detect some kneeling camels or elephants laden with white bales and coloured silks and hangings, surely more distinct here than what can be made out in many a picture by Turner since 1812? *After the Ball* (Tate Gallery) is the most bewildering of these canvases. Here one is reduced to guessing at a venture. Reality seems to have melted away into pale, aquatic dreams. The world as representation has ceased to be. The implications of the title *After the Ball* make one see here an accusation levelled at a frivolous city and its pleasure-seekers, much as Browning was to do. Is such an accusation implied in all these visions of Venice? Maybe, but that having been said, this is still magnificent painting in its own right.

J.M.W. Turner (1775-1851)
Fire at Sea, c. 1834. Oil on canvas. (67 ½ × 86¾"). Tate Gallery, London.

The phases of his art continually overlap, so that one often encounters two parallel and contradictory moods. After his return from the second journey to Italy came the paean to pure light, at Venice and elsewhere. Then he reverted to the sea, darker and more sublimely inhuman than ever. He took up the theme in 1831 with the *Vessel in Distress off Yarmouth* (Tate Gallery): a sky filled with leaden grey clouds; below, the raging sea, of a yellow cast which contrives to be luminous; and somewhere in between, a ship, its presence guessed at rather than seen, from the signal rocket bursting in the clouds.

This was followed by the *Fire at Sea* (*c.* 1834, Tate Gallery), a riot of destructive and avenging elements: strange yellow flames shoot into the sky to join the vast glow already hovering there, a cloud among clouds; below, identifiable from a mast still erect, the burning ship breaks up in a churning triangle alive with souls in torment – for each of these cataclysms is conceived, more and more, as a kind of Last Judgment.

Finally in 1842 Turner exhibited *Snowstorm: Steamboat off a Harbour's Mouth* (Tate Gallery). Forms are riven with such obsessive dynamism that the smoke of the steamer seems not so much to emanate from the boat as to swoop down upon it, like the whirlwind enveloping Hannibal's army. The ship and its funnel have been practically swallowed up, except for a glimpse of the paddle-wheel. He built up his storm with long, vehement brush-strokes, whose vast swirls seem to hollow out a chasm round the ship. Still loaded with the white he had employed for foam, his brush has traced, perhaps unintentionally, an indistinct circle or oval sweeping down from the black cloud across the sea and neatly enclosing the ship in the dead centre, amidst an ominous burst of light. To feel the force of such elemental dramas one must have experienced them oneself and this is exactly what Turner did: 'I got the sailors to lash me to the mast to observe it; I was lashed for four hours, and I did not expect to escape, but I felt bound to record it if I did.'

Chronologically, I should have spoken before of *The Slave Ship* or *Slavers Throwing Overboard the Dead and Dying – Typhoon Coming On* (1840, Museum of Fine Arts, Boston). But this picture, at once the most explicit and the most gratuitous, carries over into almost purely visionary terms what before was still reality, however much interpreted. There is no storm here: yet the slave ship, with rigging as skeletal as that of the phantom ship in *The Ancient Mariner*, stands out against a glaring sky, pursued by a metaphysical hurricane which also stirs up the sea, tinged with fiery gleams or streaks of blood. Into it, in darker confusion than in the *Fire at Sea*, plunge a mass of dead and dying men, thrown overboard by the slavers, and the hungry fish – another obsession of Turner's – are already at work on them. Sticking out of the water are some curious loops, presumably the chains of the hapless slaves. Ruskin wrote of its 'majestic intent'. Too pointed an intent perhaps. Turner had in mind actual cases, which had attracted public notice, of slavers throwing the sick overboard when an epidemic broke out. But by that time the slave trade was very much on the decline.

Turner, the truest poet of all painters, combined as Coleridge did a passion for tales of sea voyages and adventures with an obsessive sense of guilt, in his case perhaps less personal; Turner felt guilty on behalf of mankind. He stands in time between Coleridge and Melville, and his *Slave Ship* might have carried a man like Benito Cereno. Round about 1845 he painted several pictures illustrating passages from Thomas Beale's *Natural History of the Sperm Whale*, which was one of the sources with which Melville supplemented his own experience when he wrote *Moby Dick*. Out of his own head or dreams, then, Turner evoked the modern epic of whaling on the frontiers of the unknown, in abysmal seas sailed by doomed but heroic ships. It is the supernatural creation of a visionary, and like an hallucination emerges the beast in the *Sunrise with a Sea Monster* (Tate Gallery). It must be remembered that Turner in his early days was familiar with the theories of Alexander Cozens attributing inspirational power to the concentration of the eye on an accidental form. One may suppose that in scrutinizing the seas before painting them his seer's eye detected the pre-existent monster as a condensation of greenish brine. In his *Seascape with Approaching Storm*, the storm-centre in the middle of the picture is a kind of ink spot; from it emerges an apparition, reddish within yellow. For all that may be said about the natural sources of the 'sea monster', there is no denying its fantastic character. Surely there is no such fish or sea mammal as this with its eyes in front. But Turner wanted an effect of terror, which he heightened by launching the monster straight at the spectator. The picture raises, but does nothing to solve, the question of the explicit use of the fantastic in painting.

The blending of water and fire – before the latter became merely symbolic in *The Slave Ship* – had given rise first to the *Fire at Sea* of 1834 and then to the *Stormy Sea with Blazing Wreck* of 1840 (Tate Gallery). In the latter, as in the *Sea Monster*, one finds a method of construction or better a mode of vision added to a whirlwind that indeed goes far beyond mere representation: in the gaping void which is the threshold of the mystery and the omen of danger, the attention is arrested and focused on the only point where, dimly but unmistakably, something is happening which may account for this mighty upheaval. Fire alone provided a theme when in October 1834 the Houses of Parliament were burnt. The picture in the Cleveland Museum of Art (1835) may be compared with Constable's *Inauguration of Waterloo Bridge*. Constable produced a brilliant picture. Turner, at the peak of his genius, again measured his powers against the demands of the sublime in seizing on this weird and glowing spectacle. In the foreground is the mighty shape of a bridge, its arches half eaten away under the impact of light and the reflections of the vast sulphurous glow flanking the red scarf thrown across the sky, magnified and repeated in the mirror of the Thames. Everything is subordinated to this accord of intense red and palest yellow, to their blendings and gradual fusion in the greens, blues and mauves of sky and water. The fire seems to divide the mild blues of dusk on the left from the mauves of night on the right, from which emerge the dim towers of Westminster Abbey. The pictorial power of this actual scene witnessed and interpreted constitutes, I fear, a severe critique of such inventions as the *Plagues of Egypt* and *Hero and Leander*.

I have referred to overlapping developments, to moods and veins running parallel rather than successively. *The Fighting Téméraire* (1839, National Gallery) is a further example of this. At Trafalgar the *Téméraire* was the second ship of the line after the *Victory*. One evening, over thirty years later, Turner and the seascape painter Stanfield[42] were together on the packet which ran from London Bridge wharf to Margate when they saw the old battleship being towed from Sheerness to Deptford to be broken up; and Stanfield is supposed to have exclaimed that it would make 'a fine subject'. It was indeed a subject fit to strike the patriotic imagination, associated as it was with the glories of the navy. Again, and more subtly than in the *Battle of Trafalgar*, this was living history. Seeing the picture at the Royal Academy exhibition of 1839, Thackeray wrote: 'The old Téméraire is dragged to her last home by a little, spiteful, diabolical steamer. A mighty red sun, amidst a host of flaring clouds, sinks to rest on one side of the picture, and illumines a river that seems interminable, and a countless navy that fades away into such a wonderful distance as never was painted before.'

The picture elements are interwoven like a noble piece of music: the pale ship with its tall masts, the setting sun throwing a coppery glow over most of the sky, the tug with its funnel pouring out smoke and flame. In painting as in poetry, the sunset hour brings a mood of melancholy, and day's end is the symbol of other declines and other endings. Turner would not perhaps have gone so far in the direction of Claude, had it not been for the fact that both artists were so keenly responsive to a certain quality of light.

This picture was followed up and re-echoed in 1842 by another: *Peace – Burial at Sea* (Tate Gallery), representing the burial of the painter Sir David Wilkie, who had died on

J.M.W. Turner (1775-1851)

Rain, Steam and Speed — The Great Western Railway, exhibited R.A. 1844. Oil on canvas. (35¾ × 48″). National Gallery, London.

J.M.W. Turner (1775-1851)

Shade and Darkness: The Evening of the Deluge, exhibited R.A. 1843.

Oil on canvas. (31 × 30¾″). Tate Gallery, London.

board ship the year before. It is a nocturne in dark and light: under the rising moon, a great ship with black sails and red torches, under a pall of black smoke (for it was actually a steamer), with its enormous black reflection in the water, composes a fine funereal poem.

For earlier critics like Hamerton and even Finberg, the period from about 1840 is that of Turner's senility. But from this marvellous 'senility' comes *Rain, Steam and Speed – The Great Western Railway* (1844, National Gallery). Of Turner lashed to a ship's mast I have said that, for him, it was an experience, not a spectacle; for such a man, it was also an experience to be in a railway carriage (Turner loved trains). Look at his locomotive: the important thing about it is that it is bearing down upon the spectator. It drives on through rain and storm, and it was the dynamics involved, expressed in red and black, that appealed to the painter. One can well believe the anecdote recorded of him, putting his head out of the carriage window, and keeping it there for nearly nine minutes, in order to experience a torrential downpour from a speeding train. A similar sensation is conveyed here, in this vision from the viaduct of the waterscape down below, blurred by the driving rain from the sky – a waterscape which he associated with this speeding movement.

If one covers up first one half of the picture, then the other, one is struck by the clear, luminous tonality of the 'natural' part of the picture and the Rembrandtesque aspect of the other half dominated by the works of man – which in sum he did not see but invented.

The locomotive comes straight out of the picture as the sea monster did. In the *Yachts Approaching the Coast* (1845, Tate Gallery), the vessels retain something of that dynamism, marked by a shimmer of pale golden reflections coming from a white sun, a mere suggestion of a sun, such as now becomes common in Turner. This glowing streak is no longer static, being associated with the movement of the most prominent yacht: so what one has here is a typical structure.

The last years of a visionary are apt to be the most visionary of all. From this type of man there is nothing to fear in the way of fancy pictures, but what he did produce was magnificent phantasmagorias; for example, *Undine Giving the Ring to Masaniello* or *Queen Mab's Cave* (1846, Tate Gallery). The bubble (as in *Undine*) alternates with the chasm. It, too, is a threat to reality.

Goethe's theory of colours interested Turner and for a long time he had been trying his hand at it on the basis of elementary diagrams. Goethe provided him with an attractive theory based on the imaginative affinities of colours. There were those that related to shadow and tended towards black; others, the reds, yellows and greens, tended towards light and told of joy and good humour. Turner set little store by this division into shadow-colours and light-colours. But he did set store by their respective affinities with joy or sadness, and taking one with the other this resulted in the two strange Deluge pictures. First came *Shade and Darkness: The Evening of the Deluge* (c. 1843, Tate Gallery), an artistic testament in which, around the usual circle of light, swirl in more or less opaque browns – for he goes no further than this into darkness – all the storms that had haunted him since his *Hannibal*. They stir up a welter of indefinite forms and doom-stricken figures which now are quite fantastic, as if Turner had plied his brush at a venture in a waking dream, heedless of scale. On the right is an enormous animal, some wild beast perhaps; below, a horse and an ox; on the left, a prostrate human form; possibly, with skilful deciphering, still other species or inventions can be puzzled out.

J.M.W. Turner (1775-1851)

Light and Colour (Goethe's Theory): The Morning after the Deluge, Moses Writing the Book of Genesis, exhibited R.A. 1843.

Oil on canvas. (31 × 31″). Tate Gallery, London.

Light and Colour (Goethe's Theory): The Morning after the Deluge, Moses Writing the Book of Genesis (c. 1843, Tate Gallery) is perhaps the most Blakean thing Turner ever painted. A sort of mystical globe repeats this accord of yellow and vermilion, the tones which had figured in the *Burning of the Houses of Parliament* and which are used here to happy effect. All mankind, summed up by a large number of small heads, seems to be whirling round, borne up no doubt towards the light. [43]

Turner's watercolours were much appreciated and helped him to live. To say no more than that of them, however, would be unpardonable. He painted large numbers of them, because that had been his first technique in working with Girtin and in following the example of J. R. Cozens, and also because it afforded immediate contact with places, sites and monuments and direct expression of them in accordance with tradition. Constable said of him that at heart he had always remained a watercolourist. In saying that, he was alluding to the quality and density of Turner's oil paints, and indeed for a very long period between the impasto of his early work and the spirited brushing of his late pictures the pigments were thin and diluted, tending to the consistency of watercolour.

The early watercolour of *The Transept of Ewenny Priory* (1797, Cardiff) was hailed by a contemporary critic as 'equal to the best pictures of Rembrandt', and the young painter did indeed give here an admirable example of poetic yet accurate chiaroscuro, recording the peculiar quality of the light under these Romanesque arches.

Coming forward to 1819, one notes among the Venetian watercolours the *Campanile and Ducal Palace* (British Museum), which shows Turner using watercolour as a medium for experimenting with colours. Here, indeed, they are the primaries. In the watercolour entitled *Room in Venice* (1839, British Museum), there are again straightforward blues, yellows, reddish browns, beiges and violets, applied in flat areas to form a suggestive, transparent pattern; and in that pattern, instead of colour being used to define form, the little form there is serves as a pretext for a coloured construction.

In a contrary manner is *Winchelsea, Marching Soldiers* (c. 1828, British Museum), a watercolour full of spirit, gaiety and movement, but with an admirable precision in the rendering of attitudes, gestures and even faces; it shows Turner playing with his medium in masterly fashion, as if demonstrating that he could do anything with it.

He was, of course, up to all the tricks. On heavy grey or blue paper, the advantages of which had been shown by Girtin, he worked with increasingly thicker paints which enabled him to scratch and rub until he got the right tone. Then he combined gouache and watercolour in order to produce the extraordinary works inspired by visits to Normandy between 1821 and 1830 – first of all *Rouen Cathedral, West Front* (British Museum). It is not the sort of architect's design that Girtin had produced with his *Durham Cathedral*, but a hymn of light subtly consuming the detail of form, not disregarding it but on the contrary giving it a higher kind of recognition. One cannot help wondering whether Monet had ever seen this work. One *Honfleur* at least in the British Museum is handled with the precision of a miniature painter. He inserted small details which reached right into the background of the town and inserted them with a sure hand that never over-emphasized them, thus achieving an unusual and perfectly constructed work.

It was not only in the practice of watercolour that he proved resourceful, self-assured, disdainful of the common tools used by all. Like Gainsborough, he worked with anything to hand, brushes, sticks of wood, his pocket knife for scratching, his fingers for rubbing. The power of his genius is revealed in what, from the beginning, I have called his economy, his sparingness. Economy of imagination – that may suggest niggardliness. But economy of utilization – this was one of the exacting demands he made on himself. Girtin, as if knowing that he could not wait, made of each sketch a finished work (or nearly so). Turner rarely utilized his sketches as such; he sought in them such elements as he could combine in an invention of his own, whose vague title (though there are some exceptions) answered to his refusal to represent any particular reality.

What kind of man was Turner? Those who knew him, including Ruskin, have testified to his mean style of life. He kept a stock of good sherry but would serve it from a chipped decanter. He would eat whatever was set before him. His house was lighted with tallow candles. He lived in dust and disorder like some odd character out of Dickens. Ruskin, meeting him for the first time, wrote in his diary (22 June 1840): 'I found in him a somewhat eccentric, keen-mannered, matter-of-fact, English-minded gentleman: good-natured evidently, bad-tempered evidently, hating humbug of all sorts, shrewd, perhaps a little selfish, highly intellectual, the powers of his mind not brought out with any delight in their manifestation, or intention of display, but flashing out occasionally in a word or a look.' It was as if he were absent or absorbed in his art. Here, as in other things, there was a streak of parsimoniousness in him. He never gave away a picture or a drawing, nor did he have much desire to sell them either, being increasingly taken with the idea of a gallery in which the whole body of his work could be seen and studied: he bequeathed to the nation 19000 drawings of all kinds and two hundred canvases. He had always had his little vanities (he wished to demonstrate his superiority over Claude by a direct comparison of pictures) and what have been called his shopkeeper's gestures (he left a thousand pounds for a mausoleum to be erected beside Reynolds' tomb in the crypt of St Paul's). He had suffered much in childhood, and his art had been a glorious escape. He had felt the need for audacity, for the stretch of fancy, in an age when bourgeois conventionalism was on the increase. His first great painting had been sold for one hundred and fifty pounds to a greater eccentric than himself, William Beckford. But there were no more Beckfords. The sub-Hazlitts in the service of the bourgeoisie denounced his pictures ('Bedlam broke loose'), and Hazlitt himself spoke of his 'waste of morbid strength,' his 'visionary absurdities – affectation and refinement run mad.' But he went on in his own way, recording the ever varying image of his heroic clash with the elements – his perennial subject.

At twenty-five he had formed a liaison with Sarah Danby, by whom he had two daughters, but he was not a good father to them. She was superseded by Mrs Booth, a sailor's wife, in whose house at Margate he had taken lodgings in 1834. Captain Booth having died, Turner installed the widow in a cottage at Chelsea. There he became known to the children of the neighbourhood as Captain Booth or Admiral Booth. He died at his cottage, 119 Cheyne Walk, on the 19th of December 1851. His canvases were found in indescribable disorder and neglect, many of them irretrievably damaged – rolled up, stacked up, exposed to dirt and damp, even patched with wrapping paper. Matters were made no better by the fact that, like Reynolds, he persisted in a corrupt technique; for the sake of an immediate effect he would adopt any expedient, and owing to his reckless experiments in colour, time has fatally darkened some of his pictures.

It is a tribute to Ruskin's generosity and greatness of mind that he should have devoted so much time and talent to the cause of a man whose genius he had recognized. In 1836, at seventeen, he wrote an essay defending Turner against his detractors. In 1842 Ruskin set to work on the more elaborate defence of him which was to become the five volumes of *Modern Painters*. The first volume, by 'a Graduate of Oxford', appeared in 1843 and created a sensation. It was praised by Wordsworth and Tennyson, and Charlotte Brontë wrote: 'Hitherto I have only had instinct to guide me in judging of art; I feel now as if I had been walking blindfold – this book seems to give me eyes.' Turner was Ruskin's idol; but to ignore Cotman and describe Constable as one who sees 'about as much [of nature] as an intelligent fawn and a skylark' did not help Turner's cause with future generations.

Constable – at heart a Christian materialist who was deeply disturbed by this immaterial and demoniacal art – paid frank tribute to the genius of its creator: 'Turner', he wrote on 12 May 1836 (referring to the Academy exhibition of that year), 'has outdone himself; he seems to paint with tinted steam, so evanescent and so airy.'[44]

Then this great tumult passed into history. The Impressionists recognized the debt they owed him. In their famous letter to Sir Coutts Lindsay, Monet, Renoir, Pissarro and Sisley declared 'that their aim is to bring back into art a scrupulously accurate observation of nature, by striving passionately to render form in movement as well as the fleeting phenomena of light. They cannot forget that they were preceded in this endeavour by a great master of the English school, the famous Turner.'

Pissarro later summed up the matter more precisely and in a more critical spirit (letter of 8 May 1903): 'Though helpful in many ways, Turner and Constable, we soon realized, never understood the analysis of shadows, which, with Turner, are always a kind of preconceived effect, a mere hole in the canvas. As for the division of tones, Turner showed us its value as a procedure, but never its true accuracy.'

Turner's approach, then, was not scientific but empirical. Has any English painter taken a scientific approach, apart from Reynolds, who was something of a pedant, down to Sickert, who was actually a German?

9

Approaches to Pre-Raphaelitism: Genre Painting and High Art:
Wilkie, Haydon, Mulready, Landseer, Dyce.
The Pre-Raphaelite Contestation and the Deadlock of Idealism:
Brown, Hunt, Millais, Rossetti, Hughes.

For whom did all these painters paint? Hogarth no doubt for a middle class of his imagination which failed to buy his canvases. Fortunately the lower middle class bought his prints. All the painters after Hogarth, with but few exceptions, worked for the cultivated or luxury-loving aristocracy. Things were changing, society was evolving, but in which direction?

Among the exceptions, it is true, was an artist like Joseph Wright of Derby. But the class of great millowners for which he catered was only the cultivated vanguard of the society that was to be brought to power by the industrial revolution, by the age of coal and steel. These millowners, on the whole austere, earnest-minded men (much more so than their French counterparts), were suspicious of art, seeing it as frivolity, hedonism or the temptation of hedonism, a by-product liable to distract the mind from the requirements of production. This meant that in fact they were not prepared to accept the competing influence, the interference, of a serious art whose motivations (those of culture) were foreign to them; but they were, on the contrary, inclined to look indulgently on a light-weight art of no consequence which they could understand, as well as disdain, while it could at the same time reflect an increased prestige upon them. A flowering of genre painting in the early nineteenth century followed as a matter of course. At times it put on airs, for example with Sir David Wilkie (1785-1841). Born in Fifeshire and trained in Edinburgh, he began by painting scenes of Scottish life. *Pitlessie Fair* (1804, Edinburgh) shows a technical skill which is almost excessive for a nineteen-year-old painter. Teniers could not have improved on this firm delimitation of a well-ordered scene, could not have articulated the figure groups more tellingly to give the impression of a crowd or animated them more effectively by the play of bright light. What is quite lacking is any renewal or development of form. What matters is local background and associations, the recognizable portraits of local notabilities. Only the setting changes, as he went on to *Village Politics* (1806), again composed of typical characters, but this time discussing politics in the pub. He quickly won recognition and was elected to the Royal Academy in 1811, at twenty-six, while Constable had to wait until he was fifty-four. For twenty years Wilkie painted Scottish manners and social history, tending to individualize his scenes with a touch of sentimentality or sympathy appreciated by his middle-class audience. The *Blind Fiddler* of 1806 is a characteristic example. The success of Wilkie's work lay in its sentimental appeal. He was never at a loss for subject-matter. The middle classes loved their pets – which proved, in their own eyes, that they were capable of love. So Wilkie painted *Fido's Bath* (1811).

In 1805 he had moved to London, and though the character of his work did not change, it became less localized. The *Letter of Introduction* (1813, Edinburgh) may be taken as characteristic. The genre scene thus conceived represented an episode in an imaginary comedy of middle-class life, and to an even greater extent than in Hogarth the figures are actors; there is no question of regarding them as men and women moving in the current of actual life. The emotions they show are merely a series of stock responses. Thus the young man in the *Letter of Introduction* has downcast eyes and an uneasy tremble of the lips; the old man in a night-cap, sitting at his desk, holds the letter which, however, raising his head with a suspicious look in his eye, he does not read; with a sidelong glance he takes stock of the intruder and wonders what he wants. Such painting is not an end but a means.

Conceived in the same vein, *Reading a Will* was a commission from the King of Bavaria. Prints spread Wilkie's fame far and wide. After 1815 it was time to commemorate the recent victories. Wilkie himself seems to have had the idea, following a vague commission from the Duke of Wellington, of painting what is perhaps his most famous picture, the *Chelsea Pensioners Reading the Gazette Announcing the Victory at Waterloo*. Begun in 1818, it was scarcely finished when Géricault saw it in 1821 in the painter's studio, Wilkie, it was said, having just spent sixteen months' uninterrupted work on it. Géricault dispatched an enthusiastic letter to Horace Vernet: 'It would be most helpful to see Wilkie's touching expressions!... He has varied all his characters with great feeling.' It is true that Wilkie spared no pains with his *Chelsea Pensioners* and contrived to give an extraordinary variety and precision to their unanimous expression of joy. One hearty old man comes out with a burst of enthusiasm which conspicuously fails to move his sluggish, senile neighbour. A woman, noted by Géricault, alone shows anxiety as she tries to get a glimpse of the gazette, which doubtless includes a list of those killed in action. When the picture was exhibited at Somerset House in 1822, it attracted record-breaking crowds; a brass railing had to be put up to protect it. It was the first time such a thing had happened. Such, in England, was the democratization of aesthetic pleasure. But neither Constable nor even Turner ever got the benefit of it.

As Wilkie's fame increased, so did his ambitions. In the 1820s he turned to history painting and his *Knox Preaching to the Lords of Congregation* (c. 1822-32, Tate Gallery) aroused Delacroix's admiration, just as the *Chelsea Pensioners* had Géricault's. From 1825 to 1828 he travelled on the Continent, chiefly in Italy and Spain, studying the Old Masters. In Murillo, who was also a painter of expressive faces, in Van Dyck and to a lesser extent in Rubens, he found what he needed, and his debt to them is clear in a picture like *The Empress Josephine and the Fortune-Teller* (1837, Edinburgh). In spite of the historical personage, this is a genre scene of the old type conceived in the new style. But usually, from now on, Wilkie sought out dramatic subjects, often concerned with the Irish poor, and depended on chiaroscuro to express the drama. The late Wilkie thus became a Romantic, but his later work is frequently faulty in form and draughtsmanship, and the Pre-Raphaelites were wise in preferring his *Blind Fiddler* for its tonality. Eager, however, for fresh experiences, he went in 1840 on a journey to the Holy Land and died on his way home in 1841. Nothing in his life was more genuinely romantic than his burial at sea – as painted by Turner.

Benjamin Robert Haydon (1786-1846), whose unswerving devotion to history painting in the grand manner drove him to suicide, personifies romantic ambition and despair. His career has something in common with Barry's; it is a chronicle of short-lived success, cantankerousness, vanity and self-willed perverseness leading to isolation, mounting debts and imprisonment for those debts. From the age of twenty he imagined himself to have a mission: that of opening a new era marked by public recognition of the moral value of history painting. The great deeds and relics of the past touched and inspired him; hence, among many ambitious projects and undertakings, his eager campaign to bring the Elgin Marbles into the British Museum. He had lofty ideas of civic art and, as with Hogarth, this went with ideas of grand-style painting: *Wellington Meditating at Waterloo, Christ's Entry into Jerusalem*. Haydon had a streak of genius; what he lacked was talent. Between his muddled self-delusions and his confused composition, there may be some connection. In any case, if his Romantic vision did not appeal to a Wellington, it met with comprehension and encouragement from his friend Wordsworth. And Haydon's portrait of *Wordsworth on Mount Helvellyn* (1842, National Portrait Gallery, London) is not only, as the poet himself said, 'the best likeness, that is, the most characteristic, that has been done of me'; it is also, I should say, the best portrait of any of the great Romantic poets. Only in the background is the dramatic obscurity overdone, against which stand out the superbly expressive flesh parts: the hand resting on the sleeve and the head weighed down by the broad brow. A moving portrait, whose expressiveness, however, cannot conceal its technical shortcomings. Part of the bitter comedy of Haydon's life lay in the fact that he was only successful in genre painting, in the vein of the early Wilkie; there, in spite of himself, he was at one with the spirit of the times.

Verve, gaiety and movement, in the best English tradition of humorous observation of daily life, are to be found in his *Chairing the Member* (1828) – a subject, it will be remembered, that Hogarth had also treated – and *Punch or May Day* (1829), both in the Tate Gallery, though there are some strange lapses and faulty construction in the grouping of the figures. Haydon was a democrat, which cannot be said of many of the painters dealt with here, whatever the circumstances of their birth. He painted *Waiting for 'The Times' on the Morning after the Debate on the Reform Bill, 8 October 1831*. This was one form of action among others. Being a megalomaniac, Haydon imagined that he could have some influence on politics. What is certain is that he failed to have any influence on art, and it has been rightly said that the best of his work lies in his writings, not only his *Autobiography and Memoirs* but also his *Lectures on Painting and Design*.

William Mulready (1786-1863) was a pupil of John Varley, the eccentric watercolour painter and astrologer whom I mentioned in connection with Blake. He was influenced by Wilkie, who helped to turn his attention from landscape to genre scenes. His landscapes, however, are by no means without interest. They show precision, a sense of lighting and a sound disposition of the masses, as for example in *The Farrier* (c. 1810, Fitzwilliam Museum, Cambridge), and in spite of a certain static quality they deserve an honorable place in the history of landscape directly observed and rendered.

Typical of Mulready's genre scenes is *The Last In*, meaning the last boy to reach the schoolroom, followed, moreover, by a mongrel. The master bows ironically to the laggard who, one may surmise from the look of him, is seldom on time. Another scene is *Choosing the Wedding Gown* (1846); it is typical of his preoccupation with minute detail, which he carries even further than his masters and models, the seventeenth-century Dutch genre

William Mulready (1786-1863)
The Sonnet, exhibited R.A. 1839.
Oil on panel. (14 × 12″).
Victoria and Albert Museum,
London.

painters. His work rose at times above the level of rather pedestrian realism that may seem characteristic of him. *The Sonnet* (Victoria and Albert Museum) shows a pair of contemporary lovers, she reading the sonnet composed for her, he bending over with his hands at his ankles, but with his head on a horizontal plane and his back turned towards the girl. The unusual pose is easily explained: it was taken from Michelangelo's Jeremiah in the Sistine Chapel. Proceeding like Ramsay and Reynolds, Mulready drew discreetly on the Old Masters in order to enhance his subject. The result is not uninteresting, but Mulready is of more importance in the history of British painting for the fact that (unlike Wilkie) he kept to a lighter tonality, almost as light as watercolour, starting from a white ground on which the pure, vivid colour is applied in such thin coats that sometimes the preparatory drawing shows through. He was one of the inspirers of the Pre-Raphaelite conception of colour and tone.

Sir Edwin Landseer (1802-73) was one of the leading official artists of Victorian England, and the Queen's favourite painter; as such he was engaged to give painting lessons to the Royal couple. Before he was thirty he became an academician. Knighted in 1850, he was buried in St Paul's Cathedral. He is remembered as an animal painter, specializing in dogs endowed with human pathos and sentimentality. Singularly gifted, he deserved better than that.[45] Trained first by his father, the painter and engraver John Landseer, he later studied with Haydon, who set him to drawing the Elgin Marbles and dissecting animals. Géricault in 1821 was impressed by his youthful talent. That talent was still evident when, about 1836, in the Scottish Highlands, Landseer painted a landscape entitled *A Lake Scene, Effect of Storm*, a Romantic lake landscape in its mid-winter bleakness, the drifted snow in the foreground contrasting with the dark boulders and sky. The storm effect is there, but it is not overdone. Something of his talent was still evident in 1844 when he painted *The Challenge* (Duke of Northumberland), a picture of elongated format (38 × 82½″) representing a stag troating beside a broad sheet of water that spans the whole canvas, among tree-trunks to which the water gives a sinister, skeletal bareness. Across the water the mountains stretch away among the clouds. I am surprised that the arresting parallel between this painting and Holman Hunt's *Scapegoat* has not been pointed out. Landseer's *Challenge* was so famous that it was parodied in *Punch*. Hunt could hardly have failed to see it.

William Dyce (1806-64), a native of Aberdeen, was not a full-time professional painter. Had he not been made an academician in 1848, one would take him rather for a distinguished amateur, of no genius and little invention, painting intelligently conceived and competently executed pictures. A much-appreciated official, teacher and administrator, he was appointed superintendent of the school of design at Somerset House in 1838 and professor of fine art at King's College, London, in 1840. The fact that he held such positions may account for his being invited in 1844 to contribute to the fresco decorations in the House of Parliament, while Ford Madox Brown's cartoons were rejected. He was pious, and the renewal of Christian art played a well-known part in the rise of Romanticism. Like Palmer, but with none of Palmer's embarrassing excesses (Dyce was incapable of excess), he belonged to the High Church, with its love of the beauty and mystery of ritual. His frequent journeys to Italy gave him a firsthand knowledge of the sources, but his borrowings from them are handled with northern restraint; actually, the chief guidance he found for his art in Rome was that of the German Nazarenes, Overbeck and Cornelius. In front of Dyce's *Virgin and Child* (1845, Royal Collection), a score of names come to mind, between Bruges and Florence, suggested by the skilful archaism of the modelling, the graceful attitude and layout, and the ingenious idea of having the Virgin read to the Child – the book recalling the best of the Reformation, in contradistinction to Catholic obscurantism.

The great age of the Church of England was in the early seventeenth century, in the time of Donne and Herbert. Dyce's picture of *George Herbert at Bemerton* (1861, Guildhall, London) was meant to commemorate the poet's gentle, cheerful piety, but the picture fails to rise above the usual insipidity of Victorian idealization. It is otherwise with his *Pegwell Bay, Kent* (1859, Tate Gallery). This is probably one of the most interesting landscapes of the period, and one of the most characteristic of what may be called the Victorian sensibility. As often pointed out, the four figures in the foreground, three snugly clad women and a

William Dyce (1806-64).
Virgin and Child, 1845. Oil on canvas. (31 ½ × 25").
Royal Collection, reproduced by gracious permission
of Her Majesty the Queen.

child with its spade, are treated with almost photographic precision, and it is true that English painting – one has only to think of Turner's figures – had never carried illusionism of facial features and clothes to this pitch, going far beyond mere suggestion. Yet there is something curiously compelling about this imitation of visual reality, as though this degree of illusionism was necessary to make the solitude of these figures, in the pale afterglow of sunset, so strongly and deeply felt. It must be added, however, that this picture stands outside any significant art current, and that here again one comes to that deadlock in which the orthodox Pre-Raphaelites were in the end to find themselves.

Anyone dealing with the cultural history of Victorian England, in any field whatever, soon realizes that there was a current and a counter-current: the broad current of mediocrity and happy stolidity, and a thin, intense counter-current of idealistic protest. But England is not a country of group movements: individuals take their own way, and it is only later that they are brought together. The case of Ford Madox Brown (1821-93) is exemplary.

Born in Calais in 1821, he studied art in Belgium, under Gregorius in Bruges, Van Hanselaere in Ghent and, most importantly, in Antwerp under Baron Wappers, a Romantic affiliated with Delacroix. At fourteen he was already a proficient portraitist. By the age of twenty he had been oriented towards Romanticism and painted *The Giaour's Confession*, after Byron. Then he went to Paris, there becoming something of a realist, despite the influence of Delacroix. At the end of this cosmopolitan schooling, his imagination and pictorial invention appeared nonetheless intact and separate. In London, in 1844, Brown took part in the competition for the fresco decoration of the new Houses of Parliament, submitting three cartoons which show that he was turning now to historical themes; Rossetti was much impressed by one of them, *The Body of Harold Brought to William the Conqueror After the Battle of Hastings*. Here he adopted a style of linear design and flat colours, in reaction against his training and the chiaroscuro of his early paintings in (as he recounts) 'a sombre, Rembrandtesque style'. Needless to say, none of his cartoons obtained a prize. For the sake of his young wife's health, he left for Italy, stopping on the way in Basle, where he admired Holbein's portraits. In Rome he met Overbeck and Cornelius, leaders of the group of German painters known as the Nazarenes, because of the Christian, almost mystical tinge of their Romanticism and the exclusively religious inspiration of their painting. On his return to London, where he settled for good in 1846, the influence of Holbein is clearly discernible in portraits such as that of *Mr Bamford*, which he described as the first token of the new direction taken by his thoughts and feelings. It was painted on an unprimed canvas. From 1847 to 1851 he was occupied with his *Chaucer at the Court of Edward III*, of which he later executed a replica (1856-67, Tate Gallery). It is a curiously vertical composition, marked by the 'Gothic mannerisms' of the Nazarenes and memories of the tiered design of early Italian painting, that of Gentile da Fabriano or Benozzo Gozzoli, rather than by any return to nature. The crowded figures and awkward divergence of movement betray his over-eager desire to avoid a static effect. It was about this time that Rossetti applied to him for technical instruction. Brown's solitude and isolation had been such that he thought it was some kind of a joke and he awaited his visitor with a stout stick. But Rossetti only worked with him for a few months (in 1848). In the historical pictures of this period Brown sought a dramatic accent, as in *Wycliffe Reading his Translation of the Bible to John of Gaunt in the Presence of Chaucer and Gower* (1848, Bradford). Of his *Chaucer*, Brown said that it was the first picture 'in which I endeavoured to carry out the notion, long before conceived, of treating the light and shade absolutely as it exists at any one moment, instead of approximately, or in generalized style.' Brown was an experienced painter but not a committed one, having indeed no clear idea of the course he wished to take, when in 1848 he began frequenting the Pre-Raphaelites, first Rossetti, then, through him, Millais and Holman Hunt.

Brown's *Jesus Washing Peter's Feet* (1852-56, Tate Gallery) shows the same concern that appears about the same time – actually a little earlier – in Millais: to treat sacred history with accurate, painstaking realism. The veins stand out sharply on Peter's feet and Christ's hands. The sandals are exactly rendered. Judas has a thick shock of red hair and the traditional money-bag; he leans down to unlace his sandal, preparing his foot for the master's homage. All this is effectively, if not very subtly, held together by an angular rhythm. Possibly Brown owed to his new friends the use of a wet white ground, calculated to set off the colours, green, red and orange. But Brown worked slowly, so slowly that it seems unlikely that he could have made much use of a wet ground; it would have dried before he got very far. He was at one with the Pre-Raphaelites in his love of precision and minute detail, but they were probably responsible for his decisive orientation towards open-air painting: one thinks first of all of *The Pretty Baa-Lambs (Summer's Heat)* (1851-59, City Museum and Art Gallery, Birmingham). It is a fascinating work, 'painted', according to the artist, 'almost entirely in sunlight.' But again, as with the wet white ground, one wonders if this can really be the case, since the picture was on his easel from 1851 to 1859. Nor can Mrs Brown have been in the habit of wearing every day such an elaborate eighteenth-

Ford Madox Brown (1821-93)
The Pretty Baa-Lambs (Summer's Heat), 1851-59. Oil on panel. (24 × 30″). By courtesy of the City Museum and Art Gallery, Birmingham.

century gown with quilted under-skirt, similar to the one worn by Nelly O'Brien and rendered by Brown with painstaking care, square by square, skilfully and minutely recording the irregular relief of the quilting – which in itself sufficiently accounts for the time it took him. The two figures of mother and child outlined against the sky are curiously tall, the monumental effect being emphasized by the crouching figure of the maid picking grass. No Flemish master would have carried his brushwork to this point of minuteness, and Palmer himself, intent on rendering the double character of grass in sunlight, would not have gone so far in individualizing each blade of grass. Brown did not hesitate to give the summer sky a violet tinge, to rub the face and arms of the servant maid with red, to bring out the green with an emphasis that makes Constable's green seem dim and hackneyed: the result is realism carried by sheer boldness to the level of super-reality. One takes real pleasure in lingering over each detail, a lamb's fleece or a tree, and each touch of colour: the three or four blues in the same piece of material, varying with the impact of the light. Though Ruskin had something to say about Hunt's *Our English Coasts*, he never, so far as I know, paid tribute to this astonishing hymn to nature. Perhaps it was because he saw that Brown was abandoning religious, symbolical, allegorical, edifying painting. Witness Brown's own, almost aggressive statements concerning *The Pretty Baa-Lambs*: 'Few people, I trust, will seek for any meaning beyond the obvious one... I should be much inclined to doubt the genuineness of that artist's ideas who never painted from love of the mere look of things, whose mind was always on the stretch for a moral. This picture was painted out in the sunlight; the only intention being to render that effect as well as my powers in a first attempt of that kind would allow.'

In 1852, when the Pre-Raphaelite Brotherhood still had a community sense, Thomas Woolner, the sculptor, one of the seven Pre-Raphaelites, emigrated to Australia and his departure was keenly felt by all. It was commemorated by Brown in *The Last of England* (1852-55, Birmingham), depicting the artist and his wife as emigrants. In its rendering of the sad light of an overcast day and the precise effect it has on things, it is almost the counterpart of *The Pretty Baa-Lambs*. 'To insure the peculiar look of *light all round* which objects have on a dull day at sea, it was painted for the most part in the open air on dull days, and, when the flesh was being painted, on cold days. Absolutely without regard to the art of any period or country, I have tried to render this scene as it would appear.'

Brown had advanced beyond such fragmented, divergent compositions as his *Chaucer*. The background figures in *The Last of England* hardly count, and the couple in the foreground occupy nearly the whole picture, the husband with brooding gaze and tight lips, the wife sad and resigned, framed by a tilted umbrella. The Woolners having left England in 1852, they were of course unable to pose for the emigrants, who in fact are portraits of Brown and his wife. They convey extremely well the feelings of two departing exiles. They sit hand in hand: each, one feels, is now all in all to the other. They are muffled up against the chill sea air, which seems to strike at their very heart. Behind them, but like a store of meanings held in reserve which have to be sought out, and which constitute the social background of this emigration scene, one catches sight of a fist raised against the ungrateful mother country and a careless pipe.

The Hayfield (1855, Collection John Gillum) is an attempt, and perhaps a successful one, to repeat the exploit of *The Pretty Baa-Lambs*, in the way of chromatic intensity and vivid

Ford Madox Brown (1821-93)
The Hayfield, 1855. Oil on panel. (9 × 12 ½″). Collection John Gillum, Esq.

open-air effects. Brown himself explained that he had been fascinated by the contrast between the pink hay and green grass in the fading light of evening. One is chiefly struck by the touches of red and carmine. One of the horses is painted a forthright red, and so, apparently, is a head of hair in the wagon. The green of the grass has taken on an even deeper tone than in *The Pretty Baa-Lambs*. Brown preferred to paint the trees light brown in order to heighten the intensity of that green. This, undoubtedly, is an imagined pattern of colours, not an imitation of the actual tones of nature. The light is still bright, even though the full moon has already risen in the sky. Were it not for the sensible restraint with which that light is handled (though it does go beyond the closeness to nature of Linnell, for example), one would be reminded at once of Palmer and his *Gleaners (The Harvest Moon)*. The hay wagon and its team are not without a reminiscence of Constable, whose naturalism, however, was not to Brown's liking.

Carrying Corn (1854, Tate Gallery) is an evening landscape, but with daylight still vivid, dimming the full moon and throwing an intense band of green shadow across the foreground; beyond it is a bright band of green and at the back, towards the horizon, are hayricks, a wagon, a curtain of trees and a red-roofed farmhouse. This energy and splendour throws Palmer's fields into the shade.

Like the idealists of a period marked by technical progress, economic inequality and grinding poverty, and like Carlyle in particular, Brown was fully conscious of the social evils of his time, and that responsiveness underlies his glorification of work, workers and their friends. *Work* (1852-63, Manchester) is one of his most brilliant paintings. It enables one to gauge the progress he had made since his *Chaucer* with its incoherent massing of figures. It matters little that one cannot quite make out all the action of all the figures in a picture which John Rothenstein has likened, not without exaggeration, to a chapter of Zola. Everyone is in his due place, and the composition is astonishingly firm, with light and air circulating freely. One is only surprised that the workmen can get much done with so many children and dogs in the way. Constable, whose mills would obviously go round, would doubtless have told Brown that nothing in his picture functions properly: it is not a document, no more than Hogarth's *Beer Street* was, which in fact it brings to mind in its robustness, vigour and optimism. Social criticism is by no means absent. The ragged, barefoot flower girl is followed by fine ladies in crinolines and behind are a lady and gentleman on horseback. But what superb workmen! What arms, legs and muscles! Society people are there all right, but more important is the presence, as sympathetic observers of human toil, of the thinkers who were striving to build an England where it had its due place: Carlyle and F. D. Maurice, portrayed on the far right. Maurice, a leader of the Christian Socialist movement, had , with Madox Brown's active co-operation, founded the Working Men's College, where instruction in drawing and design was given free of charge by established artists, anyhow by the Pre-Raphaelites and their friends, including Brown. *Work* is a strongly and broadly coloured composition; the usual high-pitched tonality is dominated by reds and whites or near-whites, these bright but, as often with Brown, rather crude colours being set off by the dark notes of the two figures on horseback and the mass of trees in the background. Wishing there to be no mistake about the social (and socializing) intentions of the picture, he published an explanatory pamphlet to accompany it. There was nothing hypocritical or heartless about Brown; during a particularly severe winter, he installed a soup kitchen for the poor in his own home. He was a friend of William Morris, whose great object was to narrow the gap between art and life, and for the firm founded by Morris, Brown designed stained-glass windows and furniture. Then he fell back on history painting, and from 1878 until his death in 1893 he worked on twelve large wall paintings for the town hall of Manchester, recording the history of the city from Roman times; these, however, lack the vitality of his previous work.

English painting in the 1840s was at a particularly low ebb and the fact that painters of little or no talent won public acclaim not surprisingly aroused the indignation of younger artists. For example, a painter of modest abilities and insufficient sincerity like Daniel Maclise (1806-70) enjoyed great success with such works as the *Banquet Scene in Macbeth* (1840), whose unreal composition, much more theatrical than Shakespeare gave any warrant for, and unreal lighting, much more artificial than is justified by the torches allegedly providing it, passed unnoticed, while its fine monumentality and classical gestures aroused enthusiasm. The Pre-Raphaelites could not abide Maclise.

In 1847 William Holman Hunt and Dante Gabriel Rossetti, both students at the Royal Academy, often met and worked together in the studio of the youngest and doubtless most brilliant of the three, John Everett Millais. There they discussed the principles of their art. They took as their text or pretext Raphael's *Transfiguration*. 'We condemned it', wrote Holman Hunt in his history of the movement published nearly sixty years later, 'for its grandiose disregard of the simplicity of truth, the pompous posturing of the Apostles, and the unspiritual attitudinizing of the Saviour.'[46] In their eyes, this picture marked 'a signal step in the decadence of Italian art'. Raphael was thereby made responsible for the Bolognese (Carracci, Guido Reni, Guercino), as also for Giulio Romano and all the lesser lights of academic art. 'Then', their fellow students concluded, 'you are Pre-Raphaelite.'

Their criticism was both historical and theoretical. From Italy they passed on to England and came to Reynolds. As Hunt said:

> Of course, we have got some deucedly gifted masters... but I think they suffer from the fact that the English School began the last century without the discipline of exact manipulation. Sir Joshua Reynolds thought it expedient to take the Italian School at its proudest climax as a starting-point for English art... the parts of a picture which gave him no scope for his generosity were of little interest to him. Under his reign came into vogue drooping branches of brown trees over a night-like sky, or a column with a curtain unnaturally arranged, as a background to a day-lit portrait...

This in effect is one episode in the great Romantic revolt against established rules, a rather clamorous, belated and, it may seem, pointless revolt, for little had been seen of night-like skies for three-quarters of a century, nor of brown trees, in spite of Sir George Beaumont. Could the young iconoclasts have confused Reynolds and the Hogarth of the *Analysis*? In any case, Hunt denounced a number of 'rules': that figures should form an S-curve, that the composition should be pyramidal, that the highest light should always be on the main figure, that one corner of the picture must be in shadow. Hunt even attacked the gradation of colours. Yet he knew well enough that rules have never been a check to the creative artist, since he noted that 'what gave charm to Wilson's works was his departure from the examples of the classical painters whose general manner he affected.' Whatever the case with men of exceptional gifts, 'the last fifty years... have proved that his [i.e. Reynolds'] teaching was interpreted as encouragement to unoriginality of treatment, and neglect of that delicate rendering of nature, which had led previous schools to greatness.'

Looking more closely, one realizes that what the young painters chiefly deplored in their attack against academicism was the degradation of taste, the widespread preference for bad painting, the popularity of an artist like Maclise, the fact that in contemporary English painting everything seemed designed for a stage peopled with mediocre actors incapable of expressing the straightforward realities of life. The reaction against this sort of thing on the part of Hunt and his friends, though it was not to last, was all to the good. Wilkie and his peers, so much admired by Delacroix and Géricault, had come to form what might be called the school of expressive features. It was time to protest against a general phenomenon: insincerity, faulty craftsmanship, lifeless posing, artificial lighting, conventional effects and repeated imitations.

Though Hogarth was the inventor of an aesthetic system (and thus by its very nature an impediment), these young painters, probably without realizing it, were at one with him in protesting against cosmopolitanism and the vogue enjoyed by foreign artists. As Hunt pointed out, Gustave Doré had been praised to the skies in England and gained such popularity as to make a fortune there, while doing so much to corrupt English taste, and this at a time when Madox Brown was reduced to penury.

The group had barely been formed when it drew Ruskin into its orbit, and not by chance, for he and they shared a like concern for the moral basis of art. This needs to be emphasized, because the movement had hardly got under way when it was involved in contradictions, and because what is sometimes called Pre-Raphaelitism represents, it must be said, a purely aesthetic deviation running from Rossetti to Burne-Jones. The Pre-Raphaelites stood, to begin with, not only for conscious artistic aims but for social awareness. This was another aspect of their critique of academicism and academicians. Modern practice, they maintained, led to an alienation of the student, who in the past had been an apprentice and who as such had had a constant personal relationship with the master, superseded now by an aloof, impersonal system of teaching and correcting. It was important to imbue art with a revived sense of community life and a new respect for sound craftsmanship, making this a means of uplifting the soul. Such aims fell in well with those of Carlyle and Ruskin, and there was obviously but one source for the ultimate models: the Middle Ages and the creators of Gothic.

Hunt's piety was peculiar to himself: the group desired to base the renovation of art on the Christian virtues but not on revelation. 'Once, in a studio conclave', wrote Hunt, 'some of us drew up a declaration that there was no immortality for humanity except that which was gained by man's own genius or heroism.' Hunt and Rossetti thereupon compiled a list of Immortals, extending from Jesus Christ to Tennyson and Ary Scheffer, and including Raphael, Titian, Tintoretto, Poussin, Hogarth, Flaxman, Haydon and (oddly enough) Wilkie. The group had its maxims and principles: 'death to slosh' (i.e. 'Sloshua' Reynolds), no smoking, drinking or swearing, etc. There were seven of them, as in every Pleiad: William Holman Hunt (1827-1910), Dante Gabriel Rossetti (1828-82), John Everett Millais (1829-96) and those who are usually overlooked, James Collinson, Thomas Woolner, Frederic George Stephens and William Michael Rossetti. The brotherhood was founded in the autumn of 1848 and it was agreed that the members would sign their works 'PRB'.

One is struck by the movement's air of launching a small reformation – the point always being to react against a subsequent corruption and return to a previous purity, to the authenticity of innocence. Corruption had set in with the intellectualism of the High Renaissance and its aristocratic art. So a return to earlier times had to be made. Millais had been lent a book of engravings of the Campo Santo frescoes in Pisa, whose 'innocent spirit' delighted them, and they determined on a 'kindred simplicity'. 'We appraised as Chaucerian', wrote Hunt, 'the sweet humour of Benozzo Gozzoli.' Then too, perhaps even more important, there were the Flemish masters, offering the example of Jan van Eyck's Arnolfini portrait. Such a return to the sources provided a sound basis for principles. These were formulated by William Michael Rossetti, who was not himself a painter and whose devotion was such that in retrospect he seems to have lived only for his brother's sake. He summed up the aims of the group as follows: '1, To have genuine ideas to express; 2, to study

Nature attentively, so as to know how to express them; 3, to sympathize with what is direct and serious and heartfelt in previous art, to the exclusion of what is conventional and self-parading and learned by rote; 4, and most indispensable of all, to produce thoroughly good pictures and statues.'

Hunt was even more categorical, anyhow in the statements he made in his book *Pre-Raphaelitism and the Pre-Raphaelite Brotherhood*, which was published in 1905. According to him, their work was meant to be derived from nature more systematically than anything before it, and he maintained that the poetry of painting would not be destroyed by a close pursuit of the beauty of nature. Hunt admitted that their extremely minute rendering was meant to some extent as a demonstration, and that as such it may at first have been excessive, for they felt that such careful delineation was essential to train the artist's eye and hand. They were critical of the aristocratic choices that governed the artistic motivations of Reynolds. One is tempted to say that the Pre-Raphaelites anticipated a democratic art in which no privileges obtain, and for which early painting, whatever its apparent subject, provided an example. The bright manner of the early Renaissance had to be rediscovered.

Turning now to the matter of technique (and bearing in mind that, as with Constable and his natural painting, one convention is never destroyed but by another, contrary convention), it is clear that a distinction must be made between the resolve to keep close to nature and the resolve to heighten the tonality of oil painting after the example of watercolour. Hunt, from the outset, was intent on these two points. A pupil of Wilkie's explained to him how his master had painted *The Blind Fiddler* without any priming coat – 'without any dead colouring, finishing each bit thoroughly in the day.' Hunt copied the picture and adopted the method. This led to a consideration of fresco painting, which allows of no retouching and each part of which has to be painted quickly on a damp working surface which, once it has dried, is unusable. Retouching was regarded as a practice of academic art.

With the Pre-Raphaelites and their friends, one can distinguish between what might be called the ideal technique and the habitual technique. The latter included the white ground; the former was more demanding. In principle, the outlines were drawn on the canvas; then a thin coat of white paint was laid over it, all superfluous oil being removed by means of absorbent paper, and the outlines generally showing through. The colours, as transparent as possible, were applied to this coat while it was still wet. Bitumen was of course ruled out, and copal varnish enabled small, sharp touches of colour to be inserted in shadows. The first object was brilliance of colour, and in practice it meant giving a dangerous importance to local colours. After all, it was the observation of nature which had led painters, in the course of generations, to invent tonal perspective and the atmospheric veil. Probably because of a certain habit of looking at pictures, the eye is surprised to find neither in the early works of the Pre-Raphaelites, which represent the most categorical statement of their principles.

Millais had his fine gifts at his finger tips whatever he did, Hunt had his will-power, and Rossetti his imagination and his enthusiasm (as the son of a Carbonaro) for setting up more or less secret societies. It was he apparently who initiated the Pre-Raphaelite Brotherhood; and it was he – more spontaneously a writer and poet than a painter – who in 1849 proposed the launching of a periodical in which to set forth their ideas. Oddly named *The*

Germ, it included the poet Coventry Patmore among its contributors. The first issue appeared on 1 January 1850; there were only four issues in all, the third and fourth appearing with the less extravagant title of *Art and Poetry*.

The brotherhood appeared before the public with works signed PRB at the Royal Academy exhibition of 1849. Hunt showed his *Rienzi*, a solid piece of history painting but also a demonstration of their intentions and the first picture in accordance with the principles of Quattrocento art and with his own resolve to paint everything in the open air and sunlight, entirely doing away with brown foliage, smoky clouds and dark corners. There was a fig tree in it, and this he had painted 'in full sunlight, with what was then unprecedented exactness', in the garden of F.G. Stephens's father at Lambeth. 'In the foreground I painted also a patch of grass with dandelion puffs and blossoms, and over one of these last a bumble-bee hovered... Instead of the meaningless spread of whitey brown which usually served for the near ground, I represented gravelly variations and pebbles, all diverse in tints and shapes as found in Nature.' Background and faces were painted at Hampstead. 'They were done thus directly and frankly, not merely for the charm of minute finish, but as a means of studying more deeply Nature's principles of design, and to escape the conventional treatment of landscape backgrounds.' For the shields and spears he went with his canvas to the Tower of London. The Rossetti brothers and Millais sat for the figures. The members of the brotherhood had determined to avoid professional models.

Millais, in 1849, exhibited *Lorenzo and Isabella* (a subject from Keats, who was then all the fashion), showing for the first time the versatility which flawed the genius he very nearly had. A brightly coloured painting on a white ground was called for? Nothing simpler. A meticulous rendering true to nature? Each figure would portray a friend or relation, and Rossetti himself is in the picture lifting his glass at the end of the table. Historical truth? Rossetti, as it happened, had just given him an album of medieval costumes. There remained the all-important question of style. Millais brought off a veritable pastiche of primitivism; the schematized gesture of the outstretched leg in the foreground, kicking the dog, is characteristic.

Rossetti exhibited *The Girlhood of Mary Virgin* (1849, Tate Gallery), but not at the Royal Academy; whether his friends suspected his motives in showing at the Free Exhibition at Hyde Park Corner is not known, but the inventor of the Brotherhood had made the first move which would end in the break-up of the group. The picture, painted under the direction (one is tempted to say the control) of Holman Hunt, is exquisite. Keeping to a classical design, a balanced, pyramidal construction, it is at once faithful to the principles newly laid down and characteristic of the painter's early manner. The freshness and blue-mauve accent of the colouring in the left-hand side of the picture has the charm of majolica; the play of reds, from the angel's wings to Mary's embroidery, is curiously successful, marking off the gravity of colour and expression of the right-hand group. Rossetti never again painted such fine faces as those of his sister Christina as Mary and his mother as St Anne. Everything is in right angles, as if to emphasize an essential rectitude.

All these pictures were well received and found purchasers. In 1850 Rossetti exhibited his *Ecce Ancilla Domini (The Annunciation)*; again he exhibited separately and the picture does not bear the PRB monogram. There is no further reference here to the gothic style, and one could hardly imagine a fresher interpretation of a traditional subject. The angel, seen from behind with face in profile, stands close to Mary, who shrinks back on her bed, and seems to impose the lily and the tidings on her. There remain none of the details which in the previous picture marked his adhesion to the group, neither in the furniture nor the decoration nor the leafage (whose framing function in *The Girlhood* was characteristic). The angel's robe falls in straight stiff folds; he has no wings. The colouring has a paradoxical boldness. The white of robes, bed, floor and walls is but faintly tinged with grey; all this is set off by a light blue rectangle behind the Virgin; the same narrow, vertical embroidery frame as in the previous picture appears here, the lilies being now finally embroidered. The painter's judgment or instinct has avoided matching the blue with an outspoken red; the strip of embroidery has become carmine, and this rectangle has been ingeniously placed at a sharply receding angle; the eye indeed needed to be reminded that the picture had depth, a third dimension. Just as it is, with this minimum of pictorial devices, the picture is delight-ful. Rossetti had no respect for his painting and one day in a cynical mood (such as often visited him) he referred to it scathingly as 'that white daub'. Whistler would have made it into a symphony in white.

Sir John Everett Millais (1829-96)

Christ in the House of his Parents (The Carpenter's Shop), 1850. Oil on canvas. (34 × 55″).

Tate Gallery, London.

Hunt in 1850 exhibited a canvas as edifying as its title: *A Converted British Family Sheltering a Christian Priest from the Druids* (Ashmolean Museum, Oxford). Here again is the meticulous attention to every detail of the external world, to the 'true' aspect of objects, which I have noted before. This 'truth to nature' does not exclude, indeed it calls for rather, an overlay of symbolism, and as Hunt explained the vine and corn were introduced to suggest the civilizing influence of divine religion. For all its profusion of objects painted from nature, it seems to me that it would be difficult to do anything more bogus than this picture with its stage-set hut sheltering a group of figures whose dramatic poses are hardly more convincing than those of Maclise.

Millais, who had begun with *Lorenzo and Isabella*, resigned himself now to doing something in the religious way like everyone else and his picture of 1850 was *Christ in the House of his Parents (The Carpenter's Shop)* (Tate Gallery). If one accepts at face value what meets the eye, this is perhaps the most moving and imaginative picture produced in the course of the Pre-Raphaelite campaign. There is nothing here of Holman Hunt's naïve grandiloquence and awkward agitation. The design has the simplicity of near-symmetry: Joseph and John the Baptist on one side, St Anne behind the work-bench and the journeyman opposite Joseph, these four figures framing the central group of Virgin and Child. The latter, exactly as tall as the kneeling Virgin, raises his hand (and Joseph, leaning over from behind, pulls back the fingers) to show that it has been wounded. Jesus has his back turned on Joseph, but while his face is held against his mother's, he nevertheless turns away from her and holds his arm in front of his body in a gesture of separation – a most effective device. The Virgin's face (standing out like that of Jesus against a set of carpenter's tools) shows an anguished tenderness which knits the eyebrows and wrinkles the forehead. In the colouring, there is no attempt to innovate: these are the reds, blue and dark green of the Quattrocento.

This is probably Millais's masterpiece. Writing in *Household Words*, the popular magazine which he then edited, here is what Dickens, the inspired spokesman of the British middle class, had to say about it:

'In the foreground of that carpenter's shop is a hideous, wry-necked, blubbering, red-haired boy in a night-gown who appears to have received a poke in the hand from the stick of another boy with whom he has been playing in an adjacent gutter, and to be holding it up for the contemplation of a kneeling woman, so horrible in her ugliness that (supposing it were possible for any human creature to exist for a moment with that dislocated throat) she would stand out from the rest of the company as a monster in the vilest cabaret in France, or the lowest gin shop in England.' The critic of *The Athenaeum* savaged with generous impartiality all three pictures by Hunt, Rossetti and Millais, for it was now realized that they were in revolt against the taste of the day.

Millais, however, was not disposed to take it lying down. He appealed to the poet Coventry Patmore, who was associated with the movement, and urged him to enlist the support of Ruskin, who had so brilliantly and effectively defended Turner; Millais pointed out that the Pre-Raphaelites had taken their cue from *Modern Painters*. And indeed in the first two volumes Ruskin lashed out at the docile acceptance of the established masters and their conventions. He even suggested a return to the Italian artists who had lived before the time of Raphael, such as Cima, Fra Angelico and Ghirlandaio, whose works reflected their faithful love of the object studied. The second volume again spoke highly of the Florentine primitives, Giotto, Orcagna, Gozzoli, noting that for them there was no lowly object but a revelation in all things. Ruskin had thus been instrumental in bringing the primitives into fashion. He had made a strong impresssion on Hunt. Ruskin could hardly refuse to help his followers. He accordingly wrote two letters to *The Times*; in that of 13 May 1851 he vigorously defended the practice and proficiency of the Pre-Raphaelites, while regretting the choice of a name for the movement. For, as he reminded his readers (in a note added to *Modern Painters* in 1851), 'the principles on which its members are working are neither pre- nor post-Raphaelite, but everlasting. They are endeavouring to paint, with the highest possible degree of completion, what they see in nature, without reference to conventional or established rules.'

It was time for things to change, and luckily they did, for just when Hunt was almost penniless, in October 1851, the Liverpool Academy awarded him its prize of fifty pounds, with a place of honour for his *Two Gentlemen of Verona*. In the spring of 1852 Millais's *Ophelia* and Hunt's *Hireling Shepherd* were hung well on the line at the Royal Academy exhibition. Millais later paid tribute to Thackeray who, he said, 'sympathized and spurred me on when I was dreadfully bullied.' The movement was now well under way, but in fact once it had come into the open the lack of any real collective impulse made itself felt. By 1853 Rossetti was falling away, Millais had got an intoxicating foretaste of academic success and Hunt was off in the Holy Land in search of the Truth that overlays all truth.

Ruskin's two letters to *The Times* were followed by a seventy-eight-page pamphlet entitled *Pre-Raphaelitism*. He paid tribute to what he regarded as the movement's salutary reaction against the evils and vices handed down (according to him) by the Renaissance schools of art: 'indolence, infidelity, sensuality, and shallow pride'. He had seized the opportunity, which Turner, as too well-established an artist, had been unable to give him, of influencing living art; and having saved the Pre-Raphaelite movement he proceeded to give it a doctrine, earnest and demanding. He urged the artists to paint 'stern facts' rather than 'fair pictures', to return not to 'archaic art' but to 'archaic honesty'. 'Go to nature in all singleness of heart, and walk with her laboriously and trustingly, having no other thoughts but how best to penetrate her meaning, and remember her instruction; rejecting nothing, selecting nothing, and scorning nothing.' One is at a loss to understand how he reconciled such precepts with the practice of Turner. He further urged the Pre-Raphaelites to 'paint nature as it is around them, with the help of modern science.' It is not very clear what that meant either, but he encouraged the painters to take up geology; anyhow the key word here is 'modern'. He opposed 'archaic honesty' to 'archaic art': he feared that the movement might lapse into medievalism and, in consequence, into Romanism – that is, Catholicism. Hunt should have been the man for him, but Ruskin in spite of himself, in spite of his moral rigour, was only interested in genius. By a painful paradox, it was in Rossetti that he found it.

Such were the great days of the Pre-Raphaelite campaign. I have dealt with it collectively because it has seemed to me that in this phase the militant and collective aspect takes precedence. Now it is necessary to consider these painters separately.

William Holman Hunt (1827-1910), son of the manager of a city warehouse, was brought up in an austere Protestant home. His father encouraged his artistic tastes as an

William Holman Hunt (1827-1910)

The Hireling Shepherd, 1851. Oil on canvas. (30 ⅛ × 43 ⅛″). City of Manchester Art Galleries.

amusement but not as a profession and placed him at the age of twelve in an estate agent's office. By perseverance and hard work, however, Hunt got his way and entered the Royal Academy schools in 1844. There he met Millais who, more precocious and more advanced, probably helped to open and broaden his mind. But it was Hunt who had discovered Keats, despite the fact that the poet was no moralizer. His first notable work was *The Flight of Madeline and Porphyro* (1848, Guildhall, London), from *The Eve of St Agnes*, the story of two lovers who had lost no time in enjoying their happiness. But Hunt felt obliged to foist a puritanical interpretation on the poem: to him it illustrated 'the sacredness of honest responsible love and the weakness of proud intemperance' (admittedly the watchman was dead drunk). Already in February 1848 he was intent on painting from nature as much as possible; the bloodhounds in his picture he painted from a pair owned by a friend. In 1850, after his *Christian Priest Sheltered from the Druids*, he went on from Keats to Shakespeare and painted *Claudio and Isabella* in the prison (Tate Gallery), from *Measure for Measure*.

He sought out an old prison in which to work, a window beside which to hang a lute and in which to place a man in order to gauge the exact degree of light impinging upon him. The effect of reflected back-lighting on Claudio's face and crimson doublet is significant and successful. The stiffness of the two figures is a fault that Hunt never quite overcame. It is distressing in his *Two Gentlemen of Verona* (1851) and noticeable in *The Hireling Shepherd* of the same year; but the latter, not being dramatic, suffers little from it and is perhaps Hunt's masterpiece.

The subject is to be found in the shepherd's hand: he is holding a death's-head moth and showing it to his companion as a bad omen. Hunt is not Wilkie and the necessity of imparting expression to a face obviously cost him an effort; he could not always be painting

William Holman Hunt (1827-1910)

Our English Coasts (Strayed Sheep), 1852. Oil on canvas. (17 × 23″).

Tate Gallery, London.

figures who, like Claudio, stand in a jail in back-lighting. The shepherd is meant to be seen as uneasy; his companion, more successfully, as disdainful. As one might expect, the negligent shepherd and his moth are the object not of an anecdote but of a moral – 'a rebuke to the sectarian vanities and vital negligencies of the day.' He is a type (in Hunt's own words) of the 'muddle-headed pastors who instead of performing their services to their flock – which is in constant peril – discuss vain questions of no value to any human soul. My fool has found a Death's Head Moth, and this fills his little mind with forebodings of evil, and he takes it to an equally sage counsellor for her opinion. She scorns his anxiety from ignorance rather than profundity, but only the more distracts his faithfulness. While she feeds her lamb with sour apples, his sheep have burst bounds and got into the corn.' Hunt is a curious figure indeed, intent with unremitting diligence on representing the world of appearances, and yet seeing no more of it than the veil of reality. His plea was that his symbolism must be distinguished from allegory, that his meaning was reserved for those alone who could be induced to decipher it. His prime object here, as he expressly stated, was 'to paint, not Dresden china bergers, but a real shepherd, and a real shepherdess, and a landscape in full sunlight, with all the colour of luscious summer.'

One may therefore forget about symbolism and admire the intensely tangible and sensual reality of this couple. The moral behind *The Hireling Shepherd* is the price one has to pay for a picture which is as good as the *Christian Priest Sheltered from the Druids* was bad, a picture in which his stated intention of rendering actual daylight with the strictest accuracy is fully achieved. In its correspondence with the external world, the picture has none of the fascinating excess of a Ford Madox Brown. The mown field stretching away behind the trees on the left is delightfully satisfying in its measured accuracy, while at the same time bringing to mind the fields behind *Mr and Mrs Andrews*. The intensity of the green shadows is resolutely modern, yet not without a certain restraint.

But most of the critics of that day felt the same way as Dickens. Just as Millais's Virgin, in *The Carpenter's Shop*, struck them as a slum girl, so did this shepherd and shepherdess seem to bear in their blotchy faces all the tell-tale signs of habitual drinking. One critic, more technically minded, noted that faces and arms were stippled with the painstaking care of a miniaturist and coloured as if they had fed on too many raspberries. To this *Shepherd* must be added a complementary work, *Our English Coasts (Strayed Sheep)* of 1852. Here too, in a high-pitched tonality proclaiming the glow of sunlight, the intensification of the colours partakes of an ultra-realism which is the vehicle of symbolism. Here, however, I would not say that this intensity is accompanied by either restraint or any particular accuracy, in spite of Ruskin's claim that this picture 'showed to us, for the first time in the history of art, the absolutely faithful balances of colour and shade by which actual sunlight might be transposed.' In *The Light of the World* (1851-56), which was based on a text in Revelation ('Behold, I stand at the door, and knock'), the obsession with accessories was carried to a point verging on the grotesque. Hunt was led to paint diligently in the moonlight, to construct a lantern, to install a false door in his studio, etc. The picture has certainly found a better resting place in a special chapel adjoining Keble College at Oxford than its replica has in the City of Manchester Art Galleries.

In 1853 the series of edifying pictures was continued with the famous *Awakening Conscience*, exhibited at the Royal Academy in 1854 with pious quotations from Ecclesiastes and Isaiah. A kept woman sitting on the lap of her paramour suddenly rises to her feet, her face expressing, or being meant to express, her horror on hearing him sing a song that reminds her of the days of her lost innocence.[47] Outright allegory would have been preferable to this profusion of symbols, from the cat tormenting a bird to the gilded tapestry. And allegory he proceeds to produce in the astonishing *Scapegoat* of 1854. Being in Palestine, he bought himself a white goat, which he took out to the Dead Sea. There the animal died. Returning to Jerusalem, he bought another. Having brought back some salt and mud from the Dead Sea, he spread them on a platform and got the goat to tread in it. The resulting picture has a sinister power which one would not have expected him to obtain by such means. It is not only the utter solitude suggested by the goat standing alone in this bleak landscape shut in by a range of mountains beyond the thick water, full of fragments of floating skeletons; it is also the utter sense of an inescapable malediction, which makes flight and movement impossible: the guilty beast is arrested in an everlasting trance. Hunt recounts that he had thought of proposing the subject to Landseer; which seems to justify the parallel which I have drawn between Hunt's *Scapegoat* and Landseer's *Challenge*.

Hunt was a painter and remained so, one might say, in spite of himself. So that a comprehensive exhibition of his works, like that held at the Victoria and Albert Museum in 1969, is full of happy surprises, at almost every period of his career. One such, a compound of subtle technique and naïve vision, is the *Festival at Fiesole*, a watercolour of 1868, its composition dominated by the lone figure of the little boy with his drum facing the strolling ladies and the military band. This work shows Hunt's usual intensity of lighting, together with an unexpected effect of sunlight filtering through the leafage.

Hunt was too faithful to what he saw and at the same time too much concerned with the transparency of spiritual things not to be a good portraitist. His portrait of *Rossetti* (Birmingham) is a fine example of his powers. Today, however, in the renewed appreciation of his work in England, there seems to be some danger of overrating him. What he does deserve and, it seems to me, has failed to receive as yet, is full recognition as the leader of a movement whose principles, as laid down by Ruskin, he alone adhered to with obstinate fidelity; the history of that movement, however, worked itself out without him, following the deviation marked out by Rossetti.

John Everett Millais (1829-96), though undoubtedly a greater painter, is of less interest here, having availed himself of the movement rather than serving it; in spite of his close friendship with Hunt, he does not represent its true spirit. He is one of the most precocious painters of all time, winning a silver medal at nine, entering the Royal Academy schools at ten and winning a gold medal at seventeen. By 1851 he had ceased to take his Pre-Raphaelite commitment seriously. The story has often been told of the picture called *The Huguenot* (1851-52), which originally was meant to represent only a pair of lovers whispering by a garden wall (suggested by a Tennyson poem). But for the dramatic justification, it would be no more than a sentimental vignette. By combining the lovers' meeting with a hint of religious persecution, he secured for it the privileged status attached to history painting. The picture came first, then the subject, for which he cast about a good while: Millais 'paused a moment', wrote Hunt. '"I have got it," he said – "the Huguenots."' He was fond of associating himself with a poet: in 1851 he painted *The Woodman's Daughter*, after Coventry Patmore's *Tale of the Poor Maid*.

Ophelia (1852, Tate Gallery) is a work which has suffered from the assumption of insincerity that attaches to everything Millais did. It is not easy in the present case to decide where that insincerity lies. 'The combination of a Surrey stream and Elizabeth Siddal in the bath,' writes Leslie Parris sarcastically in the Tate Gallery booklet on *The Pre-Raphaelites*. But what more could he have done in the way of models, apart from procuring the actual body of a drowned woman? It may be said: he could have painted it all out of his head. But then it is the whole group that must be incriminated for its superstitious reliance on real models; if there is anything ridiculous in that, the ridicule attaches to Holman Hunt, whom Millais tamely followed, and it touches the painters more than their painting. With Millais, the gist of the matter lies elsewhere: *Lorenzo and Isabella*, *Christ in the House of his Parents* and *Ophelia* are three successive pictures, and in fact show three successive manners. Unmodelled, painted in flat tints, in an angular design, *Lorenzo and Isabella* is, if I may put it so, genuinely pseudo-primitive. *Ophelia* is genuinely Pre-Raphae-

Sir John Everett Millais (1829-96)

Ophelia, 1852. Oil on canvas. (30 × 44″). Tate Gallery, London.

lite, in accordance with Hunt's definitions, and not only because a model was found who would lie in a bathtub full of water. Ophelia is about to die in a green world of water irises and eglantines – the flowers which she had picked to give to the Queen, and which tinge her gown with blue, yellow, orange and red. She sings her last song as she floats in the water. Her role being what it is, there is simply no escaping from the stage, and it would have been labour lost for the artist to try and do something more natural. Elizabeth Siddal's fine features, copper-gold hair and milk-and-roses complexion were perfectly suited to pathos; but it does not seem possible to say that the execution is that of Millais alone. One feels that a very fine picture of 1851, *The Return of the Dove to the Ark* (Ashmolean Museum, Oxford), is even more alien to his personality. Everything here is governed by a chiaroscuro which sets off two hands, one holding the dove, and the sweet faces of two young girls, one of them wearing a kind of stole whose broad folds fall straight down, and which recalls the one worn by the angel in Rossetti's *Annunciation*.

The Huguenot was in the nature of a mystification which he did not see fit to repeat, for the public might have realized that he was making sport of it. There was no lack of pathetic subjects which would go down well enough with the Victorian middle class. Scotland plays in British history something of the part that the South plays in that of the United States: once it had been subdued, its heroism and fate touched and rent the heart. *The Order of Release* (1852-53, Tate Gallery) deals with a pathetic subject in the same broad manner as *The Return of the Dove*, but with a greater profusion of realistic details and the inevitable joyful dog, which ever since Opie and Gainsborough had been bounding from picture to picture to welcome its master. The young, barefoot Scotswoman, with her sleeping baby in her arms, hands the British jailer the paper which will restore her husband to her. The kilted Highlander with his arm in a sling, less spirited than his energetic wife, drops his head sadly on her shoulder. When the picture was exhibited at the Royal Academy in 1853, a police guard was required to protect it from the admiring crowd.

Art, Ruskin and Holman Hunt had decreed, was a matter of observing nature closely and rendering it accurately. William Bell Scott, a minor member of the Pre-Raphaelite circle, tells of an incident that shows pretty clearly what Millais's true attitude was. In Millais's rooms about 1849, Scott was examining a carefully detailed Italian print hanging on the wall, when Millais burst out: 'That's PRB enough, is it not? We haven't come up to that yet. But I for one won't try. It's all nonsense. Of course nature's nature, and art's art, isn't it?'

In saying that, he was undoubtedly right, and it is only fair to note that from 1853 to 1856 he was honestly trying to find himself and his art. But already it was clear that even in trying to find himself he was going astray, that he no longer had any serious idea of the 'serious idea' which William Michael Rossetti called for as the starting point of the work; he gradually replaced it by appealing, reassuring ideas acceptable to a positive, middle-class art. *The Rescue* of 1855 – firemen rescuing people from the flames – marks an early stage in his decline.

Sir John Everett Millais (1829-96)

Autumn Leaves, 1856. Oil on canvas. (41 × 29 ⅛"). City of Manchester Art Galleries.

In 1856, however, Millais could still paint two pictures which, though they no longer keep to the Pre-Raphaelite commandments, are none the less very fine works. One is *The Blind Girl*, a poor itinerant musician with her accordion on her lap, her beautiful face held up to catch some essence of the world around her, described by the little girl nestling against her, and of the bright double rainbow above, left by the shower that has just fallen. The accurate beauty of the landscape that lies about, unseen to her, is still worthy of the artist. The other, a final reflection of Hunt's vision but not of his manner, is *Autumn Leaves* (1856, City of Manchester Art Galleries). Hunt's vision, in other words a store of symbolism. But what does it amount to apart from the banal paradox of associating youth and budding life with dead leaves and the declining year? Four little girls stand gravely, in an atmosphere of suspense, around a heaped-up pyramid of dead leaves. Superbly posed, two upper-class girls in elegant blue gowns support the picture, like two pillars, with their imperious, almost symmetrical verticality, while two children of the people are entitled to form only a single vertical unit. They are the motionless, seemingly undecided spectators of the act solemnly performed by the tallest girl in the centre, as she throws more leaves on to the heap. The group is most effectively composed, and the girl in purple eating an apple and the girl in russet red have all the charm of a gravely expressive realism, on which, however, the picture depends less for its effect than on its intense colouring, its rich and resonant tonality: the deep blue of the gowns, the girls' hair, gleaming in the fading light of sunset, the brown leafage at the back, where the light is already extinguished, and the daringly intense blue of the landscape and the yellow sky. Here, in the heap of leaves, one finds almost for the last time in Millais that careful rendering of detail which was central to the Pre-Raphaelite creed. Becoming an associate member of the Academy, then a full academician, knighted and then elected president of the Academy, Sir John Everett Millais was buried in St Paul's Cathedral. The artist had died many years before.

Neither the puritanical Hunt nor the opportunistic Millais has much in him to appeal to the imagination. It is quite otherwise with Dante Gabriel Rossetti (1828-82), a man of dual endowment, ever torn between the two, a manifold and incomplete artist, probably a great poet, certainly not a great painter, yet a personality whose influence, curiously enough, was greater in the field of visual art than in poetry.

The son of an Italian exile, he lived in poetic communion with his private dream of Italy (which he never visited), knew and translated all the poetry of late medieval Italy culminating in Dante, with whom he tended to identify himself, at least with the Dante of the *Vita Nuova*, the great poet whose nature was tormented as much as sanctified by his love for Beatrice. It is the Dante legend, born of both his life and his writings, that forms the essential Italian source of the subjects and motifs of Rossetti's painting.

This Anglo-Italian, like an Italian-American of today, was proudly and passionately devoted to his adopted country and nationality. He left England only twice, on journeys to Paris in 1849 and 1864, and his comments on what he saw there are as insular as those of Hogarth. He dismissed Manet's pictures as being 'for the most part mere scrawls', and he

Dante Gabriel Rossetti (1828-82)
The Girlhood of Mary Virgin, 1849. Oil on canvas. (32¾ × 25¾"). Tate Gallery, London.

thought Courbet's 'not much better'. Writing to Swinburne, he summed up his impression of French painting in these words: 'A beastly slop and really makes one sick.' To his mother he describes it as 'simply putrescence and decomposition'. He was scandalized by the Cancan, and bewailed the fact that he had not seen half a dozen pretty girls during his stay in Paris. Yet his Mediterranean ancestry left its mark on him in the shape of an unbridled sensuality. The women in his life were all-important to him, haunted his mind and inspired him with an obsession for lips, hair and jewellery that bordered on fetishism. Mrs Gaskell described him as 'hair-mad'. Though no puritan, he was very much of an idealist and could

Dante Gabriel Rossetti (1828-82)
Dantis Amor, 1859. Oil on panel. (29½ × 32″). Tate Gallery, London.

never be happy in love; it was always accompanied by guilt, remorse and anxiety. All these things, forever stirring in his imagination, entered into his imagery. One English source of his romantic medievalizing was Malory's *Morte d'Arthur*, which he knew as well as he did Dante, and the Arthurian legend was rich enough in passions and guilty loves for him to project himself into it without difficulty or restraint. The result was a body of work that is symbolical but by no means allegorical.

Born and brought up in London, he hesitated already in his childhood between two muses. For a time, at King's College School, John Sell Cotman was his drawing master. At nineteen, he bought for ten shillings a now famous manuscript of William Blake, who remained a more or less discernible inspiration behind his own poetry. As early as 1844 he saw and admired some works by Ford Madox Brown: they revealed to him the extent to which painting, to which colour, could be used as a means of expressing emotion. He accordingly chose painting in preference to poetry as a career. Hampered by lack of technical skill, he applied to Brown for lessons, but Brown set him to copying pickle jars and medicine bottles. Rossetti was not the man to bear such discipline for long and he soon left. He met Hunt, who continued to impose on him the exacting study of inert models, even though human this time. Under Hunt's direction he painted the *Girlhood of Mary Virgin* (1849, Tate Gallery), then broke free. He came under the spell of the Pre-Raphaelite doctrine just long enough to attempt one work entirely in keeping with its articles of faith, though it was an effort that went very much against the grain of his nature as a painter. This was *Found*, begun in 1854 and never finished. The theme is that of a country girl turned prostitute in London. A farmer, bringing a calf to town, recognizes her, jumps from his cart and runs towards her. The fallen woman cringes at the sight of him, just as Hunt's fallen woman rises up in horror, prompted by her awakening conscience and the realization of her sinful state. Rossetti and Hunt argued as to which of them had had the initial idea for this characteristic cliché of the Victorian age, which was taken up again in 1858 by Augustus Egg, a friend of Hunt's, in his triptych entitled *Past and Present*. What must be noted is that this sense of guilt, this association of sexual love with evil, this insistence on evaluating the sinfulness and doom of the prostitute, together with the sense of the fatal, ineluctable power of woman expressed in terms of a multiplicity of female divinities all equally mournful and cruel – all this is part and parcel of Rossetti's emotional sincerity and mental confusion.

To come back to *Found*. It was not the pathetic group of the farmer and the dishonoured girl that gave him trouble, it was the calf, shown under a net in the cart. It is true that he did not buy a calf to paint it from; he did, however, find a suitable brick wall to copy at Chiswick. Then a suitable calf and cart were found at Finchley, on a farm just opposite a tiny cottage occupied by Brown and his pregnant wife, who were then (November 1855) going through a difficult period of poverty and hardship. Nothing daunted, Rossetti moved in on them and his reluctant but good-natured host gave him a mattress on the parlour floor. He stayed for weeks, making a nuisance of himself and straining everybody's nerves. Brown noted sadly in his diary: 'He paints the calf in all like Albert Dürer, hair by hair, and seems incapable of any breadth... from want of habit I see nature bothers him.' Like Blake and Fuseli, he lived in a world of the imagination. After working on the picture intermittently for thirty years, he left it unfinished, baffled, it is said, by his inability to get the perspective right. It would be truer to say that what baffled him was his inability to construct the picture on any other lines but those of a realistic space and a more or less illusionistic perspective.

As early as 1851 Rossetti began taking his subjects from Dante, and from that time, too, he found relief from the technical problems of oil painting by turning to watercolours, with the happiest results. It was in watercolour (stiffened with size and Chinese white), in a Giottesque style, that he painted *Beatrice, Meeting Dante at a Marriage Feast, Denies him her Salutation*, the *Meeting of Dante and Beatrice in Paradise*, and *Dante Drawing an Angel* in very straight and rather stiff draperies; then *Dante's Dream at the Time of the Death of Beatrice* (1856), and finally *Dantis Amor* (1859, Tate Gallery): Beatrice in the peace of paradise gazes continually on the face of the Saviour. He usually takes his matter from the *Vita Nuova*, but this last motif comes from the *Purgatorio*, for the *Divine Comedy* as a whole provided a rich store of inspiration for the painter. Also from the *Purgatorio* is *Dante's Vision of Rachel and Leah* (1856, Tate Gallery), a work that deserves to be better known. It is one of Rossetti's most delicate and graceful watercolours, one of those in which the stiffness of the fifties gives way, without slackness as yet, to the mellow curves of later years, and indeed the supple inflexions of the creepers anticipate Art Nouveau. Leah is wreathing honeysuckles while Rachel looks on. Leaving out of account the mystical, dream-like forest before which the figure of Dante is passing, this picture, by virtue of its foreground, is one of the most Pre-Raphaelite of all Rossetti's works (it was painted for Ruskin). The ideal purplish hue of Rachel's robe answers to the erotic Veronese green of Leah's. Elsewhere the motif of a cruel and guilty love is illustrated by *Paolo and Francesca* falling through the flames of hellfire.

For a time in the 1850s Rossetti taught drawing at the Working Men's College founded by F.D. Maurice. One student presumed to ask him for the name and address of the best colour shops. His reply was: 'I don't know, I generally use the halfpenny colours from the oil shop myself.' In April 1854, seeing the watercolour *Dante Drawing an Angel*, Ruskin went into raptures over it and a few days later the two men met for the first time. 'He seems in a mood to make my fortune,' was Rossetti's cynical comment on Ruskin's admiration for his work. Ruskin, while recognizing the artist's 'very noble powers', soon lost any illusions he may have had about Rossetti's unabashed egoism and constitutional indolence. To Elizabeth Siddal he wrote: 'You inventive people pay dearly for your power – there is no knowing how to manage you. One thing is very certain, that Rossetti will never be happy or truly powerful till he gets over that habit of his of doing nothing but what "interests him".' Ruskin plied him with technical as well as moral advice. In vain. The halfpenny colours carelessly handled did not always hold and in 1859 Ruskin was lamenting over his blue lady that was already going to ruin.

Ruskin, in spite of his own analysis of what the movement meant, always regarded Rossetti as the leader of the Pre-Raphaelites. It was the Post-Romantic and Pre-Symbolist vision of Rossetti that counted and not the sanctimonious moralizings of Holman Hunt. As for Millais, he was an admirable technician but had nothing to say. In 1856 a momentous event occurred for Rossetti: Burne-Jones and William Morris, then still undergraduates at Oxford, became acquainted with his work and soon admired it so much that for them he stood out as the 'chief figure in the Pre-Raphaelite Brotherhood'. Burne-Jones came to

Dante Gabriel Rossetti (1828-82)

Beata Beatrix, c. 1863. Oil on canvas. (34 × 26″). Tate Gallery, London.

London and attended an evening class at the Working Men's College for the express purpose of meeting Rossetti. His pre-eminent position was definitely established the following year, when a Pre-Raphaelite exhibition was held in a private house in Fitzroy Square: Rossetti's 'numerous contributions unquestionably constituted the main interest of the exhibition', said the *Saturday Review*. Yet he was the artist of whom Holman Hunt declared that he had never really been one of them, and who himself was to say more or less the same thing. That same year, 1857, Burne-Jones and Morris invited him to come to Oxford and take charge of the work they were about to begin: the mural decoration of the Oxford Union Debating Hall. Rossetti accepted and the work was carried out, but in tempera on unprepared, whitewashed walls, none of the young artists having any notion of the technical problems involved. This ineptitude was fatal to the murals, which very soon deteriorated. Further complications were at hand.

Since 1850 Rossetti's favourite model had been Elizabeth Siddal, who had also posed for Millais's *Ophelia*. She soon came to live with him and they were engaged. It cannot be definitely said that she was his mistress at this time. She was frigid and full of complexes. It is quite possible that he let her keep him at arm's length. Suffering from mysterious ailments, she was a prey to intermittent languors, reflected in her deathly pallor which, with her copper-gold hair, long thin arms and greenish-blue eyes, made her so strikingly beautiful. He drew her a hundred times in a great variety of attitudes and movements, sitting, standing at the window, laying the table. Some in the Rossetti circle disliked or pitied her, but she had her particular friends and admirers, Emma Brown, Ruskin and, most of all, Swinburne, who fairly worshipped her. By 1857 Rossetti, it would seem, was no longer in love with her, but could not gracefully escape from the role of fiancé which he had assumed in the eyes of all. It was then that Morris, who was steeped in Malory and presumably initiated Rossetti into the Arthurian legend, needed a model for Guinevere, a subject which he was to use in the mural paintings at the Oxford Union. He found her in a splendid brunette who was to appear later in so many of Rossetti's paintings: Jane Burden. Morris fell in love with her, wooed her and married her in 1859. From such evidence as there is, it would seem that Rossetti, too, was in love with her even then (as he certainly was later) and withdrew in favour of Morris, feeling himself in honour bound to respect his engagement to Elizabeth Siddal, whom he proceeded to marry in the following year, 1860, after courting her for ten years. The state of mind and nerves, of both Elizabeth and Rossetti himself, is all too clearly reflected in a letter he wrote shortly before the marriage: 'She has seemed ready to die daily and more than once a day. It has needed all my own strength to nurse her through this dreadful attack... It makes me feel as if I had been dug up out of a vault, so many times lately has it seemed to me she could never lift her head again... I assure you it has been almost too much for me... indeed, it hardly seems as if I should ever work again.'

But to go back to 1857. For Rossetti that was a year of such brilliant watercolours as the *Wedding of St George and Princess Sabra* and the *Tune of the Seven Towers*. The *Wedding*

William Morris (1834-96)

Queen Guinevere, 1858. Oil on canvas. (28½ × 19¾"). Tate Gallery, London.

of St George is a curious little piece (it measures 14×14″). Nothing in it is natural. All the intense and even crude colour motifs on stuffs and furniture look as if they had come straight from a book of heraldry. The dominant note is a golden green, amid an outburst of red and gold, purple and blue. The dragon's head in a chest behind St George goes to form, with the two figures, a triangular composition in which the pair of embracing lovers is neatly supported and aligned by the black diagonal of the saint's sword. Everything in Rossetti's vision at that time seemed to fall into broken angles and straight lines, even this tender love scene in which the princess cuts off a lock of her dark hair as a keepsake for the saint in his knightly adventures. What is striking is the languid and mournful expression of the lovers in the grip of a fateful passion – such no doubt was Rossetti's view of love. The *Tune of the Seven Towers* has an even more emphatic diagonal in the long lance cutting across the picture, but it does not carry the figures with it, their verticals are clearly marked by the details of their medieval costumes and further stressed by the colours. The central figure is the lady musician, of a hieratic type, seen in profile. The knight listening to her leans forward with his bowed head shrouded in shadows, a motif increasingly favoured by Rossetti. On the right is (presumably) a maid-servant, her arms hanging loose in front of her, her head bowed, with an expression both dreamy and downcast, as she listens to the music. She serves to break up the symmetry of the central pair of figures, but her attitude emphasizes the decadent aspect of the picture.

In 1860 he reverted to oil painting with *Bocca Baciata*, for which the model was a sensual and rather vulgar woman, Fanny Cornforth, for whom Rossetti conceived a lifelong attachment and who, perhaps unfairly, has been held accountable for the artist's lapses and slow decline in later years. It seems characteristic of him that in this very year, during his honeymoon, he should have painted or anyhow completed one of the most mysteriously appealing of his watercolours, *How They Met Themselves*. In vaguely medieval costumes, two lovers, wandering in a wood, meet their own wraiths: the woman swoons and falls to the ground, vainly protected by the man's unsheathed sword. This ominous meeting seems to express a schizophrenic division of self and psyche. It adds a mirror image to the Arthurian image of that same year, 1860, *Arthur's Tomb*: Lancelot and Guinevere meet on either side of the tomb, death dividing them irremediably. Lancelot leans forward eagerly to kiss the Queen, but she checks him with her hand, and the curve that should unite their two heads is broken by the fall of her veil. The mantle and shield striking against each other are like a flash of lightning. In the case of both these pictures, the historical remoteness of the theme fails to leave the ego uninvolved or untouched; on the contrary, the motifs cut it to the quick.

In February 1862 Elizabeth, chronically ailing, depressed and hysterical, died of an overdose of laudanum, taken one night while Rossetti was out – probably not at the Working Men's College. Stung by remorse, he took refuge more than ever in a world of myth and moods of deepening melancholy. In his imagination he saw, not a dead woman, but Beatrice in ecstasy. This is the subject of *Beata Beatrix* (*c.* 1863, Tate Gallery). She leans forward, her head tipped back slightly, with shut lids and parted lips, her mouth avid, but for nothing of a sensual order. This is the head of *Ophelia*, recognizably so, but how much more intense and spiritualized, straining towards a revelation. Shadows overhang and cling to her. The only light is that of illumination and vision. It sets off her hair, glows above her head, bathes the dial that tells the hours, and gleams on the bird of faded red that drops into her hands the poppy of death. Love, of the same red as the divine bird of death, and Dante stand behind and beyond in one of those Rossettian backgrounds quite devoid of perspective. All the colours, the pale or dark greenish greys, the muted golds of sundial and hair, the brownish golds of poppy, hands and sleeves, are the very reverse of the bright and forthright tones that he used from the *Wedding of St George* up to *Dantis Amor*. The dark green of the dress, faintly kindled by gleams of reflected light, forms with the red and brown the most moving colour scheme that Rossetti ever devised; the pale bronze of the rapt face tells clearly enough that here is no longer any question of flesh.

But already Rossetti was painting *The Beloved, or The Bride* (1865, Tate Gallery): an earthly face, of delicate sensuality, with 'amorous-lidded eyes', seen between two women this time, with two further women behind, in keeping with a strict symmetry. The robe under the auburn hair is of a rather crude green, proclaiming the erotic symbolism with which Rossetti invested it. The delightful figure of a Negro girl carrying roses sets off and intensifies the sumptuous texture of this vision from the *Song of Songs*. A passionate delight in colour and its power of suggestion seems to lend a particular appeal to the works of this period. The *Blue Closet* (Tate Gallery) comes to mind, rendered in harmonies of blue and green: blue tiles, blue cornflowers, turquoises in the fair hair, the green of a fur-lined robe. There came now a succession of women's heads carrying, in the title, mythological implications which the heavy features of a Fanny Cornforth or an Alexa Wilding could not always sustain. But it must be added that the point of the picture, in most cases, is an erotic temptation raised to the most fateful or ominous pitch. As in *Lilith*, a female demon, whose golden hair has held man in thrall and haunted poets, or *Helen of Troy* (1863), or *Monna Vanna* (1866), 'all sleeves', as Whistler sarcastically commented, or *Veronica Veronese*. He had a curious knack of picking up girls and models in the streets of London. Thus it was a handsome cook who sat for *Venus Verticordia*, Venus the Turner of Hearts, holding in readiness for man the enticing apple and fatal dart. Her bare breasts are quite exceptional in Rossetti's art.[48] The diadem of butterflies and the honeysuckle (always an erotic symbol) from which she emerges, together with the roses round about her, make it something of a perverse manifestation of Pre-Raphaelitism. It was all too sensuous for Ruskin; he was shocked and broke with Rossetti. The heads of Rossetti's women were likened by Ford Madox Brown to a fan of peacock feathers (which seems particularly apt in the case of *The Beloved*). Rossetti was looking forward to the fateful yet happy love to come; Elizabeth had meant only bitter illusions. But Tristan was now to find Isolde, and Lancelot, Guinevere. This took place about 1868, and no present-day student of Rossetti, in dealing with the sonnets of *The House of Life*, can help dividing those inspired by Elizabeth Siddal from those, much more numerous, more broodingly passionate and voluptuously sensual, which were inspired by Jane Morris, whose dark hair he occasionally changes to fair in order to throw the reader off the track. When he drew and painted Jane, he was fond (just as he had been before with Elizabeth) of giving her fanciful names, for example *Bruna Brunelleschi* (1878); but he could not disguise her identity. And while earlier models supplied the lips, the heavy mass of hair, the enlarged eyes and resigned gaze, it was Jane Morris, with her long majestic neck and bent head, who fixed the type of Pre-Raphaelite woman and imposed that type on Burne-Jones and many others. It occurs already in one of the figures of

Rossetti's very fine *Bower Meadow* (1872), a beautiful composition with two female musicians in the foreground, whose faces and hands on their instruments exactly frame the two female dancers in the background. As often with Rossetti, the picture has something of the organic symmetry of a flower.

Jane, her hair often adorned with a shell whose coiling pattern carries a suggestion of magic, was a woman of grave and noble enough beauty to sustain the roles with which Rossetti invested her. As she holds the deadly pomegranate, the funereal black of her hair and the strange, sombre air of her pale face made her admirably suited to the role of *Proserpine*, then of *Mnemosyne*, *Astarte Syriaca* and *La Donna della Finestra*. She incarnated *The Daydream* (Victoria and Albert Museum), one, it is safe to say, that often filled Rossetti's mind. Unfortunately she was not the model for *The Blessed Damozel* of 1875-79, which has given rise, since he wrote this early poem, to some fine things in prose and music; the head here was that of Alexa Wilding and, though purportedly leaning from the gold bar of Heaven, it is disconcerting in its fleshliness. In tracing the history of any school of painting, one is bound to meet with ill-considered practices; such, among English painters, was the practice of employing drapery assistants or landscape assistants. Rossetti's work suffered from his besetting failure to respect what, as an artist, most nearly concerned him, the organic unity of his work. His persistent habit of substituting one head for another, of painting in Alexa's head over that of Fanny, is a grievous foible. In considering his sketches, his studies and his finished pictures, one sees that one of his greatest weaknesses is his inability to retain the quality of the original sketch: it is often very fine in its beauty and gravity.

James Collinson (1825-81), PRB, was the comedian of the troupe, suddenly being converted to Catholicism and then as suddenly unconverted again. In his *Empty Purse* (1857, Tate Gallery), he shows himself to be a typical Victorian painter, delicate and timid. His *Stray Rabbits*, one black, one white, with the iridescent, enamelled greens of the undergrowth, brings to mind Holman Hunt's *Strayed Sheep*. Another original member of the brotherhood was F. G. Stephens (1828-1907). Before abandoning painting for art criticism, he had time to paint *Mother and Child*, a refined and tender genre scene.

Ruskin had not waited for *Venus Verticordia* to show his irritation, not only with Rossetti but with the whole brotherhood and its associates. After all, he may have felt, he had made them and could well unmake them. In his *Academy Notes* (1857) he criticized their way of painting hair – they were all, he said, 'under the strongest conviction that it is made of red sand' – and advised them to study Correggio. Now the *Athenaeum*, which had led the offensive against the Pre-Raphaelites in 1850, found itself defending them. Not only were they no longer alone but they had followers, in growing strength, so that by about 1860 there was a host of post-Pre-Raphaelites in the field. Even some artists of the older generation, like James Smetham (1821-89), followed these younger men, and his *Naboth's Vineyard* (1856, Tate Gallery) is at once beholden to the movement in general for the minute delineation of plant life, to Hunt for its symbolism, and to Rossetti for the figure

Richard Dadd (1817-86)
The Fairy Feller's Master-Stroke, 1855-64. Oil on canvas. (21 ¼ × 15 ½"). Tate Gallery, London.

and the spirit of the picture. Walter Howell Deverell (1827-54), an early and intimate friend of Rossetti, and soon intimate with Millais and Hunt as well, was put up for membership in the brotherhood and it is not clear why he never became one of them, for he was certainly talented. In *A Pet* (*c.* 1853, Tate Gallery) Deverell shows a knack of spiritualizing reality that is similar (minus religion) to that of Dyce; this is evident in the figure – modelled almost like a primitive, in contrast with the modern costume – of the girl holding up her face against the bird cage. John Brett (1830-1902), in a landscape like *The Val d'Aosta* (1858), which calls for a magnifying glass to take in the wealth of detail, dispenses with any suggestion of emotion, apparently from lack of imagination; this was deplored by Ruskin. The same careful treatment of detail is to be found in his luminous *Stonebreaker*. This is perhaps what induced Ruskin to orient him towards geology, despite the more imaginative, if not more formal, vision of mountainous country which is found in the *Glacier of Rosenlaui*, and which recalls Francis Towne. With William Lindsay Windus (1822-1907) one comes back to the moral earnestness of Pre-Raphaelitism and its appeal to the sensibility, as in his *Too Late* (1857-58, Tate Gallery), another guilt-ridden subject, but one less hackneyed than that of the fallen woman: it represents the belated return of a lover to the woman whom he had abandoned and whose gaunt features, seen against a sunny landscape background typical of the movement, show her to be dying of consumption. Henry Wallis (1830-1916) returned to the subject previously treated by Flaxman, *The Death of Chatterton* (1856, Tate Gallery), but now the mood of despair has gone and the features of the young poet (for which George Meredith, then twenty-eight, was the model) are singularly handsome and serene. His unavailing poems, torn to bits, lie at the bedside. It is a measure of the Pre-Raphaelite passion for accuracy that Wallis made a point of painting his picture in the actual attic in Gray's Inn where the poet died. This 'documentary' aspect of the picture is combined with the symbolism of the dying plant on the window sill and the burnt-out candle on the table, all presented in terms of a vigorous chiaroscuro. But these isolated works do not amount to an œuvre.

More strength and stamina are to be found in the career of Arthur Hughes (1830-1915), who often deals with the vicissitudes of fickle or ill-starred love. In *April Love* (1856, Tate Gallery), set, as so often with the Pre-Raphaelites, amidst ivy, the girl is shown in a moment of dramatic suspense. Her 'love is hurt with jar and fret' (lines from Tennyson's *Miller's Daughter* were appended to the picture when it was exhibited at the Royal Academy in 1856), and she turns away, in her vulnerability, from the man's head dimly visible on the right, above their clasped hands. The blue gown holds its own against the rich green of the ivy. This is a more finished work, more subtly suggestive in its colouring, than the same artist's interpretation of *Aurora Leigh's Dismissal of Romney* (1860, Tate Gallery), a theme of unrequited love taken from Elizabeth Barrett Browning's verse tale. Thrust into the shadows where the neutral tone of his clothes dims his sorrowful face, contrasting with the great triumphant lily, the lover has received his dismissal from the mild but resolute Aurora, aglow with light in her turquoise dress. The Victorian refusal of love has never been more gloriously commemorated.

Arthur Hughes (1830-1915)
April Love, 1856. Oil on canvas. (35 × 19½″). Tate Gallery, London.

The mural paintings done at the Oxford Union in 1857 had consisted of scenes from Malory's *Morte d'Arthur*, a subject probably suggested by William Morris. Jane Burden was found to sit for the figure of Guinevere. Morris, in first trying to paint her, is said to have turned his canvas towards her on which he had written the words: 'I cannot paint you but I love you.' But paint her he did, gracious and grave as *Queen Guinevere* (1858, Tate Gallery)[49] against a background of transversal hangings, in a design based, it would seem, on that of Rossetti's *Annunciation* and other pictures by him with the same telling use of greyish whites. That same year, 1858, Morris published his first volume of characteristically medievalizing poems, entitled *The Defence of Guinevere*. Under the influence of Ruskin and no doubt of Carlyle, and even while medievalism continued to inspire all his work, Morris began to take a keen interest in social questions, striving against the strong currents of commercialism, trying to revive a true community sense and to enlist art in the service of a finer, simpler, sincerer conception of human needs. To put into practice his ideas of sound design and workmanship, Morris, with several associates, including Madox Brown, Rossetti and Arthur Hughes, founded a famous workshop (1861), which strongly influenced the Arts and Crafts movement in England. But that is another story.

Sir Edward Burne-Jones (1833-98) would be of much concern here, were it not that the limits of this history have been fixed at about 1860 (except for the original Pre-Raphaelites, whose careers have been followed beyond that date); and also because of the fact that with him the Rossettian deviation from Pre-Raphaelitism takes on a character that was nearer to Symbolism. 'I mean by a picture', said Burne-Jones, 'a beautiful romantic dream of something that never was, never will be – in a light better than any light that ever shone – in a land no one can ever define or remember, only desire.' In his work, Greek and Arthurian legend are combined in an atmosphere of mystery and dream. It is no longer quite a matter of painting. But *Lancelot's Dream*, to take only one example, is superb, and with no other accessories but moonlight, a dead tree and a horse, the painter contrives to create an aura of the fantastic around the sleeping knight, lying between shadow and light. *The Magic Circle* and many other subjects from the legend of Merlin still cast a potent spell.

Certain critics are fond of saying that the Pre-Raphaelite movement began as a closer approach to reality and, with Burne-Jones, ended as an evasion into dreamland. I have proposed to assume, rather, that from the very start there were two kinds of Pre-Raphaelitism. The kind practised by Rossetti, which led on to Burne-Jones and exerted an influence outside England (as the other did not), never made any pretence of facing reality.

The case of the Clique is more piquant. It was founded in 1837 by five painters who, in the name of modernism, set themselves up in opposition to academic art. The best known among them was William Powell Frith (1819-1909). Eager to record in painting the life of his own time, regardless of convention and tradition, he was uncertain how to go about it, for he had no positive programme with which to implement his opposition to received ideas. Though a professed anti-academic, he stood in some respects in the position in which Reynolds had stood. Modern dress, with frock-coat and trousers, troubled him; it was not picturesque. At first he was violently opposed to the theories of the Pre-Raphaelites, but he may afterwards have owed them a certain boldness in his approach to contemporary themes.

Frith began as a painter of genre scenes. His true vein of inspiration lay in the use of exteriors which did not involve open-air painting; one may say that he carried on in painting the tradition of crowd scenes in English caricature. Thus in 1854 he exhibited *Ramsgate Sands* or *Life at the Seaside*, which was purchased by Queen Victoria. In 1858 came *Derby Day* (Tate Gallery). He spent fifteen months working on this picture. Of it, he himself said with engaging frankness[50]: 'The acrobats, the nigger minstrels, the gypsy fortune-tellers, to say nothing of carriages filled with pretty women, together with the sporting element, seemed to offer abundant material for the line of art to which I felt obliged – in the absence of higher gifts – to devote myself, and the more I considered the kaleidoscope aspect of the crowd on Epsom Downs, the firmer became my resolve to attempt to reproduce it.' As a popular epic, a panorama of Victorian life, such a picture is impressive and charged with a certain power. What it lacks is pictorial unity in any serious sense; its multiplicity of crowded incident remains a multiplicity of parts, and the colour remains descriptive. *The Railway Station* of 1862 (Royal Holloway College, Englefield Green, Surrey), representing Paddington Station in London, certainly has nothing in common with Monet's *Gare Saint-Lazare*; but here the glass and iron roofing prompted Frith, or forced him, to construct a limited space in which the crowd is organized in terms of strongly articulated groups. This picture is unquestionably Frith's masterpiece.

Paradoxically enough, among the five young painters who banded together in 1837, figured Richard Dadd (1817-86). If he wished to liberate art, it was certainly not in favour of contemporary life, for in 1841 he exhibited fanciful pictures of fairyland, minutely and disturbingly detailed beyond even those of Fuseli himself. In 1842 he left England on a journey through Europe and the East. He returned in 1843, only to murder his father shortly afterwards. From then on, until his death forty-three years later, he was interned in Bethlehem Hospital and then in Broadmoor Asylum in Berkshire, where he had plenty of time to paint and was allowed all the means of doing so. One can hardly imagine more favourable conditions in which to create the art he had in mind. *The Fairy Feller's Master-Stroke* (1855-64, Tate Gallery) may fitly be called his own master-stroke. It is a work that has been so admirably analysed by Octavio Paz that I cannot do better than refer the reader to his evocation of it.[51] Dadd worked on it for nine years in Bethlehem Hospital but left it unfinished. All the figures are grouped round a hazel-nut, as if in illustration of a tale which, one can only suppose, Dadd himself invented. The cracking open of the nut would appear to be an ordeal imposed by the more or less royal figures on the right, while the fine ladies strutting on the left may be the promised reward of success. A mounting series of vertical registers are divided off from each other like so many worlds between which no communication is possible. There is, however, a double scale of representation in these figures: one scale is governed by a vague application of perspective, while the other is that of fairyland. Typical of the latter is the tiny old man, with white whiskers and large bald head, sitting opposite the feller; such a figure makes one wonder whether, after all, Dadd may not have had in mind Fuseli's *Titania, Bottom and the Fairies*. Perhaps even more fascinating than its structure is the texture of the picture. (One may doubt whether it is a simple matter of oil painting here; other substances may have been mixed into the pigments.) Grainy, crackled and smooth textures alternate to delightful effect. The scene is glimpsed through a matting of aquatic vegetation, chiefly bulrushes. It may be that the whole scene was conceived of as taking place underwater. Only a madman indeed could have painted such a picture in mid-Victorian England.

A wealthy nation of shopkeepers, but one whose picture collections even in the seventeenth century were so rich as to amaze Rubens when he saw them, England has had from generation to generation an ambivalent attitude towards art. Painting here, as elsewhere, has conferred standing on its collectors, but the latter have naturally been anxious to get their money's worth. This was an attitude which, as has been seen, Hogarth, Blake and Turner all had to contend with. I have tried to indicate what changes were brought about in patronage by the industrial revolution. The fact is that the industrial revolution gave such a fillip to Capitalism and created so much wealth that some of the surplus went to the encouragement of the fine arts. Such men as John Sheepshanks, a Leeds cloth manufacturer, and Robert Vernon, who made a fortune supplying the army with horses, collected pictures in the first half of the nineteenth century. So, a little earlier, did William Beckford, the son of a wealthy West Indian planter and slave-owner. The difference was that Beckford had taste. Never had so much money been spent on pictures as in Victorian England, but often the purchaser was prompted by commercial motives. Flatow, who bought Frith's *Railway Station*, made £30000 selling prints of it. Such, it may be said, is popular art. Holman Hunt, the high-minded champion of edifying art, was paid £5775 for *The Finding of Our Saviour in the Temple*. Under these conditions, it was inevitable for art to sink to a commercial level. Millais sold his *Bubbles* to Pears Soap for advertising purposes. Not all the painters in nineteenth-century England were mad.

NOTES

1 (page 13) Ronald Paulson, *Hogarth, His Life, Art and Times*, 2 volumes, Yale University Press, New Haven and London 1971.

2 (page 15) This print, which Hogarth called *The Taste of the Town*, is also known as *Burlington Gate*.

3 (page 19) Only one of Hogarth's pictures in the grand style, *Satan, Sin and Death* (1735-40, Tate Gallery), escapes these simplifications because it is inspired by Milton and not by the Mediterranean tradition. But while there is nothing here of parody or burlesque, the characteristically Northern bent for the grotesque is very much in evidence in the figure of Satan (the very reverse of Blake's fine, sinister, romantic Satan), so much so that there is not really much difference between the 'earnestness' of Hogarth and the satire of Gillray who was inspired by it in one of his adaptations of famous history paintings with Queen Charlotte as Sin.

4 (page 21) Edmund Burke, *A Philosophical Enquiry into the Origin of Our Ideas of the Sublime and Beautiful*, London 1757.

5 (page 43) Ellis K. Waterhouse, *Painting in Britain, 1530 to 1790*, The Pelican History of Art, 2nd edition, London 1964, p. 152.

6 (page 54) Such is the Aristotelian view. Blake denounced it with the vehemence of a Platonist.

7 (page 68) It has been noted that two of Gainsborough's brothers had that single-minded passion for small mechanical devices which is often associated with nervous and even mental instability.

8 (page 68) The uncertainty largely depends on the part which his nephew and pupil Gainsborough Dupont is assumed to have played in his studio. There are a number of works which may or may not be by Dupont's hand.

9 (page 95) I refer to the 1765 version of the *Lion Attacking a Horse* (reproduced here on page 99). In the 1770 version (Yale University Art Gallery, New Haven, Conn.) Stubbs reverts to the craggy landscape and melodramatic lighting of the *White Horse Frightened by a Lion* (see page 98).

10 (page 103) It is only fair to add that George Morland often proves himself a fine landscapist. His *Seashore — Fishermen Hauling in a Boat* (1791, Victoria and Albert Museum) is one of those powerful seascapes which English painters — Rowlandson is another — can produce in inspired moments. It must also be said in Morland's favour that, after the unimaginative lighting of the common run of his drinkers, his pigs and his horses, he goes far to make up for it with a picture like *Horses in a Stable* (Victoria and Albert Museum); the well-judged balance of the composition is admirable, and the skilful handling of the penumbra and the subtle play of bluish greys over and around the horse's coat say much for Morland's natural sensibility or his technical resourcefulness, or both.

11 (page 109) The large *Holt Bridge on the River Dee* (c. 1762, Tate Gallery) is typical of Wilson's Italianized English landscapes.

12 (page 110) From *Tintern Abbey*.

13 (page 110) First line and title of this famous poem.

14 (page 110) From *Tintern Abbey*.

15 (page 111) Unfortunately the date of this Sandby drawing in the British Museum is unrecorded.

16 (page 112) A.J. Finberg, *The English Watercolourists*, London 1906.

17 (page 116) See also the interesting comments on mottled marbles or *pierres-aux-masures* by Roger Caillois in his *L'écriture des pierres*, Skira, Geneva 1970, p. 25 ff.

18 (page 131) All these Cotman watercolours are in the Print Room of the British Museum.

19 (page 142) Lord Clark, introduction to the catalogue of the exhibition *La Peinture romantique anglaise et les Préraphaélites*, Petit Palais, Paris, January-April 1972. The quotation as given here is translated from the French version of Lord Clark's introduction.

20 (page 146) Most of these oil sketches on paper are in the Victoria and Albert Museum, London.

21 (page 146) Jonathan Mayne, *Constable's Sketches*, London 1959.

22 (page 147) 'In your skies, for instance', West said to Constable, 'always aim at *brightness*... even in the darkest effects there should be brightness. Your darks should look like the darks of silver, not of lead or of slate.' C.R. Leslie, *Memoirs of the Life of John Constable*, chapter I.

23 (page 153) Translation by Jonathan Mayne, in Charles Baudelaire, *Art in Paris, 1845-1862*, Phaidon Press, London 1965, pp. 199-200.

24 (page 157) Constable's name for the *Cornfield* (1826, National Gallery, London).

25 (page 160) Letter of 8 May 1824.

26 (page 161) These views were expressed in Constable's lectures on the history of landscape painting, given at the Royal Institution in 1833 and 1836.

27 (page 161) Nothing has been said in this chapter about Constable's watercolours. Most landscape painters of that time turned to watercolour as a convenient medium for working in the open air. In Constable's case, this motive did not operate, for he was in the habit of making small oil sketches directly from nature. It was only towards the end of his life that, from age and lassitude, he turned to the lighter medium, with admirable results. These late watercolours — which are not unrelated, even in

their colouring, to the art of Dürer — are works of exquisite delicacy and aerial transparency. A fine example is *Tillington Church* (British Museum).

28 (page 163) Ellis K. Waterhouse, *Painting in Britain, 1530 to 1790*, The Pelican History of Art, 2nd edition, London 1964, p. 234.

29 (page 170) Lord Clark, introduction to the catalogue of the exhibition *La Peinture romantique anglaise et les Préraphaélites*, Petit Palais, Paris, January-April 1972. The quotation as given here is translated from the French version of Lord Clark's introduction.

30 (page 176) See, as a mild example, the *Nude Woman Listening to a Girl Playing upon the Spinet* (reproduced here on page 177).

31 (page 179) Ruthven Todd, *Tracks in the Snow*, London 1946.

32 (page 179) Frederick Antal, *Fuseli Studies*, London 1956.

33 (page 191) Letter from Blake to Dawson Turner, 9 June 1818.

34 (page 193) These lines are from Edward Young's paraphrase of *Job*.

35 (page 198) One notes the value of the word 'sleep' for Palmer.

36 (page 199) Ruskin here alludes to the painting of 1819, *Entrance of the Meuse: Orange-Merchant on the Bar, Going to Pieces*. This picture was seen by Palmer as a boy and filled him with admiration.

37 (page 201) Jack Lindsay, *Turner, A Critical Biography*, London 1966.

38 (page 204) John Landseer, *Review of Publications of Art*, March 1808.

39 (page 205) Jack Lindsay, *Turner, A Critical Biography*, p. 148.

40 (page 209) But this Mannerist elongation might also have been taken over from Claude himself; I am thinking particularly of his picture *Jacob with Laban* (Dulwich), which could have been already in England at that time.

41 (page 210) Poussin's *Polyphemus* is now in the Hermitage, Leningrad. Was it already in Russia then? In any case Turner could have seen the print.

42 (page 216) Clarkson Stanfield, much admired by Ruskin, painted *Off the Dogger Bank* (1846, Victoria and Albert Museum), whose dramatic handling brings Turner to mind.

43 (page 220) Many great painters have used a very limited palette. This was not the case with Turner; one has only to think of the indignation aroused by the heightened colouring of *Ulysses Deriding Polyphemus* when it was exhibited at the Royal Academy in 1829. Turner's paintbox and palette, preserved in the Tate Gallery, show a range of twenty-two colours; it comes as no surprise to find that they include seven yellows, four reds and only two blues.

44 (page 222) Letter of Constable of 12 May 1836 to George Constable of Arundel. It is true that Constable adds rather ambiguously: 'The public think he is laughing at them, and so they laugh at him in return.' This, interestingly enough, was the very year in which Ruskin, at the age of seventeen, wrote his first article defending Turner.

45 (page 225) Landseer squandered a fine talent on his bourgeois inanities, a talent which was capable of great strength and vision as is evident in an arresting picture at Kenwood, *Hawking in the Olden Time* (1832, 60 × 72″), the only large romantic picture which takes the air as its element, placing the spectator on a level with a fantastic bird fight, an enormous triangle of enmeshed wings and beaks, while the horsemen coming into view below are but tiny figures in the distance.

46 (page 232) William Holman Hunt, *Pre-Raphaelitism and the Pre-Raphaelite Brotherhood*, 2 volumes, London 1905.

47 (page 240) It is worth recalling the comic side of this Victorian moral tale. Annie Miller, who sat for the fallen woman in Hunt's *Awakening Conscience*, was herself no better than she should be. Hunt, however, fell in love with her and became engaged to her, then broke off the engagement when he found that she would not give up her wicked ways, in which Rossetti seems to have encouraged her. Years later Hunt accidentally met her, 'a buxom matron with a carriage full of children, on Richmond Hill,' and learned that she was now happily married. 'In real life, Annie was obviously no apt example of the moral she had illustrated in Hunt's painting,' writes Oswald Doughty in *A Victorian Romantic: Dante Gabriel Rossetti*.

48 (page 251) This unusual Victorian made no secret of his horror of Ettyism, in other words of the nude. Here he was reluctantly forced by his subject to accept it.

49 (page 254) Usually called *Queen Guinevere*, but sometimes called *La Belle Iseult*.

50 (page 257) Frith published his autobiography in three volumes (*My Autobiography and Reminiscences*, London 1887-88).

51 (page 257) Octavio Paz, *Le singe grammairien*, Skira, Geneva 1972, pp. 122-126.

BIBLIOGRAPHY

DOCUMENTS

H. CRABB ROBINSON, *Reminiscences and Correspondence*, edited by T. Sadler, London 1869. — A. CUNNINGHAM, *Lives of the Most Eminent British Painters, Sculptors and Architects*, revised edition, 3 vol., London 1879-80. — E. EDWARDS, *Anecdotes of Painters*, London 1808. — J. GREIG (editor), *The Farington Diary*, 8 vol., London 1922 ff. — G. VERTUE, *The Notebooks*, Walpole Society, XVIII, XX, XXII, XXIV, XXVI, XXIX, London 1930-47. — H. WALPOLE, *Anecdotes of Painting in England*, 4 vol., Strawberry Hill 1765-71.

GENERAL WORKS

C.H. Collins BAKER & M.R. JAMES, *British Painting*, London 1933. — C.H. Collins BAKER, *British Painting*, London 1943. — E. CHESNEAU, *La Peinture anglaise*, Paris 1882; *The English School of Painting*, introduction by John Ruskin, London 1885. — S. COLOMB, *L'art anglais*, Paris 1947. — A. DIGEON, *L'Ecole anglaise de peinture*, Paris 1955. — R. FRY, *Reflections on British Painting*, London 1934. — W. GAUNT, *British Painting*, London 1945. — W. GAUNT, *A Concise History of English Painting*, London 1964. — P. JAMOT, *La Peinture en Angleterre*, Paris 1938. — A. LEROY, *Histoire de la Peinture anglaise*, Paris 1939. — D. PIPER, *Painting in England 1500-1880*, London 1965. — S. REDGRAVE, *A Dictionary of Artists of the English School*, 2nd ed., London 1878. — Sir J. ROTHENSTEIN, *An Introduction to English Painting*, 5th ed., London 1968. — T. THORÉ-BÜRGER, *L'Ecole anglaise*, Paris 1863. — W.T. WHITLEY, *Artists and their Friends in England*, London 1928. — R.H. WILENSKI, *English Painting*, London 1945.

WORKS CONCERNING PERIODS OR ASPECTS OF ENGLISH PAINTING

O. AUBRAT, *La Peinture de genre en Angleterre de la mort de Hogarth (1764) au préraphaélisme (1850)*, Paris 1933. — G. BAZIN, *La Peinture anglaise, 1730-1850*, Paris 1938. — Q. BELL, *Victorian Artists*, London 1967. — L. BINYON, *Landscape in English Art and Poetry*, London 1931. — L. BINYON, *English Watercolours*, London 1933. — A. BLUNT, Preface to the catalogue *Le Paysage anglais de Gainsborough à Turner*, Musée de l'Orangerie, Paris 1953. — T.S.R. BOASE, *English Art 1800-70*, London 1959. — K. CLARK, *Landscape into Art*, London 1949. — D. CLIFFORD, *Watercolours of the Norwich School*, London 1965. — H.M. CUNDALL, *History of Watercolour Painting*, London 1908. — H.M. CUNDALL, *Masters of Watercolour Painting*, London 1923. — W. DICKES, *The Norwich School of Painting*, London 1905. — A.J. FINBERG, *The English Watercolourists*, London 1906. — S.W. FISHER, *English Watercolours*, London 1970. — W. GAUNT, *The Pre-Raphaelite Tragedy*, London 1942. — W. GAUNT, *The Great Century of British Painting: Hogarth to Turner*, London 1971. — W. GAUNT, *The Restless Century: Painting in Britain 1800-1900*, London 1972. — M. GRANT, *Chronological History of the Old English Landscape Painters*, 3 vol., London 1926-47. — M. GRANT, *A Dictionary of British Landscape Painters*, Leigh-on-Sea 1952. — M. HARDIE, *Watercolour Painting in Britain*, vol. II: *The Romantic Period*, London 1967. — F.W. HAWCROFT, *Englische Aquarelle des 18. Jahrhunderts, von Cozens bis Turner*, catalogue of the exhibition at the Albertina, Vienna 1965. — L. HERMANN, *Il paesaggio nella pittura inglese dell'ottocento*, Milan 1967. — T. HILTON, *The Pre-Raphaelites*, London 1970. — C.E. HUGHES, *Early English Watercolour*, London 1913; revised ed. by J. MAYNE, London 1960. — Holman HUNT, *Pre-Raphaelitism and the Pre-Raphaelite Brotherhood*, 2 vol., London 1905; reprinted, New York 1967. — J.D. HUNT, *The Pre-Raphaelite Imagination*, London 1968. — R. IRONSIDE & J. GERE, *The Pre-Raphaelite Painters*, London 1948. — Sir W. LAMB, *The Royal Academy*, London 1935. — H. LEMAITRE, *Le Paysage anglais à l'aquarelle 1760-1851*, Paris 1955. — E.B. LINTOTT, *The Art of Watercolour Painting*, London 1926. — R. LISTER, *British Romantic Art*, London 1972. — N. LYTTON, *Watercolour*, London 1911. — J. MAAS, *Victorian Painters*, London & New York 1969. — A. MAUROIS, *Chefs-d'œuvre des aquarellistes anglais*, Paris 1939. — R. MÉNARD, *Entretiens sur la peinture*, XIIIe Entretien: *Le Paysage anglais*, Paris 1875. — C. MONKHOUSE, *Earlier English Watercolour Painters*, London 1890. — J. NICOLL, *The Pre-Raphaelites*, London 1970. — A.P. OPPÉ, *Early Victorian Art*, in *Early Victorian England*, London n.d. — J. ORROCK, *On the English Art of Watercolour Painting*, London 1891. — L. PARRIS, *The Pre-Raphaelites*, London 1966. — S.H. PAVIÈRE, *A Dictionary of Victorian Landscape Painters*, Leigh-on-Sea 1968. — N. PEVSNER, *On the Englishness of English Art*, London 1956. — J. PIPER, *British Romantic Artists*, London 1947. — P. QUENNELL, *Romantic England: Writing and Painting 1717-1851*, London 1970. — R. & S. REDGRAVE, *A Century of British Painters*, London 1866, reprinted 1947. — G. REITLINGER, *The Economics of Taste*, 3 vol., London 1961-70. — A.G. REYNOLDS, *Victorian Painting*, London 1966. — A.W. RICH, *Watercolour Painting*, London 1918. — E. RICHTIE, *English Drawings*, London 1935. — E. RICHTIE, *English Painters: Hogarth to Constable*, Baltimore 1942. — J. RUSKIN, *Modern Painters*, 5 vol., London 1843-60. — J. RUSKIN, *Pre-Raphaelitism*, ed. by W.M. ROSSETTI, London 1899. — F. SAXL & R. WITTKOWER, *British Art and the Mediterranean*, Oxford 1948. — S. SITWELL, *Conversation Pictures*, London 1936. — A. STALEY, *The Pre-Raphaelite Landscape*, Oxford 1973. — B. TAYLOR, *Animal Painting in England*, London 1955. — E.K. WATERHOUSE, *Painting in Britain 1530-1790*, 2nd ed., London 1964. — W.T. WHITLEY, *Art in England, 1800-1820*, Cambridge 1928. — I.A. WILLIAMS, *Early English Watercolours*, London 1952. — G.C. WILLIAMSON, *English Conversation Pieces*, London 1931.

LIST OF ILLUSTRATIONS

PRINTED BY
IRL IMPRIMERIES RÉUNIES LAUSANNE S.A.

PRINTED IN SWITZERLAND